After graduating from the University of South Florida, Jim Hooper worked as a documentary research-writer for WFLA-TV in Tampa, with weekends set aside as a skydiving team captain and instructor. He gave up television to devote himself full time to jumping out of airplanes, logging over 3,500 freefalls and building the world's premier skydiving center in Zephyrhills, Florida. His thirst for adventure unfulfilled, he sold the business in 1984 to realize a long-held dream of being a war correspondent and author.

Within two years, his byline was appearing in publications ranging from *The Daily Telegraph* of London to *Jane's Intelligence Review*. Following publication of *Koevoet* and its American edition, *Beneath the Visiting Moon*, he collaborated on *Flashpoint – At the Frontline of Today's Wars* and was a principal contributor to the best-selling *World's Most Dangerous Places*, and its companion, *Hotspots*. The only journalist to accompany the mercenaries of Executive Outcomes on operations, Hooper recorded their campaigns in his book *Bloodsong*. The Balkan wars of the 1990s found him crossing back and forth between the Croatian, Serbian and Muslim frontlines in search of stories, the most memorable when he was captured by Muslim extremists in central Bosnia. His previous book, *A Hundred Feet Over Hell*, is the story of his brother's tour in Vietnam, and has been ranked by veterans and non-veterans alike as a classic of the air warfare genre.

KOEVOET!

Jim Hooper

O! Withered is the garland of war,
The soldier's pole is fall'n; young boys and
Girls
Are level now with men; the odds is gone,
And there is nothing left remarkable
Beneath the visiting moon.

William Shakespeare
As you Like It, I. i. 64

Helion & Company   G G Books UK

Co-published in 2013 by:
Helion & Company Limited
Unit 8 Amherst Business Centre
Budbrooke Road
Warwick
CV34 5WE
England
Tel. 01926 499 619
Email: info@helion.co.uk
Website: www.helion.co.uk
Twitter: @helionbooks
Visit our blog http://blog.helion.co.uk/

and

GG Books UK
Rugby
Warwickshire
Tel. 07921 709307
Website: www.30degreessouth.co.uk

This revised and expanded edition published by GG Books 2012, reprinted with
corrections in partnership with Helion & Company Limited
Previous editions: *Koevoet*, Southern Book Publishers, 1988; and *Beneath the Visiting
Moon*, Lexington Books, 1990

Designed and typeset by Farr out Publications, Wokingham, Berkshire
Cover designed by Farr out Publications, Wokingham, Berkshire

Text and photographs © Jim Hooper 2012

ISBN 978-0-9570587-0-5

British Library Cataloguing-in-Publication Data.
A catalogue record for this book is available from the British Library.

Contents

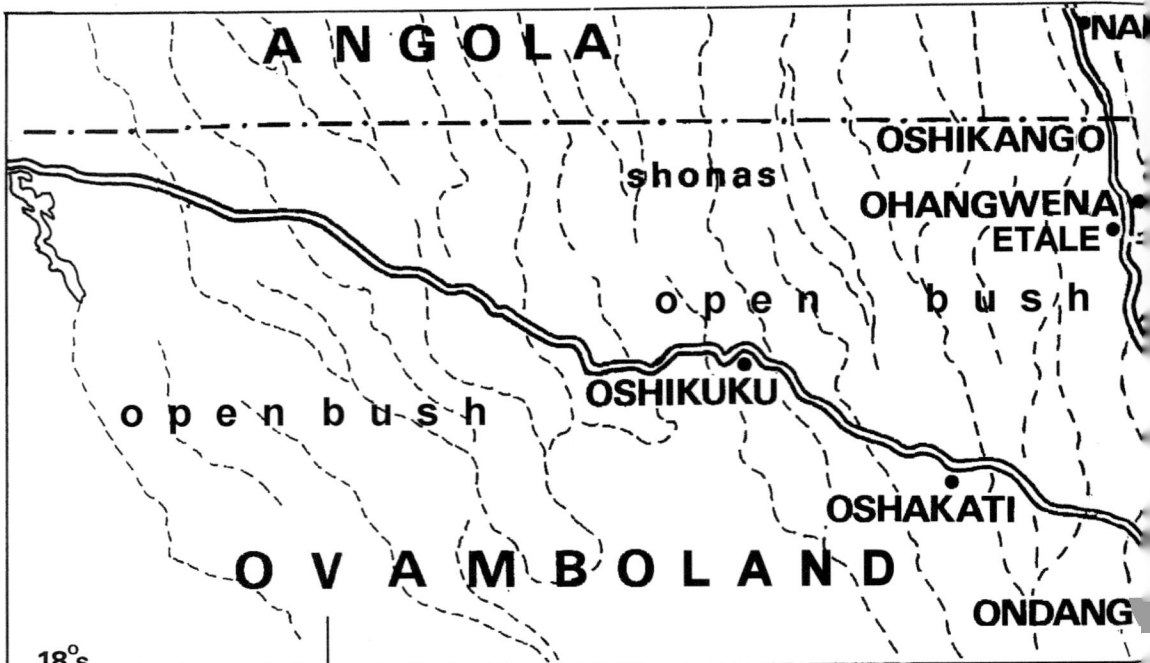

A N G O L A

shonas

OSHIKANGO

OHANGWENA

ETALE

o p e n   b u s h

o p e n   b u s h

OSHIKUKU

OSHAKATI

O V A M B O L A N D

ONDANG

18°s

15°E

0 — 80 km

0 — 50 mls

N

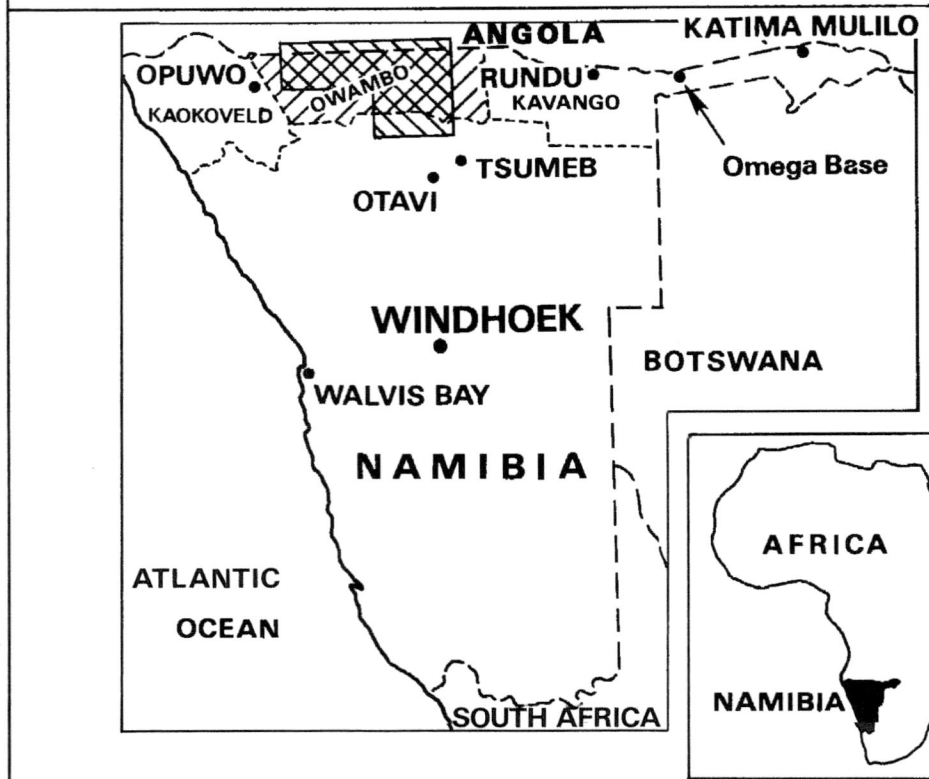

ANGOLA

KATIMA MULILO

OPUWO

OWAMBO

RUNDU

KAVANGO

KAOKOVELD

Omega Base

TSUMEB

OTAVI

WINDHOEK

BOTSWANA

WALVIS BAY

NAMIBIA

ATLANTIC

OCEAN

AFRICA

NAMIBIA

SOUTH AFRICA

Peter Redman

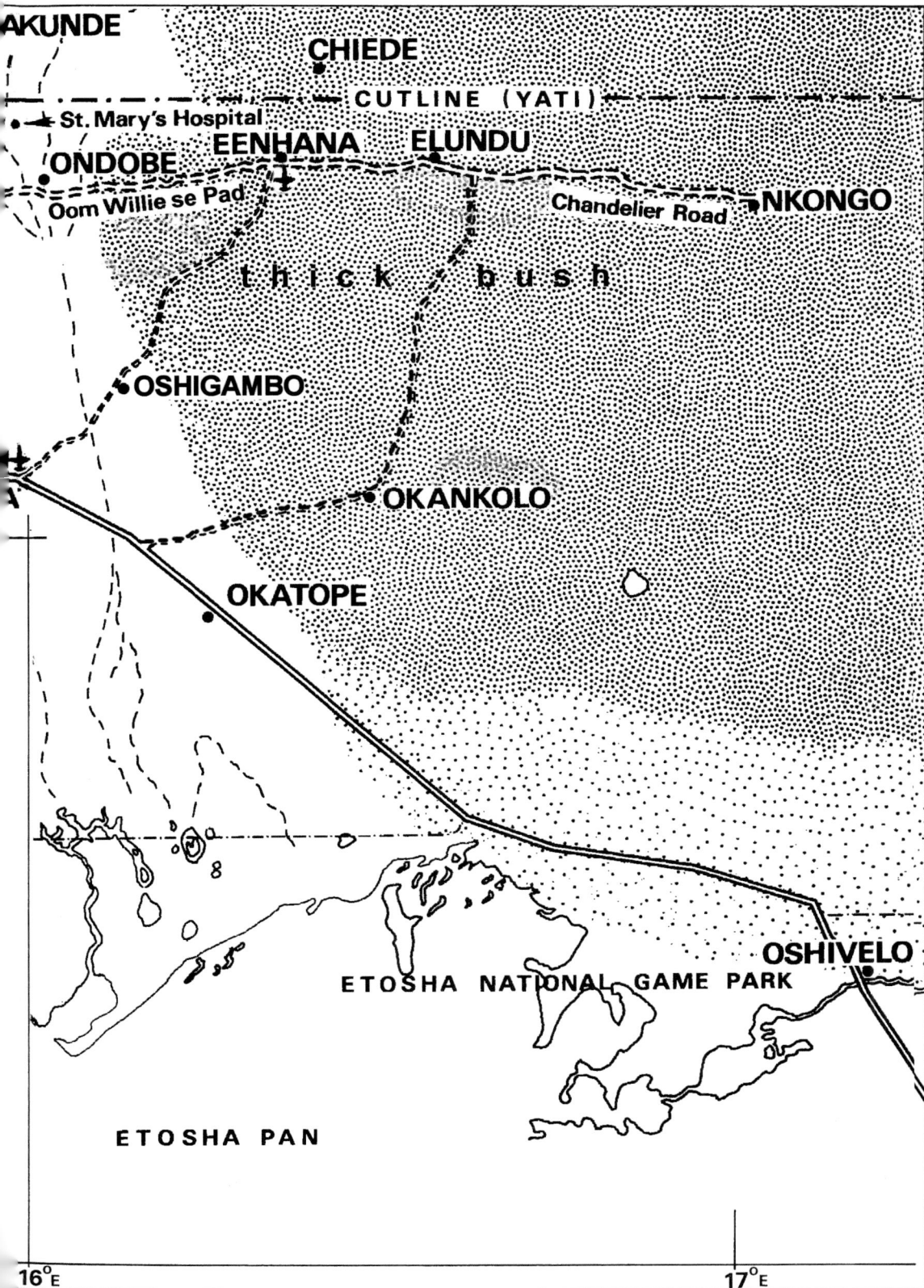

AKUNDE

CHIEDE

CUTLINE (YATI)

St. Mary's Hospital

EENHANA   ELUNDU

ONDOBE

Oom Willie se Pad   Chandelier Road   NKONGO

t h i c k   b u s h

OSHIGAMBO

OKANKOLO

OKATOPE

8

OSHIVELO

E T O S H A   N A T I O N A L   G A M E   P A R K

E T O S H A   P A N

16°E   17°E

Dedication

No author is dismayed at seeing his first work reprinted by popular demand, especially when given the opportunity to weave in dramatic material from voices that have been silent for more than two decades. Those who dug into their memories have given the story more depth and texture than any of us could have hoped for. Much credit must also go to publisher Steve Crump whose enthusiasm for the project allowed me the latitude to take this new edition several levels beyond the original *Koevoet!* and its American cousin, *Beneath the Visiting Moon*.

To answer a recurrent question from readers of previous editions, I've added the route that took me from television writer to professional skydiver to selling home and business and setting off in pursuit of a boyhood dream. Each twist and turn in the journey was marked by a cast of walk-on characters that ranged from a Chinese general to panicky CIA spooks to Kenyan smugglers. Whether helping or hindering, comical or sinister, all influenced a zigzagging trail that was as unpredictable as the final destination.

The stars came later: Brigadier Rob Crowther, Defence Attaché at the South African Embassy in London, who opened a door that led to Namibia and the United Nations' most hated paramilitary group; then-Major Bernie Ley, who championed my return some months later; and General "Sterk Hans" Dreyer, who granted me permission to spend half a year embedded with his legendary operators. My unprecedented access to one of the most politically sensitive units of the era was without restrictions, yet at no time did anyone ask to see the manuscript before publication. "You have to write what you see," Dreyer told me.

On the sharp end, it was the black and white policemen of Koevoet who showed me things never before seen by an outsider, and who kept me alive in spite of myself. I suspect I was more often than not a distraction, forever in the way and underfoot, and asking endless and tiresome questions, most of which they bore with great patience and not a little stoicism. To those who were there, thank you.

Preface

This is the story of a war in Africa. As with all such tales, it deals with the brutality, fear and sacrifice that have been the fabric of all wars and all sides since man first banded together for mutual protection or aggression. But it is a true story, though told through the eyes of an outsider, and that alone must make it suspect to anyone who opens these pages. It is an account of people caught up in a little-known conflict in an even less-known part of the world, and if my journalistic detachment faded after seeing men I knew die next to me, I hope the reader will understand.

It was my war, my beat, in that absurd and proprietary way journalists have of labelling something which has forever touched them. Mine also because I'd missed the one great conflict of my generation and went in search of its replacement long before understanding why. In retrospect, the story that emerged was as cliché-ridden as the most hackneyed B movie of the 1940s: the eager novitiate, innocent beyond his years, who is grudgingly allowed a brief glimpse of combat by a band of warrior brothers. He goes away but is drawn back to share their lives. He learns fear, receives his red badge of courage, and finally leaves to tell their story.

Although one hand still complains when the weather turns cold and wet, that too was part of the search, an adolescent fantasy lurking in the mists. But when fantasy became reality I understood it was only luck that mattered. It rode close at hand and in undeserved abundance, deflecting the ultimate reality; others it deserted entirely. The eternal question: Why them and not me? There is no answer.

What is written here will not be popular in some quarters; the line between fashionable and unfashionable truth has been very carefully drawn, and a journalist crossing it does so at his peril. In 1987, my refusal to be held to ransom by political correctness saw 22 publishers recoil from what one editor described as "a most unwholesome book." I was addressing yet another manuscript to one more publisher when the managing director of Hodder & Stoughton rang from London. "I've been trying to write you a letter," he said, "but finally decided it would be easier to call. I have to say your book has caused more dissension amongst our editorial staff than anything to cross my desk in a very long time. Unfortunately, because of the political climate, there's no way we can publish in the UK. If it's okay with you I'd like to pass it to our South African imprint."

That a publishing house with a stable of bestselling authors saw merit in the story was at least partial vindication, but the battle wasn't over. When the manuscript reached Southern Books in Johannesburg, it was passed to a freelance copy editor whose sole job was to correct spelling and punctuation mistakes. He went further, penning a furious five-page letter on why it was too dangerous to be published. He began by warning that books might soon be added to the international boycott of South African products, suggesting that *Koevoet* could contribute to such a decision. The thin veneer of altruism was soon stripped away as he got into his sanctimonious stride.

"It is indeed my contention that Southern Books perhaps acted too hastily and emotionally in accepting [this] manuscript for publication," he wrote to the managing director. "I am not suggesting SB should 'give in' to 'moral blackmail' or that SB should only publish books which take the 'correct line' prescribed from outside. But to send the rest of the world to hell and 'publish and be damned' is even more inappropriate. I believe publishers should remain calm and make sure they can defend any publication on grounds acceptable to everybody, such as objectivity, fairness, independence and quality. It is my opinion that Southern Books would not be able to defend Jim Hooper's *Koevoet* on any of these counts."

His tantrum was a classic example of the Left's position on who should be allowed freedom of expression. It also demonstrated the "correct line" in attacking critics of communist-backed liberation movements that had never delivered the many rights promised in their manifestoes. And therein lay the rub, for it was precisely the methods employed by the South West Africa People's Organization (Swapo) which convinced me that its claims of fighting for "a just society" were no more than empty rhetoric for the benefit of a deluded Western audience; the same audience—freelance copy editor included—that closed its eyes to far greater injustices in other parts of Africa. Lies, ignorance and double standards trumped the truth. His high-minded efforts notwithstanding, the book became a bestseller.

Since *Koevoet* was first published much has changed in the old Imperial German colony of South West Africa. As a *quid pro quo* for the withdrawal of Cuban and Soviet bloc forces from Angola in 1989, South Africa agreed to elections under United Nations supervision. In compliance with UN demands, all South African Defence Force units were withdrawn from

Namibia, while the men I had accompanied were reduced to the role of lightly armed police, all to ensure there was no intimidation of pro-Swapo voters.

On April 1 1989, in violation of agreements signed by Swapo President Sam Nujoma, at least 1,500 heavily armed insurgents crossed from Angola to ambush unsuspecting Koevoet patrols. Despite being taken by surprise, the unit lived up to its reputation: in less than two weeks it had broken the back of the invasion, killing over 350 invaders and sending the survivors scurrying back to their UN-protected sanctuary. At the time, I was far to the north with Jonas Savimbi's Unita guerrillas, following the events on the BBC Africa Service. It wasn't until returning to South Africa that I learned that of the 23 Koevoet members who died defending the law, I had known most.

Although Nujoma won the elections on the basis of a tribal vote, revelations of Swapo atrocities against its own members clearly demonstrated a brutal and anti-democratic nature. Testimony by Namibian refugees returning from Angola left no doubt that Nujoma's liberation movement was responsible for the torture and murder of thousands of its own people in Swapo concentration camps. Curiously, few of those who railed against South Africa and supported Swapo over the years ever voiced any criticism, the majority preferring to remain ideologically deaf, dumb and blind to the facts. It is perhaps not surprising, therefore, that *Koevoet!* was judged by those same people as supporting apartheid and the South African occupation of Namibia. Nothing could be further from the truth; nothing I can say here will change that perception if the reader is so inclined.

A Swapo-majority government in an independent Namibia has now existed for over 20 years. Its victory was due not to any military prowess but the economic collapse of the Soviet Union, which had funded, trained, and encouraged Swapo since its birth. With the death of communism and the existential threat it posed to South Africa, Pretoria was ready to allow open elections. History is a ruthless judge of ideology. The belief in a one-party Marxist state once so cherished by Nujoma and his commissars has been replaced by *realpolitik* and the gradual realization that no political system offers greater freedom than democracy wedded to capitalism. One can but pray the lesson has been learnt and that Namibia's future remains hopeful.

Jim Hooper
England
November 2011

1
In Search of a War

Part I

Not yet a teenager when I discovered Hemingway, it struck me that here was a life worth emulating. Adventure, fame, adoring women—how could any boy not want all that? By the time I was 15 I'd tried my hand at a first novel, but found it such a daunting exercise that the typed pages were quietly filed away, never to be revisited. Though the dream of being a war correspondent and author remained, the road to my first book was long and marked by detours, potholes and no small degree of irony.

A reasonable place to begin might be my four-year army service and an addiction to jumping out of airplanes, which kicked the writing into second place. Starched fatigues and whitewall haircuts were replaced by the student's uniform of jeans and tie-dyed T-shirts at the University of South Florida, and weekends set aside as a skydiving instructor. With college degree in hand, I was hired as a documentary research-writer by WFLA-TV in Tampa, where I learned the basics of doing interviews, using a camera, and stringing words together.

Though interesting, it was so riven with petty feuds and jealousies that, when the position of full-time manager for Zephyrhills Parachute Center was offered, I deserted television without a backward glance. I eventually bought the business and, working 12- to 16-hour days, seven days a week, built it into the sport's Mecca, drawing skydivers from across the United States, Canada, and Europe. In 1981, I hosted a world championships attended by teams from 28 countries, including two whose ideological collision would lead indirectly to this book.

Three years later, I was ready to give up my bachelorhood, but the marriage proposal was met with an ultimatum: it was either her or the parachute centre. I chose her, foolishly as it turned out, for as soon as I found a buyer and sealed the deal, she took another road. In retrospect, I was a lucky man. Jobless, fiancée-less and with a tidy sum in the bank, the conditions were perfect to set off in pursuit of that boyhood dream. Where, I wondered, to start? A skydiving

Reuters bureau chief who had visited my drop zone from time to time supplied the fateful answer.

Africa, he said, plenty of small wars, with one side or another wanting its story told; but, he cautioned, finding a market in the United States would be difficult. Americans had little knowledge of the continent's 50-odd countries, and even less interest in what happened there. Europe, on the other hand, with its history of colonialism, was always hungry for updates on its former possessions.

In that case I'd move lock, stock and barrel across the Atlantic. The decision was easy. Over the previous decade I'd attended annual parachuting conferences in one European capital or another and seen enough to know I liked it. Friends and acquaintances, habitués of my now-former drop zone, were spread from Norway to Italy, and as an unabashed Anglophile, England would be my new home. I'd spend a few months being free and irresponsible while deciding the next step. The new adventure was beginning. The first two years would prove immensely frustrating, but an invaluable education.

Morocco came first, a half-hearted effort, to be truthful. Still, a disappointment on discovering that the Polisario Front was not only a spent force, but that the authorities kept outsiders well away. Even Casablanca, dusty and industrialized, was unsatisfactory; not a hint of Rick's Café or a whisper of intrigue, though a Belgian girlfriend with more than a passing resemblance to Audrey Hepburn (Ingrid Bergman would have been asking too much) made it bearable.

Back in her hometown of Brussels, someone suggested that the former French colony of Chad might be worth a look. Its president, Hissène Habré, had fallen out with his previous partner-in-crime, the equally gruesome Goukouni Oueddei. In a snit, Oueddei had aligned his tribe with nutcase Muammar Ghaddafi, who had long coveted Chad's uranium-rich Aouzou Strip. Paris had sent the Foreign Legion to protect French commercial interests and drive out the Libyans. At the same time, another anti-Habré group was making a nuisance of itself in the south, where government forces were hard at work murdering anyone suspected of supporting the rebels.

This sounded promising.

"I want to report on your president's heroic fight against Ghaddaffi," I explained in godawful approximate French to the doorman of the Chadian Embassy. Clearly surprised to hear anyone say a good word about one of the more unappealing tyrants in North Africa, he offered a chair—"*Un petit moment"* —and left me to gaze at the poster-size photo of his beloved leader. He returned with mint tea, took a seat beneath the portrait and rummaged through the drawers of the desk, laying out half-a-dozen rubber stamps. *"Voila!"* he cried triumphantly, waving the one he was looking for. Carefully aligning it with a page in my passport, he applied the visa with a certain élan. I never figured out if the doorman doubled as the visa officer, or vice versa. I was reminded helplessly of Evelyn Waugh's *Scoop*.

Two weeks later I was on a UTA Airbus droning over the Sahara, rereading the printed note given to me at the American consulate in Paris.

SUBJECT: TRAVEL ADVISORY—CHAD

1. THE DEPARTMENT ADVISES AMERICAN CITIZENS TO LIMIT TRAVEL TO CHAD TO ESSENTIAL PURPOSES AND TO CONSULT WITH THE U. S. EMBASSY IN NDJAMENA CONCERNING ANY TRAVEL WITHIN THE COUNTRY. AREAS OF CHAD CONTROLLED BY THE CHADIAN GOVERNMENT HAVE BEEN THE SCENE OF ARMED INFILTRATIONS AND SPORADIC TERRORIST INCIDENTS. EXPIRATION: INDEFINITE.

I returned to my new English-French dictionary, imagining myself accompanying Legionnaires on lightning raids against the rebels. As excerpts from my journal make clear, I was wildly optimistic.

14 November 1984 Been in N'Djamena three days now, most of it trudging from one seedy office to another. There was the Ministry of Information, then la Service Censure, Sureté, Tresor (to pay my journalist's tax) and finally being handed my first genuine press card, an essential accoutrement as it turns out. The very next day whilst firing off a few snapshots I was stopped by some humourless fellows with AK-47s wanting to know Who? and Why? and Where? was my Photographer's Special Authorization?

"Vous ètes Americain, monsieur?" one asked after a close examination of the document.

"Oui."

"Alors, connaissez vous Michael Jackson?"

"Non, monsieur" Brows furrowed and bottom lips grew as my inquisitor's eyes narrowed. An American? How could I not know Michael Jackson?

Something creative was called for. *"Mais je connais son frère très bien!"* I suddenly remembered.

Faces relaxed. I knew Michael Jackson's brother. My credibility as an American was established. *"Avez vous un petit cadeau pour nous?"* The "little gift" of a few greasy CFA francs I handed round was accepted with the gravity befitting my position.

The American Embassy was the next stop. After making my way through a cordon of gloomy US Marine guards—"This place has to be the asshole of the world"—I dutifully reported my presence. Started a bit of a panic when I mentioned that what I really wanted to do was go off with the army in search of rebels. "Oh, you can't do *that*," she said. "They won't let you do that." She grabbed a pencil and began making notes. "In fact, we would prefer you really didn't do that." She made some more notes. "You could become a consular case, and the consular officer really wouldn't like that."

Okay, then, I asked in my new role of questing journalist, what about some background? Immediately everything was all-smiles-and-helpful with charts of this and that and the other thing. "As you can see," she gushed, mouth shifting up in a jolly smile, "we are fully committed to providing emergency relief."

"What about military aid?"

"Minimal," she said. "Very minimal. As you can see from the fact sheets, our primary concerns are emergency relief and training schemes."

"And the official position on human rights?"

The smile downshifted to neutral. "I would say that's an internal affair," she said, shuffling her lists together. "Our policy is not to interfere in internal affairs." She looked at her watch. She really was quite busy.

Walking back to the hotel, I ducked as a US Air Force C-141 cargo plane, landing gear and flaps down, roared low overhead. I raced to the airport fence, but Chadian soldiers waved me away with shouts of, *"Pas de photos!"* Straight back to the embassy and a request to see Anyone In Charge. An un-amused official appeared. "What's on the 141 that just landed?" I asked.

An eyebrow lifted. He cleared his throat. "Thanksgiving turkeys."

17 November N'Djamena bears its wounds with a sort of mute resignation, like a burn victim sadly yet determinedly exhibiting the terrible disfiguration. There is not a single structure unmarked by gunfire. Some lie abandoned, others have struggled back to life, yet none escaped what was a senseless and savage punishment. Steel shutters and gates hang from their hinges in the 120-degree heat, sunlight streaming through hundreds of puckered holes. Even trees died from absorbing so many bullets.

Refugees squat in the dust, along with the lame, the blind and starving, beseeching passers-by. There's the shock of fingerless palms held out by a noseless leper. The few medical facilities are staffed almost exclusively by foreign doctors and nurses. One told me of outlying villages where five percent of the population under 12 years old was dying each week.

Drought has shrivelled the Chari River, its banks littered with human excrement down to the water's edge, where people bathe, drink handfuls of the muddy water and draw buckets of it for cooking. At the river's centre hippos stand like black rocks. A fisherman poled me out for a closer look, stopping about 50 feet from them and refusing to edge nearer the beady eyes and tiny flicking ears. When one made a move towards us, the captain backed us smartly towards the shore, describing in broken French how a friend was bitten in two by an irascible bull.

30 November Patrols begin perimeter checks outside the walls of the Hotel de Tchadienne an hour before sunset and stroll menacingly through the outdoor bar and restaurant. Like a frontier fort, the gates of N'Djamena swing shut at 9pm, and no one enters or leaves 'til the sun begins its next appointed round from the east.

As dusk gathers, tables and chairs are moved from the covered patio to under open sky. Coarse white table cloths sway with a touch of warm breeze. A thin fog of the finest dust haloes the lights. White faces of N'Djamena begin to appear—staff from the relief agencies, seismic engineers, bush pilots, French army officers and NCOs. They scatter amongst the tables, each group keeping jealously to itself. Voices are subdued in this sad oasis.

The whores, gathered in tight mahogany knots near the bar or on the shadowed periphery, flash come-hither smiles and giggle amongst themselves. The more haughty and beautiful stroll languidly between the tables of mostly men, hoping to catch a beckoning eye. At the stroke of 11pm, those without a customer for the night board a French army truck and are transported to the Foreign Legion's Camp Manta to offer their services at discounted rates.

10 December Something's in the wind. More French troops slipped into N'Djamena a few days ago. Yesterday, another C-141 landed and off-loaded what the US Deputy Chief of Mission admitted were "military spare parts for the Chadian army." The American embassy—described by the State Department as its number one hardship post—is a beehive of activity. Its first permanent defence attaché has arrived, reinforced walls are going up inside the chancellery, and spooky-looking guys with no necks come and go all the time.

The problem is that even celebrity French journalists are restricted to N'Djamena; they arrive confident of success, then give way to snarls and Gallic fury before returning to Paris. The Mitterand government has undoubtedly told Habré to keep the press cloistered, wanting no inconvenient stories about its support of a regime that, according to Amnesty International, is murdering captured rebels and suspected dissidents.

Chad is obviously not where I'm going to make my name as a war correspondent, so last week I visited the Sudanese Embassy to ask about covering their war against the Sudan Peoples Liberation Army. The ambassador fired off a message to his Ministry of Foreign Affairs describing me in fulsome tones. The answer came back this morning. I will be afforded every facility. Christmas in Khartoum.

Part II

25 December
And it all started so well.

The Ministry of Cultur [sic] and Information issued my "Special Permit For Taking Cinematograph and Still Camera." A very accommodating major at army headquarters briefed me on the war and promised a seat on a flight to its southern base at Malakal, where I would be attached to a frontline unit. Everything was set. What none of them knew, however, was that they had put me on a collision course with my own country. When I eventually discovered what lay behind it, I didn't know whether to feel smug for causing a panic, or pissed off at being denied a scoop.

In 1984, the world's attention was focused on Ethiopia. Heart-breaking television images and thousands of column-inches of newspaper stories had forced Western governments and humanitarian organizations to rush millions of tons of food to the Horn of Africa. Almost as much video and ink was given to the holier-than-thou Bob Geldof and other self-serving celebrities, who, like the media, refused to acknowledge that the famine had less to do with drought than the Stalinist policies of President Mariam Haile Mengistu. Nor was there mention of international aid being confiscated to feed his army, which, with the help of Soviet and Cuban advisors, was systematically murdering anyone opposed to Marxism-Leninism.

Among those escaping war and famine were Ethiopia's Falasha Jews. Persecuted by the communists for their refusal to collectivise, some 12,000 had left their ancestral lands, of which 8,000 survived to reach refugee camps in Sudan. Three weeks before my arrival, Operation Moses, the top secret evacuation of the Falashas to Israel by Mossad and its American counterpart had been launched, with the US Embassy in Khartoum as its command centre. The possibility that I might stumble onto the story was about to make me a pre-emptive target of the Central Intelligence Agency.

Having arrived with no cash, I headed to Citibank to draw some on my credit card, only to be told it was impossible. With the overthrow of President Jaafar Niemery a few months earlier, the new Islamist-centred government was imposing Sharia law. This included the Koranic injunction against charging interest, which meant I couldn't use my plastic. Okay, how about wiring money from England? Unfortunately, the telecomms dish through which all traffic passed was broken and unlikely to be working for another two weeks. "But," the Sudanese bank officer said helpfully, "the US Embassy has a commercial telex you can use. I believe they charge $15."

And away I went to ask for help from my country's representatives. After explaining my problem I was beckoned into an office dominated by a second secretary whose size could not be camouflaged by her extra-extra-large muumuu. I explained my dilemma and asked about the embassy's commercial telex.

"This," she said frigidly, dewlaps quivering, "is a United States Embassy, not a telecommunications centre for destitute Americans."

I nodded, smiled and accepted that she had undoubtedly dealt with such people during her distinguished diplomatic career. But I wasn't one of them. I had money. In England. An unfortunate combination of Sudan's new banking laws, coupled with Khartoum being cut off from the world, meant I couldn't get it. Thus my polite request to use the commercial telex.

"This," she repeated, in case I hadn't heard her the first time, "is a United States Embassy, not a telecommunications centre for destitute Americans."

I obviously hadn't explained the situation clearly. I tried again. There was not a flicker of comprehension. Looking over the top of horned spectacles, she repeated her mantra, then pushed an official form across the desk. "But we do make provisions for destitute American citizens. If you sign this we will loan you $200, but your passport will be endorsed for return to the United States only and you will surrender it on arrival."

One more time, from beginning to end. Islamic banking laws meant no cash on the card. Big dish down for maintenance, can't wire for money, of which there's ample in my account in England. Solution: embassy's commercial telex.

A fat finger tapped the official form, the other hand held out a pen. I tried counting her chins below the blubbery lips, reaching five before noticing earlobes pushed outwards by porcine jowls. It struck me she would have found favour amongst the Chari River hippopotamuses. At which point the Mood took me. It's a personal flaw, and one I really should work on. And though the Mood doesn't appear very often, when it does, there's no stopping impetuous remarks that might best be described as ill-advised.

"Fuck you, Fatso."

She shot to her feet faster than I would have thought possible. "You can't speak to me like that!"

"I just did, sweetheart," and strode out of her office, out of the embassy and back into the heat, dust and squalor of Khartoum. A taxi carried me to the university for an interview with a courtly professor on the war in the south.

When I returned to the Acropole Hotel, a letter on US State Department stationery awaited. Offering neither hint of our little contretemps nor explanation for the sudden *volte face*, it said that the embassy's commercial telex was available after all. The cost would be 15 US dollars or 30 Sudanese pounds. I could return at 9am the following day, but would first need to speak with the embassy's regional security officer.

Right on time, I made my way past the US Marine guards and was told to wait outside the office. Half an hour. An hour. The door opened. Mr. RSO motioned me in. "Sit down." He went to his desk and signed something. He picked up another paper and signed that too. He laid down his pen, fixed me with a scowl and—*Wham!*—let me have it with both barrels. "Abuse of my staff" was the subject, and every attempt to present my case was bulldozed aside. Just like my confrontation with Ms Hephalump, none of this made sense. I felt the Mood coming on, but strangled it: the letter said the commercial telex was available and there was a story waiting. Let's not burn the last bridge.

"What are you doing in Khartoum?" I told him. Flight to Malakal. Sudanese Army. Frontline reportage. "Who authorized this?" I gave him my contacts at the press office and army headquarters. He made notes. "I'm recommending you don't do this," he said. Fair enough; I appreciated his concern. "Let me rephrase that. I'm *telling* you not to do this. In fact, I'm going to call my Sudanese counterpart and request in the strongest terms, as a favour to the United States government, that you be denied all access to their military operations."

I'm not sure if my mouth dropped open, but I was certainly stumped for words. He wasn't finished. It got worse.

"Let me remind you that as a destitute American"—this was becoming extremely irritating—"you are an undesirable element in Sudan." He jabbed a finger at me. "My word carries some weight with the authorities here. So let me tell you this: two weeks in a Sudanese jail would not be fun."

From Ms Half-ton of 1984 to Herr I've-Got-You-By-the-Balls, it was clear I'd stumbled into a world that would have made Franz Kafka sit up and scratch his head. I considered calling his bluff, but to tell the truth, that part about jail got my attention.

"You can take the hard way or the easy way," he snarled. "The easy way is that there are daily flights from Khartoum to London."

Call me a coward, but the next day, 24 December 1984, I was on a British Airways 747 as it climbed over the Sahara. Bing Crosby was crooning *White Christmas*.

Part III

Back in England, I began commuting once a week to Oxford and the Bodleian Library of Commonwealth and African Studies. The focus of my research was the conflict in Sudan, which revolved around Khartoum's attempts to impose Sharia law on the Christian and animist southerners. Equally offensive were Muslim slave raids against the Dinka and Nuer tribes. Though the British had pretty much stamped out the practice by the time they ceded independence in 1956, the Koran's justification for it saw the raids quickly resumed. It was no coincidence that the Arabic slang for a black person was *abd*—slave.

There was also the issue of Sudan's vast reserves of oil, with most of the fields lying south of Malakal, a town, I noted ruefully, the fine folks at the US Embassy had prevented me visiting. Southerners were demanding both a share of the oil revenues and independence. Khartoum had no intention of granting either. With the basic facts in hand, I contacted the SPLA's political representative in London. Over coffee in a an East End café, he assured me that if I went to Nairobi the local office of the Sudan Peoples Liberation Movement would slip me across the Kenyan border into Sudan. I believed him, but then I still had a lot to learn.

Two weeks later, I was checking into the Stanley Hotel in Nairobi, just like my hero Ernest Hemingway 30 years previously. The next month was marked by promised meetings with self-claimed representatives of the SPLA and I grew accustomed to long waits in back street cafes, sipping coffee from fly-specked cups and being aware of intruding into all black enclaves. Occasionally a promised contact did appear, always hours late, slipping into the chair across from me and whispering in a conspiratorial rumble, "Hello, my brother," followed by tales of further outrages by the Khartoum government against the southerners and urged to "tell the world."

At the end of another fruitless day I stopped off at one of Nairobi's legendary watering holes, a gathering place for white farmers, bush pilots, hunters and rogues of various stripes. My despondent appearance was cause for guffaws and loud comments about green-bloody-Yanks stumbling around Africa for the first time.

But as the evening grew wetter and wetter I wondered aloud about trying to get to Sudan on my own, which saw me taken quietly aside and given the name of someone "who might be in town, knows southern Sudan like the back of his hand"; or another, speaking into his glass in a hollow monotone: "*This* chap, only you forgot who gave you his name, see, but *this* chap, well, he's still doing a bit of poaching—been at it donkey's years old Donald has up that way. You just ask old Donald and see if he might help you along. No guarantees, mind, but give 'im a try."

More late nights saw a plan take shape. Europeans had been doing it since Dr. Livingstone, my new-found friends pointed out. All I had to do was make my way through Uganda to the border town of Arua and then into Sudan, following an old coffee and ivory-smugglers' route. Once I made contact with the SPLA I'd rely on charm and bullshit to convince them that I was just the fellow to tell their story, rather than being thrown in a cage.

Next step was a visa. A meeting with the First Secretary of the Ugandan High Commission in Nairobi gave me the official line on the country's leader, President Milton Obote: dedicated to human rights, as attested to by his honorary Doctor of Law from Long Island University in America; the people's love for him; unprecedented political stability in spite of rebel attempts to overthrow the government. In order to report all these wonderful things, I said, I'd need a visa. He shook his head sadly. "Certain lies"—read: stories of wholesale murder by the Obote regime—told by various journalists, made that quite impossible. Perhaps if I were to return next week…

I placed my passport, a £20 note peeking coyly from its side, on his desk. "Of course, for esteemed journalists like yourself, we are pleased to make exceptions from time to time," stamping and initialling the fresh visa. "What paper did you say you worked for?"

Two days later, President Milton Obote was overthrown by his chief of staff, General Tito Okello. It was a typical African *coup d'etat*. It was very bloody. By extraordinary luck, I was sitting on the border when it happened. My first story was a front-page lead. Okay, it was a hometown paper, but it had a larger circulation than *The Times* of London, and it paid real money.

The Sunday TAMPA TRIBUNE
September 22, 1985
After the coup, traveller finds it's business as usual in Uganda

The civilian government of Ugandan President Milton Obote was toppled in a coup July 27. A day later, former Tampa resident Jim Hooper entered the country. In today's Tribune and Times, he recounts his observations of the aftermath.
By Jim Hooper

Dishevelled border police blinked their surprise between yawns and scratches. I was the first white they'd seen entering their country since the coup. Inside a dilapidated shack an immigration officer thumbed through my passport.

"American," he grunted. Did I realise I did not have the correct stamps? Sighing, he drew a sheaf of dusty papers from a drawer and gave them his most serious attention. He lifted his eyes to the 200 shillings I placed on his desk, then returned to his papers. I slid 300 more towards him.

"Journalist?" he frowned.

"Teacher," I answered a little too quickly.

"I am teacher also," he smiled, pocketing the money and carefully inking my passport. "This is not corruption," he added to further my education.

A mile's walk led me past another checkpoint to a cluster of dilapidated taxis. With 11 people crammed into space designed for less than half that number, we began the jolting ride to Kampala. Roadblocks appeared at regular intervals, each a de facto toll gate. At one stop a soldier sorted us by tribe, demanding to know mine as well. "Muzungu," I joked, using the

Swahili word for white. He slipped my passport into his pocket and turned to interrogate the others.

Two women were pushed to the side. Their ID cards were insufficient. He brusquely motioned the younger one to follow him into the bush. When they returned ten minutes later, she was allowed to rejoin the group. The older woman offered him 1,000 shillings. He waved it away. His devotion to duty was eased by 5,000 shillings. Turning to me, he explained I did not have the correct entry stamp. Five hundred shillings helped him find it.

"How do you liking Uganda, muzungu?" he asked. I assured him it was my favourite holiday spot.

During a two-hour stop in Jinja, east of Kampala, a shopkeeper described the fate of Obote's local party representative.

"They dragged him from his house where he was hiding. They took him to a bar and placed him on a table. Four soldiers held his arms and legs. They cut him in half with a tree saw. We could hear him screaming from very far away."

Another told me of a mass grave containing more than 1,000 bodies. "There are many, many more such places," he said. "Obote and Amin had many enemies."

Kampala was all rumours and empty, broken shop windows. Soldiers paced the sidewalks, passers-by stepping carefully from their paths. The few drivers were obliged to halt at each intersection to await demands for money and permission to continue. Nights were punctuated by bursts of gunfire. The Ugandan family with whom I was staying knew the way of African coups. They slept on the floor, out of the line of fire through the windows, and showed no lights. As the shooting became heavier and drew nearer, they included me in their plans for dealing with looters, who would be looking for money, food and women. If soldiers came to the door, they would tell them the power was out and lure them into the house with promises of providing everything. Once inside, we would kill them, then drag the bodies down the hillside into the bushes. At first light, we would leave Kampala. Each morning found me much relieved there had been no opportunity to put the plan to the test.

It was the consensus of all I met that they were better off without Obote, though few believed the new regime of General Tito Okello would improve their lot. Amazingly, many hoped for the return of Idi Amin. As an example of African racism, his expulsion from Uganda of the Asian merchant class was much admired, despite it crippling an already badly limping economy. Only Amin was strong enough to instil discipline in the army, which, they reminded me, killed only on his orders. His strong man image was bolstered by the murder of 100,000 to 500,000 Ugandans, compared to Obote's more modest 50,000.

A Ugandan journalist just released from one of Obote's prisons told me of its horrors. "When the guards were bored, they picked a prisoner and gave him two car tyres to hold. Then they made bets about which tyre came down first. The prisoner knew he must keep them in the air, because when one touched the ground, they cut off his foot on that side with an axe."

A chance encounter with an aid worker gained me a place on a truck carrying supplies to Arua, on the border with Sudan. Forty miles north of Kampala five soldiers walked onto the road. The truck rattled to a stop. "This is bad," the driver said. "These are the people of Obote."

We were waved out of the cab. My rucksack was opened and emptied. One demanded my RayBans. I handed them over and waited for their return, knowing that the prescription lenses would make the world a blur for him. He yanked them off, examined the lenses against the sky, smashed them on the end of his AK47 and slipped the empty frames back on his face.

"Money," he said. I pulled a wad of Kenyan schillings from my pocket. Another of the soldiers shouted and pointed back down the road. A vehicle raced towards us ahead of a plume of dust. Without a word, all five turned and ran into the bush. A mutatu—African taxi van—overflowing with passengers and luggage roared past, people waving and laughing. Before the dust had settled we had we reversed course for Kampala. Sudan could wait.

Heading east through the interminable roadblocks towards Busia, I remembered a Ugandan I had met at the dusty border crossing two weeks earlier. He had fled when the coup was announced, and now waited for his wife on the Kenyan side of the 50-foot no-man's strip between the two countries. He told me of finding his home gutted and wife gone in the wake of the soldiers.

"This change will not bring law or an end to the killing. This Okello was doing the killing for Obote. He stole money from your aid programs to build his own village and pay his own army to protect him there. When will you Europeans understand that, here, there is no law? But you will soon say all is normal again in my country, and you will continue giving money.

This only makes bad people rich and keeps them in power. Why do you not understand this?"

When I finally arrived at the border and bribed my way through the immigration officer and police, I looked for the fellow. He was not there. Perhaps he found his wife. I hope so. Perhaps someday he will find his peace.

Another night in the Nairobi watering hole, where my tale of woe was the source of considerable merriment. "You're not in any ruddy Yoo-Ess-of-Aye, bwana!" shouted one sun-baked Kenya cowboy in bush shorts and sweater, slapping my back with a ham-size palm. There was a timber-shaking roar of laughter at the expense of this neophyte Africa-watcher, who was desperately trying to draw a breath. Solicitous hands leaned me against the bar and shoved a beer in my face, the accepted cure for most known ailments.

One wag, well acquainted with Uganda and who "wouldn't go back for half the bloody coffee shambas in East Africa," suggested my return in one piece was proof Someone Up There was watching over me. Which demanded another round of Tusker beer and a solemn toast to Someone Up There for delaying my early demise. This prompted suggestions of alternative routes and contacts for Sudan, and another toast to Alternative Routes and Contacts that might, after all, *hasten* my departure from this earth. Good basic types these Kenya lads.

And then in a replay of the month before, a possible new plan. "Chap I know, he has these friends. Don't know 'em myself, only heard about 'em. Run the odd load up through the N.F.D. into Sudan, no visas, no import-export, sweet eff-all and no questions asked sort of thing if you get my drift. You'd just be part of the cargo. Want me to ask if he'll put you in touch?"

Which is how I found myself on the terrace of the Stanley Hotel, with a coffee, a copy of *The Snows of Kilimanjaro* and waiting for two smugglers.

On the loading area next to the terrace, tourists posed proudly in new safari jackets festooned with bullet loops and bush hats circled with genuine fake leopard skin. Zebra-striped vans collected them in relays for a drive through the game reserve just outside the city. At an adjacent table a portly Stewart Granger-hopeful was trying to calm his wife, who was not overly eager to find herself face-to-face with "elephants and lions and things. I mean, they're not in cages or anything."

Two attractive and dusky ladies asked if they might join me. One primly introduced herself as Jeanette. "And this is Pamela," she said, opening a hand as though presenting a rare and delicate flower. Secretaries, they said in unison, explaining that they'd been accepted by "a university in America to study medical science." Unfortunately, they did not have the fare to America. Did I know anyone who could help them?

Sadly, I did not.

Jeanette's mother was "verry, verry ill," while Pamela's brother was desperately in need of an operation. Perhaps I knew someone who could help *them?*

Alas, no.

Jeanette began to writhe to the canned music. The 2000 Club was just a short walk, and perhaps we could go dancing. She loved to dance, she said, especially with American men, they were such good dancers.

I shamefully admitted I wasn't much of a dancer.

Pamela wondered if I would like to come over to their apartment to listen to music and have a few drinks. They liked meeting American men and wanted to make them feel at home in Kenya. Really at home, if I knew what she meant, leaning over to display considerable cleavage.

I was spared further offers of hospitality by a group of sun burnt Germans who settled noisily at the far end of the terrace. My new-met Florence Nightingales had a quick look in their compact mirrors and wandered towards the newcomers without a backward glance. I returned to Hemingway.

The shadows had lengthened along Kimathi Street. More working girls in high heels and mini-skirts paraded slowly back and forth on the pavement, but no sign of anyone who did business in Sudan. I looked at my watch. Three hours late. I motioned for the bill.

As I stood, two men took the chairs recently warmed by the aspiring doctors. The shorter one wore a T-shirt emblazoned with DALLAS COWBOYS, the other an expensive safari jacket. I wondered uncharitably how many ill relatives they had.

"Hello, brother. A friend have told to us you are interested to visit Sudan perhaps."

I retook my seat.

"A friend have speak to you about us, I think," said the taller one with the pockmarked face. "We are businessmen who do a little business in Sudan. Of course, this is a verry difficult and verry expensive business," he mused, looking round the terrace.

"For this, brother, we charge only 300 English sterling pounds," Dallas Cowboy said. "As you can see, it is not so much for so long a trip as to Sudan. Also, we have verry, verry many expenses."

"One hundred pounds," I said. "Fifty when we leave, 50 when we arrive."

A long silence indicated a new friendship in trouble. The pocked one flashed a gold tooth and said I should be ready to leave the next afternoon.

The next afternoon came and went with no sign of my new brothers. As did the next and the one after that. Two weeks later, I squeezed into the back seat of a battered Landcruiser. I had to admire the original, unaltered paint scheme. In the best traditions of covert capitalism, the old Toyota was resplendent in the faded colours of the International Red Cross.

Shortly after dusk the next day, we stopped in the middle of nowhere to eat and get a few hours' sleep. DC hunkered next to me. Pocked Face followed suit in front.

"Listen, brother, I think it is better you give us the other 50 English pounds now, perhaps. At the border the police or army make sometimes trouble, so it is necessary to give them a little gift, perhaps. We have never helped a white brother to visit Sudan, so perhaps there will be some little problems. With English money, I think, perhaps, there will be not so much problems. It is not so necessary for you to worry," he added, cutting off my protest, "We know these police for such a long time, it is not a problem with English money. Do not worry. You are our brother."

Pocked-Face nodded solemnly to emphasize this truth. Hardly comfortable with the turn of events, I handed over the money. Dallas Cowboy nodded. "Thank you, brother. Tomorrow we are in Sudan. For you that is verry, verry good, perhaps."

Wrapping myself in a poncho and with my rucksack a pillow, I stretched out and stared at the stars. My sense of unease was finally lulled by the snores of the other two. I closed my eyes. The sound of an engine starting jerked me awake. I scrambled to my feet and saw the Toyota moving. "Hey!" I shouted, thinking confusedly that they were forgetting me. "HEY!" I shouted again, throwing the poncho aside. There was a grinding in the worn gearbox and the Landcruiser accelerated. Unbelieving, I stared as the tail lights receded to pinpoints, and disappeared. I stood there, mouth open in disbelief, before concluding, in fact, they *had* left me. I walked back to my rucksack, sat down, stood and screamed, "You sons of bitches, COME BACK HERE!" And some other things.

With morning, I faced the sun and began walking. A pickup truck appeared behind me. It slowed and stopped alongside. The blond driver was heading to Lodwar for supplies. Did I want a ride? "Christ, yes," I said before seeing the wooden missionary's cross at his neck.

As we rattled along the rocky road he looked over. "It is not so good to walk here."

"Yeah? Why not?"

"Lions."

I decided I'd had enough of Africa for a while.

2

Hypocrisy and Contradictions

The piece on Uganda had legs and, suitably tweaked, appeared in other publications "Why," I asked in later versions, "has the horror of mass graves filled with half-a-million of Idi Amin and Milton Obote's victims received so little attention in the international media? Why are there no human rights activists demonstrating in front of the Ugandan High Commission in London?" An apologist for the continent accused me of racism and cultural bias for even posing the question. Africa belonged to the blacks and they could do as they pleased in their own lands. The real human rights violations, she said, were being committed by whites in South Africa—forced removals, no political voice, institutionalised segregation. That's where I should be reporting from.

Which was somewhat prescient of her, for that was precisely where I planned to head next. I already had a tenuous connection to the country through skydiving. The championships I'd hosted five years earlier had seen the South African Springbok team at the centre of a geopolitical storm covered by every major news organization in America. I should have anticipated the problem two years previously in Paris, when, immediately after the International Parachuting Commission accepted my bid to run the championships, the Chinese delegate asked if I planned to allow South Africa to compete. I explained that, as a member of the international body, they had every right to attend. At the following IPC meeting in England—still ten months prior to the championships—he asked again and received the same answer.

The end of that conference saw Richard Charter, the South African head of delegation, ask a favour. He'd purchased an airplane destined for Pretoria and needed a co-pilot. Would I be willing? A week later I was in the right seat of the twin turbo-prop Skyvan on the way from Northern Ireland to France, Corsica, Corfu, Heraklion on Crete, and a long leg to Luxor in Egypt. The Skyvan's wheels next touched down in Khartoum, followed by Addis Ababa, Nairobi, and Harare. Five days after departing Belfast, Pretoria's Wonderboom airport appeared on the horizon.

With so much needing my attention back home, I had only a few days in the country. But that brief visit brought me face to face with South Africa's apartheid laws. That the philosophy behind them was contrary to every Western sense of justice could not be disputed. Penalizing a man for the colour of his skin was more than immoral, it was illogical and stupid. Yet what I had just seen in Sudan, Ethiopia, Kenya and Zimbabwe left me puzzled. The grinding poverty, corruption and oppression in those countries seemed far greater than what I saw in South Africa, but I'd read no condemnations of those black governments. Never a particularly deep thinker, I put it all to one side and enjoyed the hospitality of my hosts, before grabbing a commercial flight back to America.

As the date for the championships approached there was enormous media interest in the Chinese, who would be making their first appearance in international competition. When the team landed in Tampa, a scrum of reporters was waiting. Interviews with the head of delegation, a short and stocky general, went out on every major network, and newspapers around the country took copy from the wire services. A major sports-wear company that had come on board as a sponsor was delighted by the publicity.

Three days before the meet started a cabal, led by the Canadian delegate, took me aside. You have to ban the Springboks, they insisted, otherwise the Chinese will leave, and they're far more important than the South Africans. Even the executive director of the US Parachute Association reminded me that the sponsorship money, which ensured I'd at least break even on the championships, would be lost if I didn't come to my senses. The next morning, the general and his interpreter were waiting for me. Standing to one side, Charter and the Springboks looked on helplessly: they'd been barred from the World Cup in France three years before at the insistence of the Soviets and knew what to expect.

The general followed me into my office. Ban the South Africans, he demanded, or we withdraw immediately. I thought it a bit rich for the representative of an oppressive, one-party Stalinist regime to be lecturing me on human rights. That, combined with the breathtakingly hypocrisy of those who supported the Chinese demand, saw the Mood take me. As much as I wanted to, a modicum of diplomacy prevented me telling the general to go fuck himself. The interpreter managed the first part of my answer easily—"The South Africans stay"—but struggled with—"Don't let the door hit your ass on the way out."

It was a bull-headed decision that cost me a pile of money. It would also have consequences I couldn't possibly have foreseen.

Five years had passed since that brief appearance on the international stage, two since giving up my lofty position in the skydiving world and moving to England. My first tentative steps through Africa had taken me nowhere near the adventure I was seeking, nor any closer to the book I wanted to write. I found myself becalmed, wondering where to steer next. As luck would have it, an article in one of the London papers caught my eye. Datelined Windhoek, the capital of South West Africa/Namibia, it reported a fight between communist-backed insurgents and units of the South African security forces.

I was vaguely aware of the low-intensity bush war taking place there, but had never managed to keep the details in my head. As far as this one went, little had appeared in the press beyond accusations of South African brutality and brief South African claims of having killed so many Swapo insurgents (and who the hell were they?) for the loss of so many of their own forces. I remembered stories from the Springboks, all of whom were reservists in the South African Defence Force, about the combat jump some of them had made into a place called Cassinga in Angola. Why hadn't I thought of this before now?

Rehearsing what I hoped would be a persuasive argument, I arrived at Trafalgar Square in London one winter's day and made my way through the cluster of sullen protesters outside the South African embassy. Inside, I was led upstairs to an appointment with the defence attaché, Colonel Rob Crowther. After a frosty introduction, I explained that I wanted to cover the SADF in Namibia. Crowther listened stonily and then asked what I knew of Africa in general and his country in particular. I outlined my previous travels through the continent and a skydiving trip to South Africa in 1981.

"As you probably know," said Crowther, slowly turning a pencil end over end, "foreign journalists are not exactly the flavour of the month."

I could see it coming. Sorry, chum, but no dice.

"All I can do is forward your request to the Department of Foreign Affairs in Pretoria. That's no guarantee that it will be approved. They're a little sensitive about allowing more journalists into the country at the moment." The beefy Afrikaner stood to indicate the meeting was over. "We'll let you know."

Six weeks later, Crowther and his tall, immaculately dressed air attaché, Colonel George van Niekerk, rose smoothly as I was escorted into the fifth floor office overlooking Admiral Nelson's monument. After a few minutes of small talk, the stolid army officer asked if I was still serious about covering the bush war in South West Africa. Yes, I nodded. "In that case, you'll be pleased to hear that your request has been approved. I'll send a message today, and Defence Force Headquarters in Pretoria will begin organizing a tour of the operational area."

I asked about censorship.

"As far as clearing whatever you write about the SADF, for security reasons we would prefer to have a look before publication. But we won't insist on it. Obviously, you could write whatever you want once you're outside the country. All we ask is that you tell the story fairly and with a bit of balance."

Crowther walked me to the door of his office.

"Don't expect everyone to welcome you on our side. We know we still have serious problems in our country that need to be resolved, but the international media haven't helped the situation. Instead of reporting the reforms that have been made, they've concentrated almost exclusively on apartheid and violence. And damned seldom have they made comparisons between human rights in South Africa and other countries in Africa."

"What we're saying," interjected van Niekerk, "is that we don't expect you to write that everything is fine. We know better than you that it isn't. So we're not going to throw you out for being critical. Just be honest about what you see, without distorting the facts or taking things out of context."

I left England on Zambian Airways a week later for the 11-hour flight to Lusaka. At Kenneth Kaunda International airport, passengers in transit were directed to a large, glass-fronted lounge.

I stood in front of the floor-to-ceiling windows, overlooking the runway. A shiny Mercedes-Benz limousine passed below, an East German flag fluttering on the front of it. It stopped next to a small Soviet-built passenger jet and an entourage of blacks and whites emerged to board the aircraft. I snapped a photo of the scene.

"I'd put that away if I were you, mate," someone said in a rich Australian accent. I looked around. Stretched out on a couch, a fellow traveller lifted his head and stroked a luxurious moustache. He slowly scanned the lounge. "They catch you, the least they'll do is confiscate your cameras. Around here only spies take pictures of airports and East German diplomats."

I slipped the camera into its bag.

After an eight-hour layover in the Zambian capital, I connected with a South African Airways flight. ("You mean that Zambia, one of the Frontline

States, allows the South African national airline to land there?" I had asked the travel agent. "Sure, why not?" she said.)

Pretoria hardly seemed a city under siege. Contrary to what I had seen on television or read in newspapers, there were not police on every street corner, attack dogs straining at their leashes. Instead, working-class blacks and whites mingled along the crowded sidewalks, while well-dressed black businessmen strolled shoulder to shoulder with white colleagues and shared tables in expensive restaurants. Where was the open racial hatred the media had told me about?

Dinner with Richard Charter and his wife Janet allowed us to catch up on what had happened since we last met in Florida. When I laid out my plans, he revealed that one of his companies manufactured parachutes and web gear for the South African Defence Force. "I'll make some phone calls," he said.

My initial meeting with Colonel Tim Krynauw at the SADF Media Liaison Section started off a little tensely, underscoring the complaints I'd heard in London.

"We've really gone out of our way in this office to accommodate the press by showing them all sides of the situation here," said Krynauw, "and all they've done is kick us in the teeth by reporting only the negative part. Make no mistake, there's enough of the negative if that's what someone wants to present as the only truth, but it's hard to have any trust in the so-called objectivity of the international media.

"In any case, I believe you want to do some stories about what's going on up on the border. That's being organized. But before getting you out there, we thought you might want to spend some time getting background information on the defence force here. In the meantime, if there's anything you're especially interested in, let me know."

The next few weeks went by in a whirl of side trips and interviews. One of my first excursions was to a black SADF unit at Messina, near the Zimbabwe border.

"We're essentially a quick-reaction counterinsurgency unit," said Commandant Peter Rose as we walked across the compound of the old copper-mining company. Soldiers were hammering, painting and clearing rubbish as the site was being converted into a new headquarters for the black 116 Battalion.

"This is a favourite infiltration route for ANC terrorists. They've been coming across from Zimbabwe recently to plant land mines on the roads near the border. Their aim is to chase out the white farmers along the Limpopo

River. The first victim was a black farm worker. Since then, they've killed a dozen other people. Practically an entire family was wiped out in one mine incident.

"Because the people in this area are North Sothos, we thought an SADF unit composed of the same tribe would be the most effective. So far, it seems to be working. When they see their own people in uniform being treated just like any white member of the defence force, it has a very positive effect. Without the support of the locals, terrorists have a far more difficult time of it."

I said I hadn't realised blacks were conscripted into the army.

"No non-white is conscripted in South Africa," Rose said. "They're all volunteers. And there are enough of them that we can be fairly choosy about who we take. We're still a fairly new unit, so all our company commanders and platoon leaders are still white. But most of the NCOs are Sothos, and we've just commissioned our first Sotho lieutenant, who serves as the unit's supply officer. In order to integrate our personnel more effectively, we have language classes every week for the whites. A Sotho instructor teaches the classes, and I require every white in the battalion to learn a minimum of 500 North Sotho words a year. Aside from possibly saving someone's life someday, I believe it's a matter of respect for the people you serve with."

Rose pointed at the buildings under renovation. "The first thing we planned was suitable barracks for the men and quarters for our married NCOs," he explained. "You'll find no difference between what we'll have here and those for a white unit. The same standards apply for everyone."

So why doesn't it extend to the rest of South African society? I wondered.

Rose knocked on the back door of a freshly painted bungalow. A black woman with a baby on her hip opened the door and Rose introduced her as the wife of one of his senior non-commissioned officers. She invited us in and proudly showed me a home that would have compared favourably with those supplied to an NCO in any Western army. Sitting at the kitchen table and listening to Rose ask about her house and baby was a scene full of contradictions.

Returning that afternoon to the shabby motel, I walked into the bar. A large and muscular woman behind the bar turned her back as I took a stool. Finally she faced me and asked what I "needed."

Setting the drink down with a bang, she snarled in a strong Afrikaans accent, "So why are you writing shit about South Africa?"

Somewhat taken aback, I said I hadn't written anything yet. She wasn't appeased. "We know your kind here, and we don't want your kind. Go back where you came from and leave us alone. We know how to deal with our blacks. We don't need you damned *journalists*"—the word dripped with venom—"coming here and making things worse." I started to explain that until I had a better idea of what was happening in the country... "Listen," she interrupted, "I know people who can come over here and take care of you."

Setting down my drink, I politely excused myself and walked out. Verligte—enlightened—thinking had not filtered down to some elements in the Northern Transvaal. I had already heard that it was a hotbed of white nationalism, with many open supporters of the Ku Klux Klan-like Afrikaner Resistance Movement. The next morning, I wasn't sorry to put Messina and that motel behind me.

In Cape Town, a special request to visit the South African Cape Corps was granted. One of the oldest units in South Africa—its members claim it is the oldest—the SACC was composed almost exclusively of Coloured (mixed-race) South Africans. The contradiction of non-whites volunteering for military service to defend a system that denied them a political voice was something I found difficult to comprehend. Was it a perverse anomaly, or was the apparently easy integration of black and white in the SADF a portent of things to come? Sitting behind his desk, Colonel Graham Jacobs, the second in command, clasped hands across a flat belly and explained how far things had progressed within the military.

"Up until the time I was commissioned, a white national service private could ignore orders from a non-white sergeant or warrant officer. And here I was, about to become a commissioned officer, and it was going to be the same thing. I have to tell you, it wasn't a situation I was looking forward to.

"See, I was part of the first group of Coloureds to be commissioned, and we were definitely planning to make an issue of this. We had gone through the same selection courses white officers were required to complete. And on top of that, we were volunteers, not like the whites, who by law have to serve. We were asking to be allowed to defend our country. It wasn't right that a white private should be able to ignore our orders or to actually order us around.

"Fortunately, before we completed our officer's course, the law was changed. The day I received my commission as a lieutenant in the South African Defence Force from then-Minister of Defence, P.W. Botha, was the proudest day of my life. And I've never looked back."

I asked if he had difficulty attracting new recruits.

"We've just been authorized by Parliament to form another battalion within the Cape Corps. When the news about this got out to Civvie Street, we had three times more applications than places available. Even for normal recruitment—finding new kids to replace those who have finished their two-year contract in the SACC—we have them queued up and waiting."

How much racism did he still find in the Defence Force?

"Listen, you don't change a leopard's spots overnight. Of course you still find it, though far less in the military than outside. Some of our young officer cadets have gone through rough times at the infantry school at Oudtshoorn, where they train alongside white cadets. For the good ones, the tough ones, it just makes them that much more determined to succeed.

"And I'm not saying they have problems with all, or even the majority, of white officer cadets. It's actually a minority of them. You know, a few years ago I visited your military academy at West Point, and the American black cadets there said it was the same: a minority of whites who didn't like them just because they were black.

"My own opinion is that integration within the SADF is one of the best things to have happened in this country. When a white troopie up in the operational area in South West Africa finds himself sleeping side by side with a Coloured or a black in the bush, eating out of the same mess tin, depending on each other in combat—well, when he comes back, there's bound to be an attitude change. He's been educated in the real world."

3

Colonizers, Revolutionaries and Churchmen

As the flight to Windhoek moaned steadily over the Kalahari, I ordered a whiskey and soda and dropped the seat-back tray in front of me. Pulling out the collection of files, I settled into reviewing the history of the country I was heading towards.

Hardly unusual in terms of African tribal and political complexities, South West Africa/Namibia was as intriguing as it was little known. Since Diogo Cão planted his cross on the barren Skeleton Coast in 1484, parts of this vast and sparsely populated land had seen Portuguese, Dutch, British, German and South African explorers, colonizers and administrators. Over the years they had been allied with, occasionally at war against, often simply ignored by, the indigenous Ovambos, Kavangos, Hereros, Caprivians, Tswanas, Damaras, Namas and Bushmen.

Less than a year after the outbreak of the First World War, South African forces captured German South West Africa and proclaimed it the South West African Protectorate. In 1920, the League of Nations formally confirmed the country as a "C" Mandate to be governed as an integral part of the Union of South Africa, then part of the British Commonwealth.

Following the Second World War, the new United Nations charter ended the mandate system and established an international trusteeship on a voluntary basis. When the Union of South Africa refused to surrender South West Africa to the United Nations, the issue was submitted to the International Court of Justice (ICJ), which ruled that Pretoria should continue its administration of the territory under the terms of the original mandate.

In 1960 Ethiopia and Liberia instituted proceedings against South Africa over the South West Africa issue. In 1966 the ICJ judged that neither Ethiopia nor Liberia had the necessary legal right or interest in the matter and rejected their claims. In 1971, however, a reconstituted ICJ decided that South Africa was illegally occupying the country. This claim was rejected out of hand by Pretoria as being both illegal and illogical.

Apart from its commanding geo-strategic position in the era's increasingly hot Cold War, the mineral wealth of the country was a crucial factor in South Africa's economic health. Most important were the off-shore alluvial fields, which constituted a major source of the world's diamonds. There were also rich deposits of uranium, lead, zinc, tin, silver, and tungsten, as well as profitable gold mines. There could be no question of Pretoria relinquishing its hold.

The liberation movement that prompted Western demands for change was one of many that sprang up throughout Africa in the 1950s. First founded as the Ovambo People's Congress in 1958, the South West Africa People's Organization officially came into being in 1960. By 1962 Swapo, under the leadership of Sam Nujoma and funded by the USSR, began recruiting fellow tribesmen for guerrilla warfare and sabotage. These young men were sent to the Soviet Union, China, Algeria, Ghana and Tanzania for training.

In 1966, a unit of Swapo's military wing, the People's Liberation Army of Namibia (PLAN), made its first cross-border infiltration from the Portuguese colony of Angola to establish a base camp in northern Namibia. The local Ovambo people reported its existence to the South African Police, and on August 26 of that year, the first shots of the bush war were fired.

Both Lisbon and Pretoria were agreed that the Soviet Union's support for anti-colonial insurgents constituted a serious economic and political threat. Portugal's colonial army, made up mostly of resentful and demoralized conscripts, was already fighting three Soviet- or Chinese-backed guerrilla movements in Angola, and another in Mozambique. As a result, its ability to control the thousands of square miles bordering on South West Africa— which, with its primitive infrastructure, they called "The Land at the End of the Earth"—was limited.

For the South Africans, the threat intensified when a communist junta seized power in Lisbon and declared that Portugal's colonies would be granted independence. Though paying lip service to the democratic process, the junta pre-empted elections by recognizing the Soviet-backed MPLA as Angola's new government.[1] With the withdrawal of Portugal's colonial army in 1975 and the immediate support of the new Marxist regime by thousands of Cuban troops, Swapo established permanent bases in southern Angola. Taking advantage of Cuban, Soviet and East German instructors and virtually unlimited supplies of East bloc weapons, PLAN began preparations for larger-scale operations.

---

1   Movimiento Popular de Libertação de Angola—People's Movement for the Liberation of Angola

Still, as late as 1977, South African and South West African security forces referred to the conflict as the "corporals' war," a reference to the highest-ranking member of the standard ten-man border patrols. On October 27 of that year, however, the situation changed dramatically when PLAN sent a 100-man unit across. In a three-day running fight, 61 insurgents were killed for the loss of five members of the SADF.

Although this would not warrant more than a footnote to accounts of larger conflicts, for the security forces the implications were clear: Swapo was preparing to escalate the bush war. The conventional response would have been to increase its forces along the border. But unconventional tactics and strategy have been the hallmarks of the Afrikaners' military thinking since the Anglo-Boer wars at the turn of the 20th century. Rather than waiting for the incursions, the South Africans decided to hit their enemy where they trained and planned their infiltrations. In May 1978 the SADF launched Operation Reindeer, a surgical airborne assault against Cassinga, Swapo's operational headquarters 250 kilometres inside Angola. The operation was spectacularly successful, and Swapo lost many experienced PLAN members among the 600 dead. In its aftermath, Nujoma claimed that Cassinga was a refugee camp and that the dead and wounded were all non-combatants.

Subsequent punitive and pre-emptive cross-border operations by SADF and South West Africa Territory Force (SWATF) units followed. Each was successful to varying degrees, and substantial quantities of East bloc equipment were captured and returned to Namibia. In the course of one operation in 1981, two Soviet lieutenant colonels were killed and a Soviet warrant officer captured when a joint Swapo-Angolan army base was overrun by the SADF's elite 32 Battalion.

The effect of these well-planned attacks was twofold: not only were large numbers of experienced insurgents killed, but bases and logistical infrastructure so severely disrupted that Swapo was forced to move its bases farther from the Namibian border. Under conditions of great secrecy, SADF and SWATF units remained in southern Angola to intercept insurgents on their way south. Although this interdiction strategy was probably less than 50% effective, it substantially reduced the number of PLAN fighters reaching Namibia, where specialized counterinsurgency units dealt with those who slipped through the net.

The political landscape was less straightforward. In 1978, the United Nations passed Security Council Resolution (SCR) 435, which called for UNsupervised elections. Under pressure from the Non-Aligned Movement, whose anything-but-non-aligned members were ideologically closer to Moscow than the West, the UN Security Council refused to grant observer status to any party other than Swapo during proceedings on the Namibian question. The United Nations' insistence on recognizing only Swapo and none of the other parties in Namibia meant there was little probability of free and fair elections ever occurring under UN supervision. Excluded from the debate, the South Africans refused to accept the conditions of the resolution. Their country faced an existential threat from communism, and the spectre of yet another Soviet-backed, anti-South African country along its borders sent Pretoria's political strategists to the drawing boards.

At the end of 1978, South Africa startled outsiders and further complicated the situation by holding elections without UN involvement. In spite of its invitation to participate, Swapo chose to boycott the process. A multi-party conference made up of elected representatives eventually led to the creation of the multiracial Democratic Turnhalle Alliance (DTA), which took control after the elections. This gave a degree of administrative control to the various minority parties as well as to representatives of all the tribal groups in Namibia. The United Nations, still backing Swapo as the "sole and authentic representative of the Namibian people," refused to recognize the legitimacy of the new government.

The first Namibian National Assembly formed from the 1978 elections eventually collapsed as a result of bitter infighting among the eight political parties. It was replaced with a South African administrator general. Before being dissolved, however, the infant government passed sweeping anti-apartheid laws. The government died a premature death, but the new laws survived.

In 1985, Pretoria, eager to take the edge off UN demands, allowed a transitional government of black and white Namibians to be seated, but on its own terms. Those political leaders elected in 1978 were installed as ministers and assembly members by the South Africans. One of the new ministers, Andreas Shipanga, previously had been Swapo's minister of information before being arrested and jailed in Tanzania by Swapo president Sam Nujoma.

In 1983, SADF and SWATF forces withdrew from Angola after an agreement with the Angolan Marxist government that Fapla[2], the Angolan

---

2   Fapla—Forças Armadas de Popular de Libertação de Angola—People's Armed Forces for the Liberation of Angola.

army, would cease all support for Swapo. Within weeks of the withdrawal, however, PLAN insurgents were again using Fapla bases not only as supply depots, but as staging points for infiltrations into Namibia.

Unwilling to expose itself to further international criticism, South Africa clamped a news blackout on the conflict and re-established bases in Angola, which were secret in name only. If the Angolan government was unwilling to abide by its agreement to deny support to Swapo, Pretoria was equally unwilling to wage a limited and strictly defensive counterinsurgency war. Further, those security force units tasked with patrolling the Namibian side of the frontier were authorized to cross the border in hot pursuit of fleeing insurgents. Although the details of the conflict were little understood by outsiders, it soon became a minor *cause célèbre* among Western liberals.

The echoes of those first shots in 1966 were still being heard when I arrived in Windhoek on a hot April morning in 1986. As I ducked out of the still-cool airliner with my camera bags and clumped awkwardly down the steps, I had no idea that I was on my way to seeing the bush war more closely than had any other Western journalist in its 20-year history.

At army headquarters in Windhoek, a South African sergeant escorted me to the press liaison officer. Major Zorro Kariko was not having a good day. He had lost a German television crew. They were supposed to be at the airport right now for a flight to the operational area. The driver who had been sent to pick them up at the Kalahari Sands Hotel couldn't find them. They'd gone shopping for souvenirs. He was on the telephone, saying that he'd looked everywhere. The flight crew was calling from the airport to say they didn't give a damn who they were, they had a schedule to keep.

"What tribe are you from?" I asked, pencil poised.

Kariko's eyes narrowed. "Take the phone!" he shouted to the white lieutenant in the adjacent office. He dropped the receiver into its cradle and gave me the look my question deserved.

"Black Namibian," he said slowly. "Next?"

"Well, as a…uh, black Namibian, how do you feel about white South Africa's control of your country?" Incisive, right to the heart of things.

He sighed and looked at the ceiling. I'm sure he didn't roll his eyes; he just looked at the ceiling. They lowered to me.

"How much of Africa have you seen?"

"Well, a bit of it," I said.

"So have I. So let me tell you that I'll take the present situation for the time being, rather than see us turned into another Angola or Mozambique." He leaned forward and placed both forearms solidly on his desk. "Of course, I was only born here, so obviously I don't know as much as the foreign press. You always let us know what's best for us, don't you?"

Things hadn't started off at all well.

"I understand Swapo maintains an office here in Windhoek," I said. "I'd like to get their side of the story. Can you give me their address or phone number?"

Kariko cleared his throat and thumbed through his Rolodex file. He scribbled on a slip of paper. "These are the two people who run their office here. Give them a call and see what they have to say. I'll be surprised if they agree to speak with you. Unless you're on their approved list, they're not too eager to give interviews.

I stopped in the lobby of the Kalahari Sands Hotel and rang the first number Kariko had given me and asked Danny Tjongarero for an interview.

"I don't think so. I'm quite busy writing a report at the moment. I won't have any time free until next week. You can call my colleague, Mr. Nico Bessinger, and ask him."

Replacing the receiver, I dialled the second number. Bessinger's response was the same: he was far too busy working on a financial report to grant an interview. I explained that I would be in Windhoek for the next few days and that I would be happy to cancel any other appointment to meet him.

"Absolutely not," he said. "There is no way I can make any time available for you."

"Mr. Bessinger," I pressed, "I'm trying to get some sort of balanced picture of something I know very little about. I think we can agree that the South Africans aren't going to tell me anything that's against their interests. And I'd prefer not to have to write that while they'll talk to me, you won't."

"If you do that, it will be a lie, an absolute lie. And anyone who knows the true story about the South African racist regime and what it's doing in Namibia will know it's a lie."

"Then would it be possible for us to get together, at your convenience, for a chat and a drink, perhaps? I'll be here for the next three and a half days and I'm more than willing to work my schedule around yours."

"No, I'm sorry, but I'll be entirely too busy for the next week, working on reports for the Council of Churches. You can call Mr. Tjongarero, perhaps he will have time for you."

"But I've already called him and he suggested I call you, so ... "

"Sorry, I am too busy. If you will excuse me, good-bye." Click.[3]

Puzzled by their antagonism, I walked up the hill to the Tintenpalast, the old imperial German fort that now served as the country's administrative centre. I had an appointment with another Swapo activist.

Paul Helmuth was the very picture of an elder statesman. Dressed in a sombre three-piece suit, he started by telling me of his days as a founding member of the South West Africa People's Organization.

"I suppose my political awakening came after I returned from World War Two," he said. "I left Namibia illegally and went to Cape Town in South Africa, where I was able to find work on a ship. At that time, South Africa was rather progressive compared to Namibia."

The winds of change were stirring in a post-war Africa, and Helmuth was profoundly affected by the new spirit of national liberation. By the late 1950s, he was serving the newly formed Ovambo People's Congress as a secret courier between Cape Town and Walvis Bay.

In 1961, Helmuth was spirited out to the Soviet Union. Sponsored by the United Nations Educational, Scientific, and Cultural Organization (UNESCO), he spent the next four years studying Russian and political science in Moscow and Kiev. More studies followed in Tanzania before he was sent to Sweden. "Twenty-five percent of my time was spent studying and the rest lecturing on the occupation of Namibia by the racist South African regime," he said, "and UNESCO paid for it all."

Helmuth returned to Tanzania in 1969 for a Swapo conference. "You have to understand that I was a committed nationalist and revolutionary. I had dedicated 15 years of my life to the liberation of Namibia for all its people. But I saw things which shocked me. Because of tribal politics, many of our Caprivian brothers in the struggle had been imprisoned by the Swapo leadership. Food and clothing donated by the UN were being sold by senior people, while Namibian refugees—our own people who had escaped from South African oppression—were starving and dressed in rags.

---

3   Author's note: When *Koevoet* was first published in 1988, a furious Tjongarero walked into Security
     Branch headquarters in Windhoek, slammed a copy on the duty officer's desk and snarled, "Is this
     some kind of fucking joke?"

"I started asking questions and pressing for an investigation. What I had seen was completely contrary to the principles on which we had founded the movement. Tribal politics was just another word for racism, and that was something we had all sworn to destroy. One night a friend told me that I was going to be arrested because of the inquiries I was making. The leadership had secretly denounced me as someone who could no longer be trusted."

Marked for arrest and imprisonment by the very organization he had helped to found, Helmuth escaped and returned to Sweden, where he was granted political asylum. In 1977, with guarantees of immunity from the South Africans, Helmuth accepted an invitation from another disillusioned revolutionary to return to Namibia. In 1986 Paul Helmuth was a member of the black-majority National Assembly of the Transitional Government of National Unity (TGNU) in Windhoek.

From the other side of the fence, Helmuth was viewed as a traitor for his involvement with the TGNU. On my return to England a month later, I spoke with Jacob Hannai, Swapo's deputy chief representative for Western Europe. "Paul Helmuth is among the defeatist elements," Hannai declared acidly. "I cannot finish naming the whole list, but he is among those. And, of course, what he is telling you about is to suit the situation where he is now. Because that institution where they are—the interim administration—was actually established at the expense of South Africa. They are saying they are working against the racist South African regime, but actually they are working for it. You cannot expect much from those cowardized elements."

I asked Hannai about Misheke Muyongo, who had founded the Caprivi Africa National Union (CANU). In 1966 he and his followers left the Caprivi Strip in Namibia and joined Swapo, Muyongo becoming its vice-president. In 1985, however, citing tribalism and oppression at the hands of the Ovambo-dominated party, Muyongo and most of CANU accepted amnesty from the South Africans and returned to Namibia.

"It is the same for Misheke Muyongo as Paul Helmuth and the others," Hannai said. "Muyongo, he had been vice-president of this movement and a member of the Politburo of the Central Committee of Swapo … but eventually, of course, some people like him and like many others … became too tired to fight for the cause which Swapo had been pursuing all these years. They thought they would fight today and they will win independence tomorrow. So they became defeated, demoralized, and went back to Namibia. They preferred to go back and work within the enemy rather than fighting for their cause and win a just solution, which will be satisfying to the people of Namibia. So they are defeatists."

Hans-Eric Staby was a white minority member of the National Assembly. Tie loosened and sleeves rolled up, he sat in the office of his architectural firm in Windhoek and stared out the window. "You know, in November 1978 we held our first elections based on one man, one vote. Representatives were elected on a racially proportional basis to sit in a national assembly. But since the United Nations recognized Swapo as the 'sole and authentic representative of the Namibian people,' they refused to accept the results. The fact that Swapo refused the invitation to take part made no difference."

Some months later in England, I spoke with Peter Katjavivi, who had been Swapo's secretary of information and publicity until 1979. Working on his doctorate at Oxford and still a committed member of Swapo, Katjavivi responded by saying, "How can someone invite us to come and partake in the so-called Interim Government, which is imposed by the government of South Africa? In other words, we have to participate in something which is already defined for us. We are rejecting it because it's ... not going to enable us to achieve our objective of being truly independent."

When I asked which political system he envisioned for Namibia, he explained that, "Swapo is a nationalist movement dedicated to achieving independence for Namibia and allowing a truly democratic society to take place." He paused for reflection. "But if I think a bit more with respect to Namibia, I would say this: my own view is that I would like to see a one-party state to come about through a natural process. There's nothing wrong in having a one-party state, per se. It has worked well in other countries." The examples he cited were the Soviet Union, East Germany and the Peoples Republic of China.

The West German-based International Society for Human Rights—described by Swapo as "a right-wing element supporting South Africa"—claimed to have evidence of "executions and the systematic maltreatment of Swapo opponents in Swapo refugee camps in Angola and Zambia." While admitting to holding "a few traitors," Swapo condemned South Africa for quashing opposition by detention without trial, but made no apologies for doing the same.

Sitting in the garden of Queen Elizabeth House in Oxford, Katjavivi rationalised the contradiction. "We are operating under abnormal conditions. We are in the neighbouring countries of Angola and Zambia, which culminated in the infiltration of South Africa into those countries, aimed not only against Swapo but also against our host African countries. We are a responsible movement. We are sensitive to some of these issues."

Somewhat provocatively, I mentioned that even apartheid South Africa's judicial system exercised habeas corpus and due process. Nelson Mandela's trial, for example, was held in open court and covered by the international media.

"I don't think Swapo rejoices over holding a few traitors without trial," Katjavivi said. "This is a hard decision. These are the lessons of the kind of struggle we have reached. I think none of us, when we studied the armed struggle in 1965 from the writings of Ho Chi Minh, for example, anticipated to have to deal with these kinds of cases."

In Windhoek a group calling itself the Parents Committee began investigating the allegations of torture and executions in Swapo-run refugee camps. Erika Beukes, a dedicated Swapo activist for many years, was a founding member of the committee.

"For the past year," she told me, "we've been meeting with Namibian refugees who escaped from the camps and they told us stories so terrible we could hardly believe it." A letter she showed me from a Namibian living in Zambia read in part:

The leadership should tell or bring about the group of young Namibians who were forcefully rounded up from the Boroma concentration camp in Kabwe ... amongst those killed are Jackson Hamupembe, Teodor Shongola, Halleluya Ambunde, Limpumbu Shongola, Vilho Komemaya. and many, many others...It is rumoured that Shilonga Ilya Shilonga was seen in one of the prison camps in Zambia, especially in Kabwe, and had one eye.

"Many of us had long been members of Swapo," said Beukes. "We still support the goal of an independent Namibia, free of South Africa, so we were careful to keep our inquiries out of the press. We didn't want to damage the movement many of us had belonged to for many years. All we wanted to know was what happened to our children and relatives. I was desperate to find out about my brother, who had disappeared. I had talked him into joining Swapo, and I felt responsible."

When their requests for information were ignored, the Parents Committee approached the Council of Churches, where Beukes worked as a secretary.

"It soon became clear that the CCN had no intention of investigating the allegations. The president of the council told me that they couldn't act on 'rumours.'"

The general secretary of the Council of Churches of Namibia, Dr. Abisai Sheyavali, at first declined to comment when I reached him by telephone.

"Dr. Sheyavali, all I'm asking for is your position on the accusations being made by the Parents Committee. Can't you just give me a simple statement on these allegations?"

"Well, of course, we cannot imagine them doing anything like what's been suggested."

"But have you investigated them?"

"No, we have not asked officially about the situation."

In 1987 at the European Parliament in Strasbourg, France, members of the Parents Committee confronted Swapo President Sam Nujoma, asking him about the fate of Namibian children in Swapo camps in Angola and Zambia. According to the London *Daily Telegraph*, Nujoma, defender of freedom and human rights, slapped one of the members and told her, "You will die."

The following document, reproduced as written, was found on the body of Josatu Tutaleni, Swapo's intelligence secretary for the Central Region. He was killed by Koevoet on September 20, 1985.

Copy No 02

RHQ [Regional Headquarters]
NF [Northern Front]
17/03/85

TO ALL DET COMMISAR

Dear CoMr.ades,

Our liberation struggle is now approaching ... another stage of criticality which of course created by the powerful forces of occupation with the sole purpose of the independence of our country Namibia.

The RHQs has critically tried to analyse the situation in Namibia and in our operational sector in particular and drawing examples from our many setbacks and the work of our political department in regard with the political mobilization of the masses and political work among our Combatants were reassessed. Viewing the facts of the past we concluded that drastic measures should be taken to regain the support of the masses. The RHQ put emphasis on our organization standing through these difficult times. The following guides should be followed during the Political Mobilization among the masses and own troops.

-Try to make the masses understand the critical situation for PLAN and they must stay in high morale for the future.

-The use of force is allowed on those who do not want to support the organization.

-Enemy propaganda should be countered as soon as heard or dropped in an area of our jurisdiction because we cannot allow a further drop in morale.

-Meetings should be conducted to individual persons or collectively whenever applicable but always remain vigilant of the large number of puppets and agents of our regime in our midst.

-Murder should be limited only to suspected enemy agents and supporters.

-Large numbers of children if possible a whole village or school must be captured to rebuild our organization.

-A revolutionary has always a goal to achieve. To be cruel in the struggle is to do good for the future.

-We must [not] expose the atrocities committed by our own people, but side them to the enemy. Therefore atrocities should not be committed in front of masses.

-The firing squad will be re-implemented for cases of desertion among own troops. Only detachment cmdrs are authorized to judge and execute after recommendation by det cmsrs. Personal belongings and statements must be sent with monthly report. This aforementioned is the task that is on the shoulders of all det commisars and their substitutors to be carried out through the struggle.

-The revolutionary movements which is separated from the people will not in any way win Victory, or it victory cannot last long.

EVERYTHING FOR THE STRUGGLE, ALL FOR FINAL VICTORY

MAPAYA YA MAPAYA RC [Regional Commander]

4
White "South West," Black Namibia

Henk Rheeder, a gangly South West Africa Territorial Force sergeant, had been assigned as my escort for a tour of the operational area. A former South African journalist, he had settled in Windhoek two years earlier. "I may go back to the States someday," he said, using the popular term for South Africa, "but I kind of prefer the way of life here. Things are a lot more relaxed than back there." It was a refrain I would hear over and over from transplanted South Africans.

The night before we were to start driving north, Henk took me on a pub crawl. Our first stop was the NCO mess, where we bellied up to the bar side by side with black and white members of the SWATF. A steady stream of American Country and Western music twanged in the background. As a foreign journalist, I came under close scrutiny. Willi, a black sergeant on the bar stool next to me, bought my first beer and asked the usual first question about how I liked Namibia.

I admitted that I had seen only Windhoek and really not much of that, since most of my time had been spent on interviews. The white bartender, three horizontal stripes of a sergeant on his sleeves, leaned on the polished surface.

"I tell you, this is a good country. God's country. I'm South African, but I don't want to go back there to live. It is just easier here, the whole situation between blacks and whites. Genuine. I tell you, I am an Afrikaner, brought up on a farm in the Northern Transvaal, believed in apartheid. I didn't dislike blacks, I just believed you didn't socialize with them. I came out here five years ago with the SADF, and when it was time to go back to the States, I transferred into the SWATF." He pronounced it, like everyone else, Swa-tee-eff. "I tell you … excuse, I'll be back just now." He straightened up and turned to serve some newcomers.

Willi nodded towards the bartender. "Gysbert, he is okay, but he talk a lot," he said, feeling his way through English. Afrikaans was the lingua franca of both the SADF and SWATF, and for many of the soldiers, English was a little-used second or third language.

Gysbert returned and took a reflexive swipe at the bar top with a towel. "Yeah, I tell you, South West is a good place. I live in a neighbourhood with blacks, we have braais together, it's not a problem. We don't have apartheid here. Genuine."

He pointed towards Henk, who was talking with a group of black and white NCOs at the other end of the bar. "Henk there, he's got a black boss, Zorro Kariko, and he doesn't seem bothered by it. If a man can do the job, what's the difference whether he's black or white?

"Willi here, he and I couldn't have a drink together five years ago in the States. Even if I wanted to. In the sergeants' mess, yeah, okay, but not outside on Civvie Street. It's a lot better now, back there, but they still have a long way to go to catch up with us. No, I became a Southwester when I joined the SWATF. This is my country now."

I asked him to set up another round. Willi shook a finger in my face with mock severity. "It is against the regulations. You're civvie. Can't buy unless you a ... ," he looked at Gysbert. "Hoe sê jy 'lid' in Engels?"

"Member," Gysbert translated.

"You can't buy here unless a *member*," and pushed a bill across the bar, scribing a circle with his finger to indicate a new round for the three of us.

"Look," said Gysbert, "if you're in a restaurant and a black sits at the table next to you, and he's not bothering anyone, what's the problem? You know what I mean? If you get up and leave because he's there, who's the fool? That's what I found out here. Genuine." He poured out three brandies. "This is on me." We drank. "Anyway, that's what I found out."

Henk walked over. "Let's go see what's happening at the Air Force club."

I gave my hand to Gysbert and Willi.

"See you," said Willi.

"See you," said Gysbert. "Hope you get the stories you are after up in the operational area. Not much happening right now. Rains are late." Willi shook his head again at how much some people talked. I followed Henk a little unsteadily out the door.

When we entered the air force club, the *There I was, thought I was gonna die* stage had already been reached, with the speaker flying his helicopter through heavy ground fire in Angola. About 30 seconds after we walked in, he crashed. The accompanying hand movements and sound effects depicting his last moments in the air were impressive. It called for a drink.

He noticed me at the bar. "How's it?" he asked. I'd sat in on a briefing he'd given to a foreign television crew a couple of days earlier. "You getting the information you wanted?"

I rocked my hand back and forth. "More or less," I said. "Lot of things I didn't know, but it sounds pretty much like the standard sort of stuff put together for wandering journalists. Nothing exactly earth-shattering."

"Yeah," he said, "but there's not a lot happening right now. And there's not much infiltration going on up north. Rains are late. But the Russians and Cubans have been pretty active." Among air force personnel, the first language seemed to be English rather than Afrikaans. "They just brought in a few more MiG-23s, along with a number of instructor pilots with lots of experience in Afghanistan. We think those are just the first ones, that they'll have some more there before too long."

"Sounds like they might be expecting trouble. You guys ever penetrate Angolan airspace?"

There was a tiny pause. "Certainly not."

"Then what about that South African C-130 they claimed to have shot down last month? That was quite a way up in Angola."

"Well, I'll tell you, after the first couple of press releases out of Angola, everything suddenly went real quiet. Seems someone got confused and shot down a civilian Hercules that had been leased from an American company. Dangerous flying in Angola. That's why we wouldn't think of it." He drained the last of his brandy and Coke, swirled the ice, and ordered another.

I looked around the bar. Unlike the army canteen, there were no blacks. "Does the air force have any black pilots?" I asked.

"Not yet, but we will sooner or later. As long as they meet the same standards, I certainly wouldn't mind flying with a black pilot. There may be some who wouldn't. In fact, I know there are some who wouldn't want to. But things are changing. Maybe faster than some people want, but things are definitely changing." Apparently, I didn't look too convinced. "Look," he said, "how many non-white officers have you seen in the Defence Force?" A few, I said. "And have you seen any evidence of apartheid in the officers' mess? Were they sitting at separate tables?" I allowed that they were sitting with white officers.

"And have you noticed white troopies not saluting them?" I conceded that non-white officers were afforded the same military courtesy as white officers. "You know," he continued a little testily, "you Americans tend to forget that until the Korean War, blacks in the U.S. military were only in segregated units. It was Eisenhower who pushed through reforms by ordering that they be integrated into white units. The same thing's happening here. The colour barriers are falling fast in the military. They have to."

"Okay, look," I said, "I accept all that. And maybe it will have a major effect on the future of South Africa. But if it's happening so easily in the military, why can't the same thing happen at the same time outside—in civilian life? Is it so different?"

"Of course it's different. Ours is a pretty rigid society. That old Dutch Calvinist thinking is a big part of our heritage. Whites, blacks, Coloured, Asians, they've all been neatly categorized by the old Voortrekkers' interpretation of the Old Testament. In the military, though, new concepts are appearing out of basic necessity. Suddenly you have all colours in the same uniform, eating the same food, sharing the same barracks, living under the same rules. When that happens, it's inevitable that attitudes are going to be altered. It's a practical starting point for change."

"How long's it going to take for that thinking to spill over into the Afrikaner society back in South Africa?"

"Well, it's not all going to happen overnight. It can't, not with our history and the way we've lived. But if non-whites are going to volunteer to defend South Africa—and they're all volunteers—then they're going to have to get the same respect as a white, in and out of the military. The only apartheid in the Defence Force," he said, "is based solely on rank. How about a drink?"

Too many beers later I climbed out of Henk's car, stepped straight into a pothole and felt something crunch. The rest of the night was spent watching the ankle swell and turn fascinating shades of black and blue. You stupid son of a bitch, you get this far and blow it. This had ruined everything.

Looking decidedly delicate, Henk collected me early the next morning. Our first stop was the hospital. Henk asked for a few aspirin, and I asked for an X-ray plus something stronger than aspirin. The X-ray showed a hairline fracture and for the first time in my life I was modelling a cast. Henk asked if I still wanted to go. I threw some painkillers down my throat and nodded crankily.

Having started four hours late, we didn't reach Otavi until shortly before dusk. Henk drove unerringly along the dirt streets to the local army canteen. A couple of beers down the hatch to cut the dust, and we wandered into town for a meal.

The restaurant and bar of the Old West-style hotel were still quiet when we walked in. There was a pause in the plank-floored room as heads turned, and a dozen pairs of eyes watched curiously until we settled at a table in the corner. I leaned the unfamiliar crutches against the wall and propped the cast on an adjacent chair. Two pool players chalked cue sticks and went back to their game. The regulars sitting at the bar picked up their conversations again. The whole room seemed to shift slightly and heave a quiet, collective sigh before returning to whatever they were doing or saying before we came in.

Between posters of Marlboro cowboys and others extolling the virtues of Lion, Castle or Windhoek Lager beer, the walls were hung with spears, bows and arrows, knobkerries and curiously shaped drinking gourds. An old fan turned slowly overhead, thin strips of blue plastic trailing weakly from the blades. From the jukebox Whitney Houston crooned *Saving All My Love For You*.

The owner, a young, modishly dressed Greek, arrived to take our orders. I mentioned to Henk that perhaps we could sit on the terrace where it was cooler. Henk and the Greek exchanged looks.

"The mosquitoes are pretty bad tonight," the owner said.

"I think we'd be more comfortable in here," Henk added.

I leaned back to look out onto the terrace. Then I understood: everyone there was black. Institutionalised apartheid might not exist in Namibia, but, like many places around the world, was alive and well on a de facto basis. It was also a scene that I remembered from my boyhood in rural towns in the American Deep South.

I was 19 years old, riding a Grayhound bus from Tampa towards Detroit that Christmas season in 1962. It stopped after midnight in Macon, Georgia, where I had to change buses. Moths fluttered around the bare light bulb over the screen door that squeaked open and banged shut behind me as I walked into the waiting room. I stopped. There was something wrong here, and I didn't know what it was at first. Then I understood. I had walked into the "coloured" waiting room. Everyone in the shabby, dimly lit room was black.

I had never seen it before, never come into contact with enforced segregation. I started backing up, and then turned to go. My hand was on the door handle when I was stopped by a voice. A wizened little black woman— her prune-wrinkled face set off by white hair and gentle eyes—had risen from a scarred bench behind me. She put her hand on my forearm.

"You don" hafta leave, chile, ain't nobody in here gonna hurt you."

I stared at her for a moment and mumbled, "I—I'm sorry."

I turned and fled, the screen door banging shut behind me. From outside I saw the faded sign: Coloured. It matched the one over the drinking fountain and a third pointing towards hidden toilets. To the left were the others, all crisply lettered: Whites Only. Ashamed of my cowardice, I stood alone on the loading platform and shivered in the cold Georgia night until my next bus arrived.

Henk and I set off early the next morning and two hours later we'd reached Oshivelo and the military checkpoint on the "red line," the southern border of the operational area. While Henk handed over his identification to the guard and signed the required forms, I hobbled over to the sign that greeted everyone entering Ovamboland.

Due to the possibility of
mines or ambushes being
laid along the road to
Ondangwa by Swapo with
the intention of injuring or
killing innocent civilians, the
road is patrolled by the
Defence Force each morning
at 06h30. The gate opens at
07h30 and closes again at
18h00 in terms of the curfew
announced by proclamation
of A.G.8
Try to travel in groups of
not less than four vehicles.

"We haven't had any problems this far south for a few years," Henk assured me as he floored the throttle. Accelerating past the speed limit, he gave me a smile. "But you can still drive as fast as you want from here up to Ondangwa. If there are any terrorists around, the faster you go, the more difficult it is for them to hit you." He reached under his seat and placed a pistol between us.

Approaching Ondangwa, the first town of any size, I was struck by the number of blacks in uniform. White soldiers were definitely in the minority. Brown Casspir armoured personnel carriers full of black troops in brown army uniforms and Ratel and Eland armoured fighting vehicles moved in both directions along the road. Occasionally, Casspirs in green camouflage paint passed us.

"Those are Koevoet," said Henk.

"Koofoot?" I repeated.

"Yeah, that's the police counterinsurgency people. Afrikaans for 'crowbar.' Cause us all kinds of problems. Animals."

"Oh"—seeing another go by and dismissing it as irrelevant. On the northern edge of town was an air force base. A four-engine C-130 was high above the base in a steep spiral. Two helicopters chattered low over the flat ground beyond the perimeter.

"Choppers are in case there's a terr out there with a SAM-7 missile," Henk said, watching the French-made Alouettes. "Keeps their heads down." A bulldozed berm topped with razor wire and guard towers hid the runways. "All the casevacs are flown into the hospital there before sending them down to the States."

That within a year I would come to know that hospital with more intimacy than I wanted was the furthest thing from my mind. At the moment, there was something else to address. Henk looked over to see me cutting off the cast.

"What the hell are you doing? Don't you think you should keep that on for a few more days at least?"

"If I show up wearing this thing, there's no way they'll let me go on ops," I grunted. "And that's where the story is, Henk. So be a buddy and don't say anything about it, okay?"

"But they're not going to let you do that anyway. It's not part of your programme."

"Well, at least I can ask 'em, and the worst they can do is say no." Tossing the cast and cotton wadding out of the window, I wrapped the ankle with an elastic bandage, propped the foot on the dash, and returned to watching the passing landscape.

Tall makalani palms and massive anthills jutted above scrub that clung tenaciously to the sandy earth. Henk stopped and swore regularly as long-horned cattle ambled across the road. Another 12 kilometres brought us to the outskirts of Oshakati. Ramshackle buildings began to appear, Ovambo-owned bars, auto-parts businesses and markets. The names of the drinking establishments competed with each other for exotic flavour. There was the Beverly Hills Bottle Store, OJ's Mississippi Satisfaction, the Los Angeles Inn, and California Auto Spares and Bottle Store. The Jamaica Inn wasn't far from the Picadilly Circus Bar. Nationalists might frequent the Namib Inn, while those with budding relationships could head for the Famous Lovers Bar. And depending on one's frame of mind, there was a choice between The Happy Bar and The Sorry Bar.

Perhaps it was the proliferation of drinking establishments that led to at least an equal number of auto repair shops. Many of the Ovambo soldiers, most having grown up tending cattle at their fathers' traditional kraals in the middle of the bush, had been able to buy cars with their army pay. Their lack of driving experience, compounded by beverages with more punch than homemade sorghum beer, apparently made these repair shops particularly lucrative.

The Continental Hotel, Bottle Store, Auto Parts and Supermarket, all owned by an Ovambo entrepreneur reputed to be the wealthiest man in Namibia, included a service station and Datsun dealership. Whites shopped alongside blacks here for what couldn't be found at the SADFI (commissary) on base. Smaller markets and open-air butchers—fresh meat hanging from hooks in the heat—were tucked among the other businesses along the road. It was obvious that war had brought a degree of prosperity to Ovamboland.

We rolled through the gates of Oshakati Base and directly to army headquarters for my first scheduled briefing. A well-rehearsed team had all the facts, figures, graphs and answers to anticipated questions at their fingertips. The emphasis was on Communications Operations—COMOPS in SADF-speak—a sophisticated hearts-and-minds programme designed to draw the rural Ovambo population away from Swapo.

According to a short, bespectacled major, the war for hearts and minds was essentially won. "If we had elections today, I can promise you Swapo would lose," he declared, waiting for the logical question.

I decided to play along. "Then why haven't there been new elections?"

"Some people aren't as sure as we are," he answered with an annoying smugness. "Or maybe they're afraid of losing their soft jobs," in a transparent reference to members of the transitional government.

Before departing on a tour of the operational area, an introduction to Brigadier Jakes Swart, Commanding Officer of Sector 10, gave me the opportunity to present my case for seeing the war firsthand. "It's really the only way I can report on it with any authority or credibility," I said. He listened courteously, but was noncommittal. After a few minutes of polite conversation, Henk and I took our leave.

"I told you it wasn't going to get you anywhere," Henk said as we headed for the next appointment. "It's not on your programme."

What I didn't know was that Richard Charter had already spoken to Swart about me. Given the sensitivity of the SADF's operations in Angola, permission to cover them was impossible, but there was another unit in Oshakati that might be more receptive. My telling a fat Chinese general to get lost had not been forgotten.

The next morning Rheeder and I thumbed a ride in an air force brigadier's twin-engine King Air. "American?" he asked in a very plummy English accent as we buckled into our seats. "Yes, sir," I admitted, wondering if I was in for another chiding about the media's reporting on South Africa.

Instead, Dick Lord flashed a welcoming smile and for the next 45 minutes reminisced about his first trip to the USA in the late '60s. Though born in South Africa, he began his military career in the Royal Navy as a carrier pilot. In recognition of his exceptional skills as a fighter pilot, he was selected to join a US Navy Phantom squadron as part of a long-standing exchange programme. Arriving in Washington, DC, then-Lieutenant Lord completed all the requisite formalities and, rather than taking a commercial flight, opted to drive the 3,000 miles to San Diego. The first leg of the cross-country journey took him to Chicago, where he picked up the legendary Route 66. It was a great way to get a feel for the country, though the fighter pilot in him chaffed at the 60 to 65mph speed limit. A law-abiding citizen by nature, he grimly kept to it; it wouldn't do for an officer in Her Majesty's Royal Navy to be arrested for breaking the laws of the host country.

Four days after setting off from Washington, he reached the Texas panhandle. The first town had a speed limit of 25 miles per hour, "but I was still doing about 40 when I crossed the town's main intersection," he said with a rueful grin. Within seconds, the Texas Highway Patrol was at his six o'clock, siren wailing and lights flashing. When Lord climbed out of his right-hand drive British Rover, he came face-to-face with an enormous Texas lawman wearing the obligatory ten-gallon Stetson, silver badge, and pistol. The image was a far cry from the phlegmatic, unarmed British bobby Lord was used to.

At the time, a UK driver's license carried no photo, and Lord was sent back to the car for his passport. Both he and the Rover, its British license plate and Great Britain sticker the first ever seen by the Texan, were watched suspiciously. The lawman compared the passport photo with the polite Englishman in front of him and nodded. Then his eyes fell on the opposite page. Unlike American passports, there was a heading for "Profession", under which was written "Government Service". ("Being listed as military could cause problems in some countries," Lord said in an aside.) The Texan pondered this for a moment and turned to the page where the holder's name was recorded. First and middle names were written in longhand with the last name below them in underlined capital letters. His eyes widened on reading:

Richard Stanley
<u>LORD</u>

The Texan froze, mind whirring through the implications of having just stopped Lord Stanley of the British aristocracy. Hadn't at least 12 Englishmen died at the Alamo, defending Texas? He deferentially returned the passport. Anglo-American relations restored, he led his VIP out of town with blue and red lights flashing. At the city limits, he pulled over and jumped out to offer a polite salute as the Rover went by. The errant Englishman-South African fighter pilot acknowledged the salute with a regal wave.

"I have often wondered what stories he told the other Highway Patrolmen about how he nearly booked one of Britain's blue-bloods," he laughed as the King Air's landing gear clunked down on the long, straight-in approach to Rundu. The flight and tales of Texas had ended all too quickly.

"Hope you get the stories you're after," Brigadier Lord said as we stepped onto the tarmac. "If there's anything I can help you with, give me a call in Windhoek."[1]

---

1   During his tour with the US Navy, Dick Lord helped to establish the Fighter Weapons School—better known as Top Gun—at Miramar, California.

A bakkie—pickup truck—was waiting. Henk and I climbed into the back and were whisked directly to Sector 20 headquarters and another prepared briefing. I had to give the South Africans high marks for efficiency.

"Swapo infiltration into the Kavango began in 1980," said the next briefer, tapping the wall map. He had given the rundown to so many hacks that he was starting to sound like a tape recorder. I also had the feeling that he wasn't crazy about Western journalists.

"It peaked in 1983," he droned, "by which time insurgent activity had extended 80 kilometres to the east of Rundu. This was an unacceptable situation. We realised that a strictly military solution was not the answer, so efforts were concentrated on instituting a COMOPS programme built around the specific needs of the local Kavango population."

A tall, solidly built officer walked into the room and leaned against the wall. Colonel Dion Ferreira had spent much of his career in counterinsurgency operations. His camouflage beret marked him as the Ferreira who had commanded 32 Battalion, the elite Portuguese-speaking unit made up of ex-FNLA Angolan soldiers.

"Hell, it's too easy to forget the basics of revolutionary warfare," he interrupted, waving the briefer away. "Mao Tse-Tung wrote the book on it. 'The peaceful population is the sea the guerrilla swims in.'" He reversed a chair and straddled the seat, his arms resting on the back.

"It was the local population—because of intimidation or inclination—who were making it possible for the terrorists to operate. The terrs can't operate independently; they need food, shelter and information if they're going to be successful. And the only place they can get all that is from the local pops.

"The only answer, then, was to go to the people with our Kavango soldiers from 202 Battalion. We showed them that we had more to offer than Swapo. We built schools, sent medical teams to the kraals, drilled boreholes, held meetings and generally managed to discredit Swapo by openly inviting them to participate in these projects.

"We knew we were winning when the locals started informing on the terrorists. We knew we had won when we heard that a local headman had stood up to a group of Swapo and told them to leave his kraal, that they weren't good for his people. When they threatened to kill him, he told them to go ahead but promised that his clan would kill them as soon as he was dead.

"One of the advantages we had was that Swapo is basically an Ovambo organization with very few Kavangos in it, and the two dozen terrs operating here were all Ovambos. Tribalism worked against them. By the middle of 1985, we had cleared all of Sector 20 of insurgent activity, and we've kept it cleared. I can promise you that this is one of the safest areas in the country."

Captain Alois Gende, 202 Battalion's operations officer, settled in the chair across from me, favouring the leg he'd recently broken playing rugby. He carefully propped the cast on another chair. I felt a certain kinship.

"I was the first Kavango selected for officer training. I started with the black 21 Battalion in South Africa and came back here as a corporal when 202 was being formed. Before then, all the officers in 202 were white and most of the NCOs. Now 80 percent of our senior NCOs are Kavangos, and by the end of 1987, we'll have at least ten new lieutenants, all Kavangos, serving as platoon commanders. Things are progressing."

As if to emphasize how safe the Kavango was, we travelled by bakkie to our next stop in Sector 20. The four-hour drive in an unarmoured and unescorted vehicle seemed proof of Ferreira's claim that this part of Namibia was safe from terrorist activity; the SADF wasn't going to risk having a foreign journalist blown up by a land mine or ambushed by infiltrating Swapo insurgents. Our overnight stop was the strikingly beautiful Omega Base, home of the 201 Bushman Battalion. Still commanded by white officers, 201 was manned by Vasekela Bushmen from Angola and Barangwena Bushmen indigenous to the Kavango and Western Caprivi. The Vasekelas were essentially refugees. Their once-peaceful existence in Angola had been threatened in the late 1960s when Soviet and Chinese-backed insurgents fighting the Portuguese began crossing the border from Zambia. Many of the Vasekelas were abducted and forced into military service at the hands of their traditional black enemies.

Faced with the choice of fighting alongside or against these groups, the Bushmen began joining Portuguese units. The 1974 military coup in Portugal and the subsequent abandonment of Angola by the Portuguese Communist junta left the former Bushman soldiers unprotected. In late 1975 they escaped into Namibia and asked for asylum. The local Barangwena Bushman tribe eventually gathered in the same area, and 201 Battalion was formed.

Commandant Johann Jooste had commanded the unit for two years. "These are some of the finest men I've ever worked with," he said in the open-air officers' mess. "They are capable, quick to learn, and their loyalty is unquestioned."

If Sector 20 was free of insurgent activity, I asked, what was the function of 201 Battalion?

"Trackers," said Jooste. "Half the unit is on operations at any given time, working alongside SADF or SWATF units in Ovamboland. In their own environment, they may be the best trackers in the world, and their endurance and stamina are unbelievable."

I wondered if it wasn't a pity that such an essentially happy and, well, simple people should be made into soldiers.

"These people aren't simple. Unsophisticated, perhaps, by some standards, but I don't know any white whose knowledge of the bush is as complete as the Bushman's. He's highly sophisticated in his world. And as far as making them into soldiers, they're volunteers. We haven't forced them into anything. They can leave any time they want. They're paid well, given education, medical care and housing. And that extends to their families also. We're lucky to have them."

Our final stop on my tour was Katima Mulilo, headquarters for Sector 70. Located at the eastern tip of the Caprivi Strip near the Zambian border, Katima was a sleepy border town spoken of with nostalgia by those who had served there.

"About the only excitement we get around here," admitted Commandant Frans Verfuss, "is when Ould Gertie wanders into town." Old Gertie was a one-tusked elephant that enjoyed nibbling at well-maintained gardens.

"I couldn't get to work one morning last week because she was standing in front of my garage picking flowers off a vine! And I couldn't shoo her away. She wouldn't budge. Last year the game department chaps were going to shoot her, until almost everyone here signed a petition protesting against it. Wouldn't be the same in Katima without the old girl."

Although one of the early Namibian liberation movements, the Caprivi African National Union, emerged here, Sector 70 had been free of overt insurgent activity since 1978, when Swapo launched a standoff mortar and rocket attack from Zambia. Ten SADF soldiers were killed when a 122mm rocket hit their barracks. The predictable South African response was a punitive cross-border operation. This not only neutralized the immediate threat, but also encouraged Zambia to henceforth deny Swapo the use of its soil for attacks against the Eastern Caprivi.

(There is a story about the determined Zambian border guard who halted the invading column of grim-faced South Africans with up-raised palm and a demand to see their passports. His style, if not his common sense, was so admired by the SADF commander, the story goes, that he was picked up and removed to the side of the road under guard while the column rumbled past.)

The two indigenous tribes of the Caprivi, the Mafwe and smaller Masubia, Verfuss explained, were among the least aggressive and politically radical peoples of the region. Their major points of contention harked back to the late 19th century when Leo von Caprivi, the German administrator of the area, arbitrarily appointed chiefs and demarcated tribal boundaries, giving the Mafwe ascendancy over the Masubia. Complicated intertribal disputes based on decisions made by an obscure Imperial German officer 100 years earlier were still causing problems.

"The recent political scene here is a little complicated, so I'll just give you the bare outlines. Feel free to interrupt if there's anything you don't understand. As I've explained, there are two tribes in this area, each tracing its background in different directions and each a little contemptuous of the other. Not long after Swapo was formed, the Masubia-based Caprivi African National Union—CANU—was founded. In 1966 its membership of something like 250 or 300 left the Caprivi to join Swapo in Zambia and Angola.

"CANU President Misheke Muyongo became vice-president of Swapo. Ovambo dominance of the organization, however, led to a lot of tribal problems, and quite a few of the CANU members were accused of being South African spies—the standard charge against anyone not agreeing with Nujoma—and imprisoned by Swapo.

"We took advantage of the split by offering amnesty to anyone who wanted to return. The only condition was that if they had committed crimes against the civilian population, we would prosecute them. If they had carried out attacks only against the security forces, there wouldn't be a problem. Over 125, mostly Masubias, returned. Right away, they started to reform CANU as a legitimate political party.

"In June 1985, Muyongo, a hereditary chief of the Mafwe, accepted amnesty and immediately involved himself in politics, attempting to consolidate the older Caprivi Alliance Party and the newly reformed CANU under one banner. His two old CANU lieutenants in Swapo, both Masubias, also accepted the amnesty offer and followed about a month later to prevent Muyongo from cornering the political marketplace in the Caprivi. Muyongo succeeded, however, in merging CAP and CANU into the United Democratic Party. Right after that, he affiliated his UDP with the Democratic Turnhalle Alliance in Windhoek." Verfuss paused. "Okay so far?"

"So far, so good," I confirmed, scribbling in my notebook. Verfuss nodded and continued the history lesson.

"His old lieutenants in the armed struggle weren't very happy with Muyongo's dominance and the fact that most of the United Democratic Party's senior members were Mafwes, so they decided to continue an independent CANU.

"Then the previous Caprivi Alliance Party representative in the transitional government in Windhoek also fell out with Muyongo and continued the CAP as a separate, independent party. The next move was to start planning a Masubia CAP-CANU alliance to counter ex-CANU-president and ex-Swapo-vice-president Muyongo's United Democratic Party, which had been the Mafwe CAP-CANU alliance."

"Listen," I said to Commandant Verfuss, "would you mind running all that by me one more time? I think I'm confused."

In an area of 500,000 square miles, more than half of Namibia's population of 1.2 million was represented by the Ovambo people, who lived within the 30,000 square miles of Ovamboland. If the Kavango and Caprivi were free of armed infiltration, this traditional tribal area certainly was not. It was here that the winds of change era gave rise to the Ovambo People's Congress and its descendent, the South West Africa People's Organization.

With over 300 kilometres of open, heavily bushed border and a population generally sympathetic to Swapo, Ovamboland was the scene of regular incursions. The number of insurgents south of the border at any given time seldom exceeded 50, but their presence demanded a disproportionate response from the South Africans.

In spite of wildly exaggerated claims of success, however, Swapo had little to boast about militarily. Its victories had been limited to sabotaging telephone and electric poles, occasional standoff mortar and rocket attacks against Oshakati and remote bases, and the rare ambush against patrolling security force units. According to the SADF, over 12,000 insurgents had been killed or captured since the beginning of the war. Security force deaths for the same period were less than 450.

Jacob Hannai, Swapo's representative in London, scoffed at these figures. "It's what you always hear being mentioned because the South Africans are in control of the media," he sneered. "But I can tell you that the People's Liberation Army of Namibia have been very much successful. This year alone, they have eliminated quite a lot of racist troops. They have destroyed enemy bases at Eenhana, Ongwelume, Ruacana, Okahana, Tsandi, and Oshakati." (I forbore mentioning that I'd just returned from Namibia and that they were unscathed. Actually, I lied by saying I was going to Namibia and wanted to know the truth before I got there.)

According to Hannai, "The South African Defence Force have among more than 100,000 racist troops in Namibia a number of specialized military units who are, in fact, instructed to carry out what they call counterinsurgency operations.[2] They have a unit, which is known as Koevoet, and this Koevoet consists of some members of the South African Defence Force and all those elements that have been defeated in the war for liberation in Zimbabwe, and they are committing all types of atrocities.

"As I said, this Koevoet ... in 1982 they have wiped out a village at a place called Oshikuku, and all these years they have been kidnapping people, they have been killing people in cold blood, and they have destroyed crops. Most of the civilian population in the rural areas have been complaining about their crops being destroyed by the racist army running over their fields. And the Koevoet specialise in specifically to eliminate the supporters and members of our organization, Swapo."

When asked about charges that many Namibian civilians had been killed by Swapo-laid land mines and that his organization had committed its own share of atrocities against the civilian population, Hannai dismissed it out-of-hand. "That is what one is made to believe. I could not see a situation where the freedom fighters of our movement ... can indulge in planting land mines. But what I'm telling you is that those who have been involved in the atrocities against our people are the South African Defence Forces. I have already told you that the Koevoet have indulged in a number of campaigns in order to discredit Swapo. Sometimes have been planting land mines, sometimes have been killing people, sometimes have been committing all types of atrocities against the people, and immediately after the acts have been committed, then they say it is Swapo. It is a systematic campaign to discredit the movement.

"We are not committing atrocities. We don't see any situation why we have to go and kill our own mothers, brothers, and sisters, because we are fighting for them. Because these South African Defence Forces, the way they are doing that is to suppress the will of the people, and they really do it all expenses."

---

2   There were 20,000 to 25,000 soldiers and police in Namibia at the time.

In spite of Hannai's claims, Swapo's losses were appalling, but their amateurish efforts were forcing South Africa to maintain a military presence along the Angolan border at a cost of over $3 million a day.

"We really can't afford it," an SADF officer told me, "but we don't have much choice. We're not going to risk having another Marxist country along our borders. No way."

After eight days of bases and briefings Henk and I caught a flight from Katima Mulilo back to Ondangwa Air Force Base. When we landed, the army lieutenant meeting us shook his head gravely.

"Brigadier Swart wanted me to tell you that authorization just came through an hour ago; you leave tomorrow for a week in the bush with Koevoet." The look on his face indicated what he thought of the idea. The look on Henk's face was astonishment. I would have needled him about it "not being part of my programme," but I was too annoyed to say anything.

Koevoet? I tried to hide my disappointment, deciding that I'd been stuck with them as a sop to a pushy, wandering journalist. It was proper soldiers who were fighting this war—like 101 Battalion, which I'd heard plenty about—not some knuckle-dragging, off-the-wall police unit.

At the Driehoek guest quarters in Oshakati that night I was treated to the army's opinion of the outfit I'd be spending the next week with. Koevoet, Afrikaans for crowbar, went by the official designation of South West African Police Counterinsurgency Unit—SWAPOLCOIN. Ninety percent of its operational personnel were black, the majority locally recruited Ovambos. Most of the whites were South Africans, with a sprinkling of white "Southwesters." Comprising barely ten percent of the total security force presence in the operational area, they accounted for well over 70% of the contacts with Swapo. Things suddenly seemed a little brighter.

"But, man, those guys are animals. No discipline, long hair, all they do is drink and get into fights with the army and make problems for our COMOPS people. Okay, maybe they shoot a lot of terrs, but they're a real headache in Oshakati, I can promise you. Genuine. And a lot of them have been brought up on charges."

"What sort of charges?"

"Oh, you know, minor stuff like murder, torture, rape.

"And what's been the outcome of the trials?" I asked.

"Most of them have ended with not-guilty verdicts, but I think a couple of their people were convicted for murder. I'm not sure if they swung or not."

"You're kidding. You mean … *hanged*?"

"Like I said, I'm not sure. Ask them about it."

"You heard the joke about them?" asked an army major.

I shook my head.

"No, it seems there was this huge crocodile up on the Cunene River that was a real problem, see, eating a lot of the local pops. So General Meiring, head of the SADF, tells his chief of staff to sort it out, that he's got ten days to take care of this croc. Well, after an all-night planning session, the air force sends in the photo Mirages to locate it. Next, the Reconnaissance Commandos go in and come back with all the info about where he suns himself, where he eats and sleeps. So then a major operation is jacked up, with the Parabats, artillery, armour, 61 Mech, everything—and on the tenth day, the Defence Force delivers the crocodile to General Meiring.

"Well, next day, info comes down that there's another man-eating croc causing big problems along the Cunene. The Defence Force has used up all their assets, so the general tells Koevoet they've got ten days to sort out this crocodile. Well, they sit down and drink for nine days. On the morning of the tenth day, they jump in their Casspirs and start racing for the Cunene. About two miles out of Oshakati, they see this lizard. They jump out of their Casspirs, run over and grab this lizard, see, and then beat the shit out of him until he admits he's a crocodile."

There was a hearty round of laughter and knowing nods. It was obviously a favourite army joke about the police. "Man, that's the way those people operate," said the major. "Genuine."

"But all they're going to do is run you around in the quietest area they can find," a visiting journalist from Windhoek said. "You actually think they'd take a chance on getting a foreign reporter killed? No way." Not knowing whether to be relieved or disappointed, I finally wandered off to bed.

I awoke from the nightmare at two in the morning. Outside the tent-topped guest hut, rain, lightning and thunder battered Oshakati. Lying under the mosquito net, I lit a cigarette and listened to the storm. In spite of the drop in temperature and the cold spray driven through the windows, my chest and back were soaked with sweat. I flinched at the crackling hiss of lightning and simultaneous explosion of thunder. Was it a premonition? Was this really what I should be doing tomorrow? No, it was today already; today I was going out. No, just a bad dream. But it was a long time before I fell asleep again.

5

Koevoet: An Introduction

Captain Chris Pieterse, Operations Officer: "When Bernie Ley told me that a journalist was going to be embedded in our unit, I thought that the Old Man had gone soft in the head. Had he considered how much trouble one of those could cause if he happened to be at the wrong place at the wrong time?"

Warrant Officer Marius Brand, team leader, Zulu Alpha: "I was walking past the Koevoet admin section when Bernie Ley called me into his office and said that the boss wanted me to take an American journalist on patrol the next day. And that's all he says. Just like Koevoet. No briefing on what I'm supposed to say to this guy. They probably expected me to give him the official line about operating only inside Namibia, not chasing and killing 'freedom fighters' deep inside Angola. Well, I'd go over the border if I had to. Was I supposed to think this guy was really journalist? Probably from the FBI or something and was going to reveal everything about how we worked. That's it, I thought, the war's over. Swapo will be taking over soon. Maybe this is Pretoria's way of civilizing us before taking us out of the bush and back into society. The general didn't pick me for this because I was one of the best Alpha Group commanders, but because I could speak English. I decided that I'd take things very casual and check the situation out carefully."

Thys Loedolff, car commander, ZA-4: "When I heard that the General was allowing a journalist to join us in the veld, I knew the guy must have high up connections in the CIA or whatever. Personally I did not have a problem with it as he would be taking his own risks accompanying us to the operational zone and also possibly into Angola. What did worry me was that everyone would be super sensitive to every nuance of right and wrong, which might cause us to miss out on the action, or that we could become show offs and in the process endanger our own and our buddies' lives."

Luggage in hand, I waited outside the guest quarters as the sky lightened. A battered, mustard-coloured bakkie with one white and two black policemen in camouflage uniforms shuddered to a stop on the washboard road. One threw my bags into the back and motioned me to take his place in front. My small talk was met with stony, hung-over silence.

A short drive brought us to Okave, the sprawling headquarters of the South West African Police Counterinsurgency Unit. Feeling distinctly self-conscious in the new olive-drab uniform I'd been given, I wandered into the green maze of modular structures. Clusters of dirt-encrusted men in stained olive drab, obviously just returned from the bush, lounged along the shaded central walkway. From the guttural and incomprehensible Afrikaans, I caught the words "contact," "terrs" and "kills."

Unsure of where I was supposed to go, I paused alongside a group to ask the way. Conversation came to a halt as I was examined from head to foot. My camera bags triggered ill-concealed smirks. It would take a while to learn that visitors of any stripe were categorized as *uitlanders*—outsiders—and viewed with a mixture of suspicion and contempt. Following the directions of one glowering giant with a jagged scar across his cheek, I limped down the passageway and knocked at the door of Captain Bernie Ley's office. There was a growled, "Yeah, come in." Stocky and bearded with a quick-moving energy, Ley was already up to his eyebrows in paperwork when I entered. I was subjected to another slow scan.

"So you're the one the army pushed on us, eh?"

"Well, yeah, I guess so," clearing my throat.

"Terrific."

Frowning, he shoved the pile of paperwork to one side, found a form in his top drawer and got down to business. "Blood group? Next of kin? Your group leader will issue you with a weapon. Ever fired an R5? You understand that neither the South West African Police nor the government of South West Africa can be held responsible for any injury you may sustain while accompanying this unit on counterinsurgency operations? Got that? Good. Sign here."

Damn, I thought, leaning forward to scrawl my name.

After I'd answered the rest of his rapid-fire questions, I mentioned what I'd been told the night before about being kept away from any area where there might be a contact. "Look," I said, still dismayed at being stuck with a bunch of heavy-handed cops, "I appreciate the opportunity to see how you guys operate, but I really don't want to go out on some Boy Scout camping trip."

Ley fixed me with a withering look. "Listen, pal, we're sending you out for the next week with one of our best groups. That's four Casspirs, a Blesbok, almost 40 men and a helluva lot of experience. Our job is to stop the terrs. If you think we're going to waste all that on a media-relations exercise just for you, you're out of your mind."

"Oh," *sotto voce*. Then, brightly: "Do I need to take any identification?"

As I was asking, Captain Roelf Maritz, one of Koevoet's operations officers, walked through the door. I caught a quick, private look pass between him and Ley. *Where did this one come from?* it said.

"I don't think any terr's going to be too impressed with your press cards, pal," said Maritz.

I was making a real hit here. "Right." A map showing all police and army bases across the operational area covered one wall. "Okay if I take a picture of the map?"

"No."

This was getting better and better. *Well, they're South African cops, aren't they? What did you expect?*

Next to the map was a plaque with "Koevoet" at the bottom. It was the first time I'd seen it spelled. "Covet?" I asked, giving it an English pronunciation.

" '*Koo*' "—Ley said in exasperation—"and 'foot.' Got it? 'Koo-foot.' Don't you have any Afrikaans at all?"

I shrugged and shook my head. At least I'd brought an English-Afrikaans dictionary.

"Okay, come on," he said impatiently, "let me introduce you to the boss." I followed obediently in his burly wake. Across the open-air passage was Brigadier Johannes G. Dreyer's office. We found him standing outside his door, hands on hips and chatting with some of his men who had just returned from a week in the bush. Ley made the introductions and charged back to his office, shaking his head at the kind of people he had to deal with.

Dreyer, greying and lean with a bristling moustache, gave the impression of a man accustomed to taking command and getting what he wanted. Even the army referred to him by his nickname of "Sterk Hans"—Strong Hans. It was rumoured that he would already have been commissioner of the South African Police had he been willing to accept an assignment away from the fearsome unit he had founded eight years earlier. Dreyer's devotion to his men was legend—and, as I would learn, returned in full measure.

"I believe you're going out with Zulu Alpha this morning. That's one of our most experienced groups. Marius Brand, the group leader, is one of our best operators. I think you should find it interesting. If there's anything you need, please let me know."

Those clustered around him gave me stony stares and shifted impatiently. The interruption was not appreciated. I excused myself and wandered outside. A steady stream of men moved from storerooms to the Casspir armoured personnel carriers, carrying personal weapons, grenade launchers, medical kits, hydraulic jacks, crates of ration packs, tools and spare parts. A bewildering collection of South African and captured Soviet-bloc machine guns were being fitted to pintle mounts or placed inside with muzzles touching gunports. The amount of ammunition being stowed in each car suggested a serious intent.

"Maximum firepower," said a voice behind me. I looked around. It was Warrant Officer Marius Brand. "You can have too little, but you can't ever have too much." Tall and lanky, Brand moved with the loose-jointed swagger of a western gunslinger. "In a contact, you gotta overwhelm the terrs, break them up and kill 'em now-now. Especially in an ambush—you drive straight into them with maximum firepower." He smiled, but his eyes remained as cold as the *ndevandele*—cobra—on Zulu Alpha's team patch.

Marius Brand, ZA-1: "Ok! So now I have this journalist! I will try as hard as I can to be as straightforward and civilised as the situation allows, but we aren't angels and this is a war, not a Sunday school picnic. One of my worries is Kanjunga. If we catch any terrs I just do not know if we will be able to stop him from killing them. He is from Angola and suffered a lot from communism and hated the 'freedom fighters' for supporting it. If we aren't quick he'll shoot them as soon as he lays eyes on them."

Thys Loedolff, ZA-4: "The brigadier selected us to take him into the bush because we were the best: the highest spoor-kill ratio, most cases, least land mines, and best of all, all of us stayed alive from the time I joined the team until I left. (This I believe was because we were consistent in opening with scripture reading and prayer every single day. So we had to be protected.) But he also said that he would kill us if any harm should come to him. If we had known how reckless he was we would have objected."

Brand heaved my rucksack into the back of the Blesbok supply vehicle and I followed him to his command car. "You can take that seat across from Otto," he pointed, introducing me to an Ovambo warrant officer. The young man shook my hand in the African-style of palm grip, thumb grip, and palm grip again. Eight more Ovambos crowded into the Casspir. Magazines were inserted into R5 assault rifles that were then wedged between the seats. The black policemen hoisted themselves to the rim of the open-topped vehicle, legs dangling inside. By 11 o'clock, we were rolling, the men laughing and waving to friends along the dusty road.

Sitting in my assigned place, I examined what would be my home for the next week. Five moulded rubber seats and backrests lined either side, each separated by small, spring-loaded gunports—"pigeon holes"—topped by a row of thick, bullet-proof windows. Above the green-tinted glass, the armoured body sloped sharply inward on both sides, leaving a long rectangular view of the sky that stopped two feet short of the doors at the rear and one foot short of the forward-most seats. A pair of gunports was set below two smaller windows in the hydraulically-operated doors at the back. The narrow aisle running from the doors to the driver's and co-driver's seats was filled with machine guns, packets of ammunition, and tools. Between the open section overhead and the enclosed driver's cab was a separate hatch occupied by Brand.

Nine pairs of canvas boots swayed around me. I followed suit and lifted myself to the rim of the open well, holding on to the back plate behind Brand. Sitting across from me, eyes narrowed against the wind, was Warrant Officer Otto Shivute. Just 23 years old, he had been with Koevoet for six years. When we stopped to wait for one of the Casspirs to catch up, I asked him through Brand how many contacts he had experienced. He smiled shyly, shrugged and said simply, "Baie." A lot.

"Hoeveel?" I pressed, trying out a little Afrikaans from the new dictionary. How many?

Shivute spoke quickly to Brand. "He thinks it's around 100 or 120. He hasn't kept count."

"Why did he join the police?"

There was a brief conference. "No, he says had relatives killed by Swapo because they refused to support them. After that, he knew that the terrs didn't believe in all the things they claimed they were fighting for. Killing people because they disagree is not freedom or democracy. He also says he likes the work. Perhaps someday he'll find the terrs who killed his relatives. Otto's good, damned good," he added, for whom all his geese were swans. On open road, the armoured cars picked up speed. "We're killing them faster than they can be replaced," he shouted over the wind. "They're having to kidnap recruits and train them against their will." It was a story I'd already heard and discounted as propaganda.

We headed southeast to Ondangwa. Just before the air force base, the column turned onto a fork that branched north towards Oshikango, the border post between Namibia and Angola. Ten kilometres south of it we were brought to a halt by a crater surrounded with fresh debris. Insurgents had blown up the culvert running under the road. Men hopped out to examine the verges for possible land mines. When they signalled that it was safe, we turned off the tarmac and down the shallow embankment.

"When they got back to Namakunde they probably told their detachment commander they'd destroyed half a dozen Casspirs with that," Brand laughed as we regained the hard surface on the other side of the hole. "When you see the claims they make, you wonder what they were smoking. They exaggerate the hell out of what they've done to make themselves look good when they get back to Angola. And the commissars are happy to believe them. Sounds good in their press releases."

We passed a well-maintained dirt road on the right. "That's the Oom Willie se Pad," Brand said. "Goes east to Eenhana." Half a kilometre further, a small army base sat on the other side of the tar road. "Etale. It belongs to the army. There's some sappers there, too. They sweep the roads every morning for mines." Just beyond the base, we slowed and eased down the embankment again and into the bush, driving through low mopani thickets and uprooting small trees. We broke out into a clearing. In the middle of it stood a traditional kraal of upended tree trunks surrounding half a dozen thatched huts. The doors hissed open at the back of the Casspir and I followed the trackers, making the long step to the ground. We entered the kraal through an opening in the timber circle. Brand gave me a quick lesson on the interior layout. The thatched and wattle huts to the left, he said, were for the young men, while those on the other side were for girls who had reached puberty. The senior wife had her own hut, another accommodated younger wives.

He pointed at another hut on the west side inside its own separate compound. "That belongs to the head of the family. No one enters without his permission. He can drink his beer there without the women bothering him." Skulls of cattle were tied one above the other to the kraal fence by strips of tough bark. "Cattle are their wealth," Brand said, "and they only kill them for special occasions. The more skulls you see, the more it says about how rich and generous the family is."

Tall conical baskets of tightly woven bark sat on stilts a foot above the ground. Lined with clay as a barrier to ants and termites, they held stores of *mohango*, the staple crop of grain sorghum. Fields of it sometimes extended for 100 metres or more around a kraal. Brand explained that because the security forces were forbidden to drive through the crops, Swapo often used them for hiding places. "But I can promise you that if my buddies find spoor going into the mohango, they're not going in without fire support from the cars. We'll roll in with them, and to hell with the army's COMOPS."

I asked about the degree of support the insurgents enjoyed.

"Depends. Around here, which is where you find the heaviest infiltration, a lot of them are pro-Swapo. The further you go west or east, the less support you find. There are certain kraals we know where the local pops help them, but there are others that are definitely anti-Swapo. We get most of our info from the PBs. They might not like us, but a lot of them like the terrs even less."

"Sorry, but what's a 'PB'?"

"Plaaslike bevolking. Afrikaans for local population."

A dozen men, women and children emerged from the huts. All were dressed in shabby, Western-style clothes set off by traditional bead necklaces and bracelets. There was neither fear nor welcome on their faces, rather a stoical acceptance of the intrusion. Taking individual family members by the hand, the constables separated them to question each about the presence of any Swapo in the area. Shivute came back to say that three insurgents had been seen or heard about in the last two days. I was surprised. In spite of the blown-up culvert and the weapons everyone carried, it was difficult to believe there was a real war here.

"I can promise you there are at least a dozen Victor Yankees within ten klicks of here," said Brand. "The bad thing is, if they hear we're in the area, they sit tight or get the hell out. They're really scared of us."

Not wanting to test Brand's patience, I scribbled "Victor Yankee?" in my notepad. I'd eventually learn that it came from the first two letters of "vyand," Afrikaans for enemy.

Leaving the kraal behind, we drove another few kilometres to a village of corrugated tin shacks, where a group of flashily dressed young men stared with open hostility. Each immediately drew the attention of two or more policemen, pressing up close and demanding to see identity documents. The intimidation quickly cowed even the most belligerent. Eyes dropped and heads shook meekly. When their interrogations were complete, the trackers crowded into a dirt-floored cuca[1] shop to buy soft drinks. Brand and Shivute shared a litre bottle of warm Coke while discussing where to go from there.

We climbed into the Casspir and Brand spoke to someone on the radio. "We'll RV with Zulu Mike and go north," he said. "Maybe we'll have better luck up there."

A quarter of an hour later, I caught sight of a different type of armoured vehicle parked in the shade of a maroela tree. Nearby were three more of the big Wolf Turbos and their Strandwolf supply vehicle. Brand and Shivute climbed down to join Zulu Mike's team around a map spread on the ground. Heads nodded in agreement. They stood, brushed sand from knees and reboarded the cars. Ten diesel engines rumbled to life, exhausts blew black smoke, and both groups turned north.

Crashing through heavy undergrowth, we suddenly burst out of shadow into the bright glare of a 50-metre-wide clearing that ran straight as a die as far as I could see to the east and west. Shivute, one hand on the raised hatch behind Brand, saw my head swivel left and right as I took in the peculiar feature.

"Yati," he said.

I plucked up my courage and leaned forward. "Marius, what does 'yati' mean?"

"Cutline," he shouted, without looking back. Must be a firebreak, I decided. The column of Casspirs and Wolf Turbos paralleled the southern edge until Brand shouted a command to the driver and we turned to cross it. Otto lifted his chin towards the approaching tree line. "Angola."

Did he just say *Angola*? No way. The SADF briefers told me that the security forces crossed the border only in hot pursuit. We entered the trees and plunged back into shadow. I thumbed though my pocket dictionary. Finding the word, I tapped Shivute on the leg. "Wragtag?" Really? I asked, pointing around us. "Angola?"

He lifted his eyes from the passing ground and nodded. "Ja."

Shit! Unless I missed something, we weren't chasing anyone. Which meant we'd just invaded another country *looking* for someone to chase. In this case,

---

1   The name comes from a once famous but no longer available Portuguese-Angolan beer.

Swapo. Which, by permission of the Angolan government, had the legal right to be here. By extension, we were breaking every international law in the book by an armed incursion across a sovereign nation's border.

The deeper we drove, the more vehicle tracks I saw, tracks—I turned to look behind us—identical to those we were making. They were everywhere. It was obvious the South Africans not only entered the country at will, but with complete impunity. This was certainly turning into more than a Boy Scout camping trip.

Just before sunset and almost 50 kilometres north of the yati—"border" in normal English—we stopped near three deep, hand-dug wells. Crude winches of worn tree trunks drew buckets of sweet, cool water to top off the cars' tanks. One bucket came up containing a long-dead rat. The contents were emptied to one side and the bucket sent back down. When the tanks had been filled, we moved another few kilometres and the cars manoeuvred into a laager, guns facing outward.

"We'll set up our TB here," Brand said. He saw my puzzled look and sighed. "Temporary base. This is where we'll sleep tonight."

By the time food and bedding were unloaded from the Blesbok and Strandwolf supply vehicles a dozen cooking fires were already going. The trackers filled their mess tins with water and began lathering faces and torsos. I wet the corner of a towel and started to wipe off the day's sweat and dirt. Sergeant Dean Viljoen, on temporary duty from Zulu Delta as ZM's leader, laughed at my efforts. "It's something you get used to. We usually don't bother. You won't believe just how good a hot shower feels at the end of a week in the bush." I thought it would feel pretty good after one day.

As the camp was being organized, I turned to inspect the cars. Both types were similar, though the Wolf was wider, higher, four tons heavier and powered by an engine with three times the horsepower of that in the older Casspir. Aside from the angular surfaces, their most distinctive common features were the exposed axles and drive shafts outside a V-shaped hull. Starting about four feet above the ground, the sides sloped sharply inward to a narrow keel designed to deflect the force of exploding land mines. I'd eventually hear stories of cars rolling over as many as four mines stacked one on top of the other, the blast sheering off wheel and half-axle and lifting the front of a Casspir ten feet or more off the ground. Fatalities were rare, the worst injuries mostly limited to broken arms or legs.

Shivute and Sandsak, Zulu Alpha's second Ovambo warrant officer, hunkered down with Brand and discussed the next day's movements before going off to check on their men. When they had walked away, Brand told me that Sandsak was a hereditary clan headman with a price on his head. He'd had two pickup trucks blown up by mines or hit by Swapo gunfire and been seriously wounded by an anti-personnel mine.

Viljoen and another white joined us. "Porky wants to know what cameras and lenses you're using," Dean said, introducing his gangly partner. A born-and-bred Southwester, Ryk "Porky" Erasmus had only recently completed the Koevoet selection course and was on try-outs, gathering experience with different teams. His English was marginal, which seemed only to compound his natural shyness. Tall, painfully thin and quiet, this beardless 18-year-old with the quarter-inch haircut and jug ears looked like he should be back in high school, practicing his hook shots on the basket ball court, rather than driving through the bush behind two machine guns. He showed me a new 35mm camera he'd saved for a year to buy. I answered his questions about films, lenses and filters and offered what advice I could while Dean helped with the language barrier.

The other whites, almost as shy and quiet as Porky, kept to themselves. Zulu Alpha's Thys Loedolff, 25 years old, from Sasolburg in South Africa's Orange Free State, was newly married to his high school sweetheart, Topsie. Christo Schutte, even taller and lankier than Brand, was from Bethal and went by the nickname Skim—Phantom; getting a single word out of the 22-year-old was like pulling teeth. And finally, big, dark, and bearded Jacobus Andries, 23 and from Paarl, known to everyone as Apie—"Little Ape."

At the moment Apie was preparing a potjiekos. Like almost every South African, he had his own secret recipe for this traditional Afrikaner stew—even, such as now, when ingredients were limited. (Many years later, Chris Pieterse was moved to correct my description of Apie's culinary effort. "Proper potjiekos," he explained, "is a stew with real meat made in a cast-iron pot over a fire. What we did in the veld was to throw together various tinned products from our rat packs and call it a 'potjienaai'—a 'potfuck'. Maybe it doesn't translate too well, but you get the idea.")

After a critical taste, Apie added a good measure of Tabasco sauce, stirred his creation with the air of an artist, and raised the spoon for a taste. Frowning, he emptied what was left of the hot sauce into the pot. His expression after another delicate sampling suggested he had outdone himself. Eyes watering, he made a quick grab for a canvas water bag. A superb, if somewhat lively, *pièce de resistance*. Skim watched his sudden contortions with silent fascination.

Being in the middle of Indian Country with fires blazing seemed a touch unorthodox, but Brand explained that the insurgents were too frightened of Koevoet to even think about hitting us, worse luck. For one thing, they'd need to have a force already near a TB, the location of which was impossible to predict, and enough men to take on up to 40 battle-hardened Koevoet operators—twice that number if two teams shared a TB. One could but hope those circumstances arose, he added, because then, by God, they'd leave spoor we could follow in the morning and get some kills. Thinking he was joking, I almost laughed, but then realised he was serious. No security as an incentive for insurgents to attack was a tactic I'd never heard of. Brand's confidence was strangely reassuring. On the other hand…

By the time the last of Apie's spicy creation had been scraped from the pot the fire had burned down to embers. It had been a long day. Conversation lagged, replaced by yawns. One by one, the car commanders muttered "Lekker slaap" and stepped away to their sleeping bags. I found mine, pulled off my new canvas boots and slipped into it gratefully. Shortly after midnight, I was awakened by a hand on my shoulder. I raised myself on an elbow, thinking confusedly that it was already time to get up. Brand and Shivute were kneeling next to me.

"The boys just told Otto there are some people out there in the bush," Brand whispered. "Probably just some of the local pops looking for something to steal. We're going to scare them off. Stay where you are and don't move," and he disappeared in the direction of his car.

A few seconds later there was the hollow thunk of a mortar tube and then the pop of an illumination round bursting high overhead. Descending under its small parachute, the magnesium flare threw a harsh, blue-white light over the camp. I heard the unmistakable sound of a machine gun being charged and cocked, then a series of bursts, the tracers arcing high overhead to disappear into the night. The firing ended when the flare burned itself out, followed by the sounds of people running panic-stricken through the undergrowth. There were hoots and laughter from around the camp. Silence returned—except for someone snoring.

Apie had slept through it all.

Two days later we were back in Namibia, raising dust along the Oom Willie se Pad, the laterite road that ran east from the tar road near Etale to the SADF base at Eenhana. To either side, the bush had been cleared back for 20 or 30 metres, hardly far enough to put us out of range of concealed insurgents. Otto was thumbing through an Oshivambo-Afrikaans-English dictionary. Finding and writing down the words he wanted, he put his hand on Brand's shoulder. The whiplash thin commander shifted his eyes from the passing trees, looked at Otto's notepad, laughed and nodded.

Shivute turned to me with a smile and read them carefully in Afrikaans-accented English. "If we lucky, ambush!" I glanced at Brand who was again concentrating on the thick bush, one hand on the spade grip of the .50 calibre Browning. I looked back at the smiling Otto. No security around a TB. Hoping for an ambush. Was this really the crowd I should be hanging out with? It was obvious no one here was thinking on all cylinders.

Groups operating from Opuwa in the west to Rundu in the east kept Zulu 1 and Zulu 2—the Koevoet operations rooms in Oshakati and Eenhana—advised of their progress. If a team was on a "hot" spoor, Brand translated the Afrikaans transmissions into English for me, especially if a contact appeared imminent. When we heard that helicopter gunships had been scrambled to act as airborne spotters, he explained that the trackers reckoned the spoor was no more than 15 minutes old. Sometimes the attention-grabbing "Contact!" would come through unexpectedly, leaving everyone hanging until the outcome was relayed.

The worst calls were for a casevac chopper to take out the wounded. Who? How bad? Ops K was a tightly knit family and everyone held his breath till the extent of the injuries was known.

It soon became obvious that stealth was not part of the tactics. A Koevoet group on the prowl could be heard for hundreds of metres around. There wasn't only the sound of engines and drive trains that revealed our presence. Added to it were radios on high volume, the incomprehensible chatter of the trackers, the scraping of tree branches and low bush over and around the cars, ammunition belts clacking back and forth in their metal boxes and the rattle of whatever was loose in the cars. It was a blurred and constant sea of noise. We certainly weren't going to sneak up on anyone.

Brand took the handset away from his ear. "One of Zulu 5's teams has three spoor about 50 klicks west of here.[2] Terrs came across last night, grabbed ten kids and headed back towards Angola. The spoor's about eight hours old, but with all those kids, the gooks aren't going to be able to move very fast."

The first good sign Zulu Alpha's *spoorsnyers*—trackers—had was soon lost on hard ground, found, lost, and then found again. Side by side with Zulu Mike, we followed it most of the day, the Ovambos pointing out the signs with trimmed branches, "walking sticks." Where the tracks were clearly visible, the black policeman moved at a dead run, often outstripping the APCs in the thick bush. They would go until winded, drop back to the Casspirs, and their places taken by others who jumped off the sides of the rolling cars and took their place.

I watched Shivute running easily, the R5 slung under his arm. Occasionally, he stopped, dropped his chin and carefully examined the tracks. His eyes lifted to scan the bush ahead. Then he was off again, sprinting almost effortlessly through the soft sand.

Marius Brand, ZA-1: "This is what I wanted this journalist to see: Otto, Kanjunga, Linus, Leo, Caboy and Zula Alpha's other top trackers during a follow-up. Super athletes. The rhythmic running for hours and hours on those tracks. When one of them came to my Casspir for water, I gave him my water bag; this was how close we were. Racism didn't work here. We trusted one another with our lives. When I think back to those days, I was closer to my Ovambo people than to most of the other white policemen. They would go through hell and back as long as I was next to them. All those wonderful men! We took on the enemy together and each time came out victorious.

"The drivers, too—Fillip, Daniel, Pieta, Elusmus Johannes—and the way they could circle an ambush area and break the enemy's defence lines by driving straight into them, then swerving and turning while keeping the battle formation. 'Professional chaos,' someone described it, 'executed with precision.' This is what Koevoet was about. Camaraderie and teamwork. In the last two years we'd been in almost 50 battles and not lost anyone killed or wounded. All of these things were part of the story I wanted this journalist to write."

---

2   Zulu 5 was the western-most Koevoet detachment based at Opuwa in the Kaokoveld.

Where the spoor faded, the cars would stop and everyone disembark, fanning out to search. What they could tell from an imprint I could barely see was astonishing. "This one old man—short steps," they'd say, touching the ground with a walking stick; or "This is woman carrying baby;" or "This one Swapo—man with gun walks proud. You see?"

"Ah, yes, mm-hmm," I nodded, seeing nothing I could remotely identify as a footprint.

In thick bush there were frequent stops to clean leaves and twigs from the radiator grills and allow over-heated engines to cool. We stopped almost as frequently to change tyres punctured by stumps or thorns from acacia trees or pepper bush. I was busy with my notepad during a tyre change when Brand squatted next to me with a cup of coffee.

"You know those kids I told you about—the ones the terrs took? I just heard that four of them have been found. Apparently they couldn't move fast enough, so they were left behind. The Zulu 5 group following the rest thinks they're only a couple of hours behind them now.

"By the way," he asked out of the blue, "ever fired an RPG?" I shook my head. The only ones I had even seen before this trip were in photographs. "We have a few extra rockets if you'd like to shoot one off."

I slipped the notepad into a breast pocket. "Okay. But what would I shoot at? There might be someone wandering around in the bush."

"Just shoot it into the air. It'll automatically explode about 500 metres after you fire it."

Apie walked towards us, launcher in one hand and a rocket-propelled grenade in the other. Setting the flared bottom of the launcher in the sand, he screwed a bright-green booster into the bottom of the warhead, slid the booster down the muzzle and settled the Soviet-made weapon on my shoulder. He cocked the hammer and backed away, a deadpan expression on his face. I looked to my left and saw Skim and a few Ovambo constables with hunched shoulders, grins on their faces and fingers in their ears. A glance to the other side showed Brand, Apie and Shivute doing the same.

"I just aim it into the sky and pull the trigger, right?" I asked a little nervously, looking at Brand. The launcher swung with my shoulders and the men either side shifted smartly.

"Right," answered Brand, fingers coming out of his ears for a second, "but not too high or the back blast will burn your legs." I swung back. The two groups of men shifted again.

Based on sketchy information from the local population about Swapo insurgents, Otto Shivute and Marius Brand confer on which direction to take the search.

This typical complement of weapons includes personal R5 assault rifles, three Russian PKMs, and a Belgian FN MAG.

Christo "Skim" Schutte, Dean Viljoen, Marius Brand, Ryk "Porky" Erasmus, and Nick Coetzee discuss taking their teams across the cutline into Angola.

Zulu Mike's Strandwolf supply vehicle tucks in behind a Casspir
in the thick bush between Eenhana and Nkongo.

Under the protection of Marius Brand's guns, Zulu Alpha's
men follow anti-tracking spoor left by insurgents.

An early morning start – Apie and Skim in their command
hatches on the Chandelier Road outside Nkongo.

At a waterhole in Angola the team questions the PBs – local
population – about the presence of Swapo insurgents.

Skim Schutte and Jacobus "Apie" Andries enjoy a brief respite
in the shade before continuing the search for spoor.

Zulu Mike's Koos Combrinck jokes with Marius Brand, who is loathe
to leave his sleeping bag at a TB 50km inside Angola.

Leaves and early morning dew cover the main armament of a GPMG mounted alongside a .50 calibre Browning heavy machine gun. The GPMG on the left is fired from inside by the co-driver with cable-operated trigger.

Marius Brand in ZA-1 keeps pace with his men as they search for enemy spoor.

As their Casspir flanks colleagues on the ground, these men
prepare for the first sight of fleeing insurgents.

Jacobus "Apie" Erasmus and Thys Loedolff barely contain their frustration
at being stuck in a shona a few kilometres inside Angola,

Zulu Alpha's trackers Leo, Sebio, Josef, Otto and Mfewê prepare
for a silent follow-up 15km north of the yati.

Koos Combrinck, ZM

Chris Pieterse, ops officer

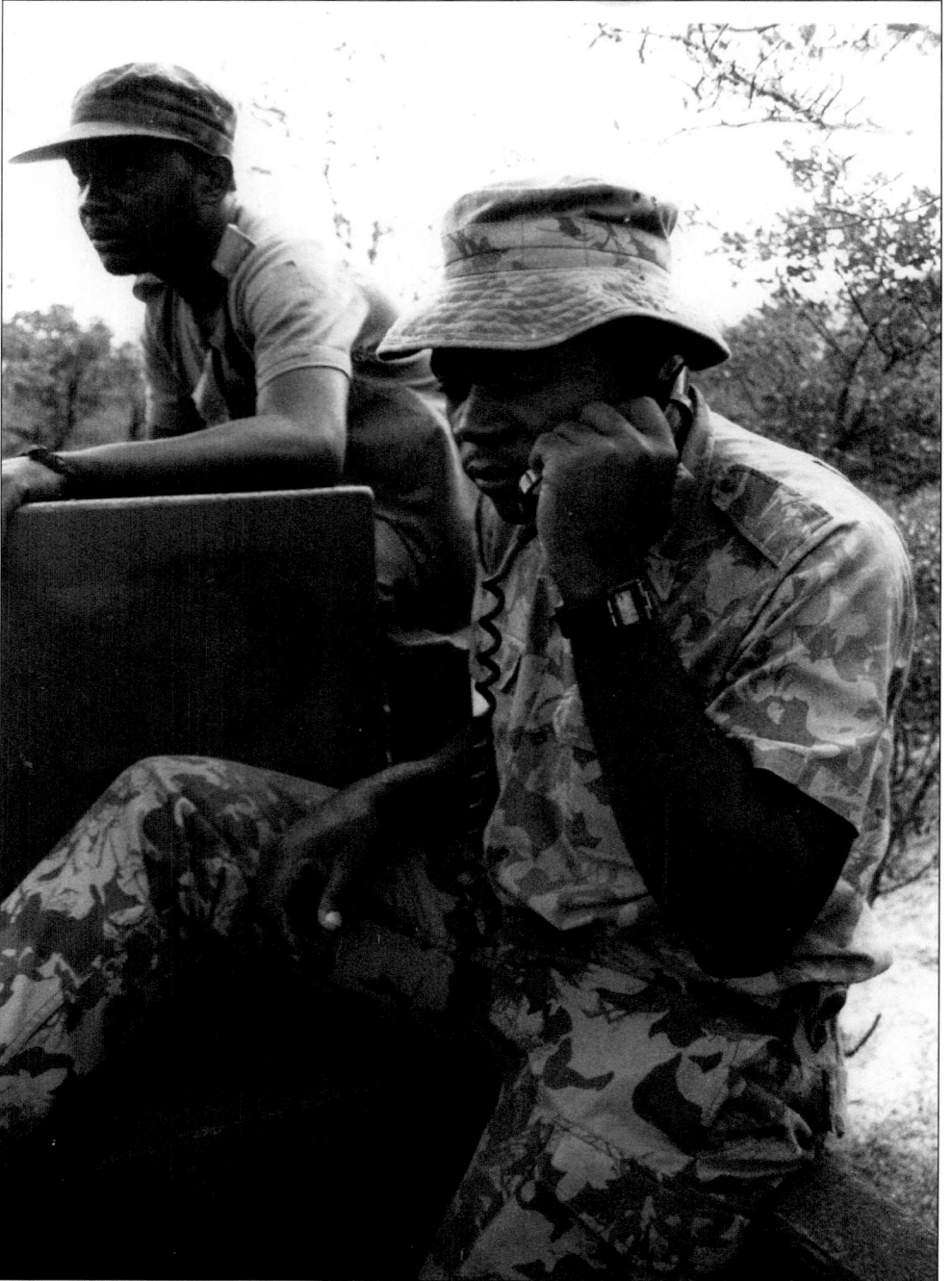

Lukas Kilino, the most senior black warrant officer in Ops K,
gets updates from Zulu November's other cars.

Jim Durand and the trackers of Zulu November put down suppressive fire during a contact.

From left, Yugoslavian "heatstrim" anti-armour rifle grenades, slender "pencilstrim" anti-personnel rifle grenades, AK-47s; at top, a Chinese Type 69 bounding mine and POM-Z stake mine with TNT charges.

Pierre Botha, author, Lukas Kilino, Thomas Kambanza, Boesman, Jansen Heputa, Didipunye Dawedapu, and Thinus Pretorius. Kneeling: Sidute, Kangiki Tjiuma, and Futo.

Pierre Botha, ZN

Samuel Pedro, ZN

With the Eenhana Z-2 operations centre in the background and SAAF ops tent and sleeping quarters to the left, Roelf Maritz, Jasper Genis, Herman Grobler, Marius Gouws, Botes Botha and Flip Fouche discuss where they will work for the day.

Zulu Foxtrot's Marius Gouws and Flip Fouche in the command hatches of their Wolf Turbos, with Zulu Hotel's Jasper Genis in his Casspir, wait for the rest of their teams to arrive before crossing the yati into Angola.

A tracker in Zulu Foxtrot's command Wolf Turbo watches as an Alouette gunship searches for Swapo insurgents 30km inside Angola.

Zulu Foxtrot marks fresh spoor for a following team, before racing ahead on voorsny to pick it up again.

A contact has been hit a few hundred metres ahead and these Zulu Foxtrot men look for targets.

Flip Fouche, Daniel Taiko and Botes Botha display AKM assault rifles
and equipment taken from the bodies of three Swapo insurgents.

Marius Gouws, ZF

Old Tom Cornelius, ZF

Haifeni Wilibard, ZF

Flip Fouche, ZF

"What if Dean sees it?" I asked, looking at Brand again. Everyone moved with me. "Won't he think something is happening?"

"No, no, I've already called him to let him know."

"Oh, okay," I said, swinging back. Out of the corners of my eyes I saw the men move again, fingers still in their ears. "Okay, here goes." I centred the optical sight on a cloud and squeezed the trigger. It was the loudest, sharpest and most physically painful *bang!* I had ever heard in my life, leaving me with ears ringing in a cloud of grey smoke. Grass and dirt blown up by the back blast settled over me. There was a black puff of smoke when the warhead exploded downrange.

I worked my jaw to clear my ears. The trackers were laughing and slapping their thighs while Brand and Apie fought grins. Brand said something.

"What?" I asked, my own voice sounding hollow and dim through the ringing.

Loud, isn't it? I read his lips.

Another day came to an end as we climbed out of the cars in front of the SADF base at Elundu. A watch tower and VHF antennas rose behind the sandbags and earthworks. As the Casspirs and Wolfs drove off to the fuel depot to rebunker half a dozen of us walked through the gate, the dirt-caked policemen swaggering menacingly. A fresh-faced army private quickly raised the red and white striped pole and averted his eyes under their glares. I squared my shoulders and worked on my own swagger.

We entered the sandbagged canteen and passed through an archway into the officers' and NCO mess. A few lieutenants, sergeants and corporals were at the tables. The hum of conversation died. There were sidelong glances as meals were hurriedly finished, and the diners left through a door on the opposite side.

> **Marius Brand, ZA-1**: "Because of Koevoet's reputation as the best counter-insurgency operators in Ovamboland, there was a lot of professional jealousy, and that led to a few scraps with both the Security Branch police and the army. But I was so good at what I did that my general covered for me each time I 'mishandled' any of them. We were basically untouchable and took full advantage of that."

A young soldier, downy fuzz covering his upper lip, squeezed behind the rough-sawn bar top and dispensed cold Castles. There was a symphony of pops and hisses as the beers were opened, followed by sighs and smacking lips when the first swallows hit bottom. Two freshly showered corporals in starched army browns entered and did a double take when they saw the green Koevoet uniforms and filthy faces. Eyes turned towards them and narrowed. There was a tangled about-face as they jammed the door in their eagerness to leave.

"What's the matter with these guys?" I asked. Here was a perfect opportunity to talk with army professionals who had to know more about bush warfare than some small police unit. The only problem was that they didn't want to join us.

"I don't know," Brand said, taking a drag on his cigarette.

"The army doesn't like us too much," volunteered Viljoen with an air of undeserved injury.

"Why's that?"

"Well, we just don't get along with them too good," Apie said.

"Why?"

"Well, there was this fight a while back…" His voice trailed off. I waited expectantly. " … but no one was killed."

"Killed?"

"No, genuine, no one was killed. I mean, after they started it in the canteen at Eenhana they were getting the worst of it. So when they went for their Casspirs, we had to go for ours. You know," he shrugged as though it was only natural.

"I don't understand," I admitted.

"You know, when they started using the guns on their Casspirs, we sort of had to defend ourselves."

"Hold on. You were shooting at each other? With *machine* guns?"

"Yeah, but no one was killed."

"But why?"

"No, well, I guess because it was dark and everyone was pretty drunk."

Thank God for night and lots of alcohol, I thought.

"Fucking army," Dean growled. "Make no mistake, man, we get most of the kills and they get the credit for it. All you see in the press releases is 'the security forces killed so many terrs.' Everyone back in the States thinks it's the army doing it. That's bullshit, man!"

"But aren't you all on the same side?" The pause that followed confirmed they bloody well weren't on the same side at all. I felt a pall of suspicion settle over me.

The base commander appeared at the door. As if to show they were the innocent parties, the policemen generously waved the lieutenant into his own canteen and handed him a beer. Dean made a show of standing and offering him his bar stool, checking sidelong to see that I noticed. Moments later, the medical officer peeked round the door and was greeted with rare bonhomie. He stepped in cautiously and a bar stool was immediately vacated for him. See what good guys we are? A beer was placed in front of him, and I was introduced.

For the next two hours, Brand, Viljoen and the others told stories of contacts and kills, obviously for the benefit of me and the two other outsiders, pausing to politely answer questions. As I listened and watched the rapt faces of the base commander and his medical officer, I began to suspect that maybe these guys were more than just cops.

After much handshaking and thanks for hospitality, we made our exit. Walking out through the gate, which lifted smartly for us, one of our number cleared his throat. "No, we get along fine with the army. It's them who cause the shit every time. But those guys were okay; they didn't try to start anything."

"Yeah," someone sighed in the dark. He sounded disappointed.

On the fifth morning, word came over the radio that "Charlie Tower," a small outpost near the border had been "revved"—mortared—in the middle of the night. Quickly breaking camp, we headed for the scene of the crime. When we arrived an hour later, three other Koevoet groups were already there. Walking over the area, I noted that many of the mortar rounds had failed to explode, their tail fins protruding from the hard ground. The aim wasn't very good, either. All had impacted at least 100 metres short of the intended target, an elevated concrete reservoir guarded by a squad from the South African Cape Corps. Taking a back bearing from the angle of the half-buried mortars, the trackers soon found where the tubes had been positioned. A message was scrawled in the sand: "Boer dogs. If you are looking for us, we will be in Namakunde."

The spoor of at least 40 insurgents was found and the groups fanned out, racing off in a cloud of dust to pick it up further ahead. The dust came to an abrupt end as we ran into a series of *shonas*—low-lying areas with a foot or more of water. The cars slowed to a crawl.

Brand told me the attackers were probably already back inside Angola and heading for Namakunde, 13 kilometres north of the border. An official policy of hot pursuit meant that the fighting groups were allowed to chase them to within eight kilometres of the Angolan army base. A terse radio call from Brigadier Dreyer gave a stern reminder to go no closer. I wondered if it was because of my presence.

By late afternoon and a little over two kilometres north of the yati, it was obvious Koevoet had lost this round. All four of Zulu Alpha's Casspirs were stuck fast in the middle of a particularly soft-bottomed shona. Branches were cut and jammed under the tyres and shoulders put to the cars. The wheels spun on the slippery bottom, spraying the pushers with mud, and settled a little deeper.

Before the cars had clouded the water, the soft imprints left by dozens of feet walking north had been clearly visible. The initial excitement of the chase soon turned to impotent rage. Zulu 1 eventually radioed to say that intelligence sources confirmed 58 insurgents had made their escape and were now safe in the Namakunde base. The unwelcome news elicited explosive oaths. This was in direct contravention of agreements between Angola and South Africa that Fapla would in no way support Swapo.

Brand radioed our predicament to Viljoen and then fired a "thousand-footer" flare to mark our position. A few seconds later, we saw an answering flare streak into the air far to the southeast. Viljoen would try to reach us before dark, but at the moment he was having his own problems getting around the shonas. It wouldn't do for both groups to get stuck.

As sunset approached, the trackers began unloading bedrolls and weapons, wading to a dry spot in the middle of the stagnant water. When I saw them laying out illumination rounds next to a mortar tube and positioning machine guns, it finally hit me that we were there for the night. I slipped on a sweater against the drop in temperature and sat on the warm bonnet of the Casspir. The things one went through for a story.

The sun disappeared. As if on cue, the quiet was broken by the bass burps of frogs declaring their love for each other. I shifted uneasily on my hard perch. What a dumb place to be. A furred and feathered orchestra of other unseen creatures added their night calls. *Tweet, burp, chk-chk-chk, burp.* Having spent some of my childhood years in Texas listening to tales about the Indian wars of the 1870s and '80s, I suddenly had a mental image of Apaches slipping into position around the cavalry.

Viljoen radioed again to say that it was too dark for him to continue and that they were stopping for the night. He fired a last thousand-footer to mark his position for us, and Brand answered it with another. They blazed into the blue-black sky, reaching their zeniths, then slowly descended and dimmed before winking out. It brought our predicament into unwelcome focus. We were stuck. In Angola. At night. No other group was near enough to help. Not all that far away were at least 58 armed-to-the-teeth Swapo insurgents holed up in a Fapla base. And with another Fapla border post at Oshikango less than five kilometres to the east, they had to know exactly where we were from the flares.

I climbed over the machine gun and into the Casspir. Clearing my throat respectfully, I mentioned these minor points to Brand, wondering what the plan was if the bad guys slipped on down tonight and laid into us with some serious pyrotechnics. A few mortars. Maybe an RPG or two. Not that I was worried or anything like that. No, just curious. Besides, I was sure he already had everything worked out: some brilliant piece of police work which would handle any eventuality.

He slapped at a mosquito. "Fuck 'em," he said through a yawn, "they can't hit shit anyway."

I stared silently at him for a moment. There was a lengthening pause neither of us saw fit to interrupt. Stretching out across the seats, I zipped up the sleeping bag he tossed at me and tried to fluff up a rock-hard ammo vest for a pillow. You were right: these people must have been brain-damaged at birth. Totally out of touch with reality. Barking. The night passed without incident, though it was a bleary-eyed and much-relieved non-combatant who saw the eastern sky finally touched by dawn.

Late in the morning, Viljoen and his Wolf Turbos reached the edge of the shona. Two of them backed into the water, being careful to stay on reasonably hard bottom. The second pair remained on dry ground, positioning themselves, like the first two, in tandem. Cables were run between the four Wolf Turbos and then to the nearest Casspir. The rest of Zulu Alpha's cars, bogged down in a neat line, were similarly attached to each other. With all eight APCs hooked together, engines roared and belched smoke, cables tightened, and the chain of cars slowly dragged itself, link by link, from the clinging mud.

Back on solid ground, we stopped to brew coffee and dry socks and canvas boots over a fire. I was digging a thorn out of my foot when Brand walked over. "I just heard on the radio that they finally rescued those kids," he said angrily. "The terrs left them and started running when the group got too close. Didn't help them. Floored all three of the bastards."

"So what's wrong?" I asked.

"No, the oldest kid, a 15 year-old girl who's a real little Swapo sympathizer, when they took the kids back to their village, she told everyone that *our* people had kidnapped her and the others. Shit!"

The next day, we responded to the scene of another mortar attack. By the time we arrived, two other groups were already there. Again, spoor was found, this time from eight insurgents, but lost on hard ground, found again—just as before. At least in this area we had no shonas to wade through.

In the middle of a field of rumbling cars, Brand asked if I'd like to ride with the "Brig," who had come out for the hunt. He pointed to a Wolf Turbo sporting the letters BD. I grabbed my camera bag, hopped out and ran to the spotlessly maintained Wolf. Climbing through the rear doors, I thought I had the wrong car; there was no sign of Brigadier Dreyer. Then I caught sight of him in the driver's seat.

"If he has the time, you can't keep him out of the field," one of his staff said admiringly.

As the sun sank, we stopped outside the police base at Ohangwena. Officially known as 21D, it was, like Elundu, surrounded by earthen walls topped with razor wire. Manned by Security Branch personnel doing their annual three-month border duty, it sat just east of the tar road that we had followed from Ondangwa on my first day. Five kilometres further north was the Oshikango border post. As the TB was being organised outside the berm, we walked through the gate to accept the hospitality of the house.

The young lieutenant in charge passed beers around and we took chairs on a concrete patio alongside a large wire cage. Inside it, two vervet monkeys leapt from branch to branch of a dead tree, chattering for attention. The commander reached into his pocket for a few peanuts and tossed them through the wire. To the other side, a pair of shoats raced after two young dogs. Barks and oinks overlapped as one species was bowled over by the other.

"Those damn pigs think they're dogs," he said. "In fact, they're better than the mutts as watch dogs." Then he pointed across the parade ground. "But those are the best." I followed the direction of his finger and saw two baboons, one sitting at the foot of the berm, the other pacing back and forth at the top. "Anything comes close at night, they go crazy."

Were they tame? I asked. He tilted his hand back and forth. "So-so. The female is okay, but Bobba the male can be a little aggressive. We had to get the army dentist to pull his fangs."

"He's fine," Brand said. "Go say hello."

I slung a camera over my neck and wandered across. The female sidled up timidly and began grooming the hair on my legs. There was a commanding bark from the male and she sped away as her companion loped towards me. He rose on his back legs and pulled the cassette recorder from my breast pocket. I took it back. Then he grabbed the camera, almost yanking me off my feet. I pulled back, and there was blur of motion as he dragged me forward and buried his teeth in the crook of my right arm. We were rolling in the dust, when one of the Ovambo policemen charged in with a raised stick. As quickly as he'd attacked, he was gone. I was left sitting on the ground, blinking in surprise and looking very foolish. Behind me, Marius, Thys, Apie and Skim were in hysterics.

Inside the infirmary, the base doctor cleaned up a long, deep scratch on my shoulder and was finishing the second stitch on two punctures in the arm. "That's why we had to pull Bobba's incisors," he said, snipping the thread and reaching for the antiseptic. "He does that all the time."

Wearing bandages and blotches of red-orange Betadine, I returned to the patio. Brand handed me a fresh beer. "Africa's a tough place," he said straight-faced. I got the distinct impression I'd been set up. Again.

The week with Zulu Alpha came to an end. Swapo, through fortune or skill, had managed to keep out of the ZA's way. Groups working other areas of Ovamboland's 30,000 square miles found what they were looking for. Seven Swapo insurgents had fallen to Koevoet's guns. After more than 600 miles of patrolling, we rolled back through the gates of Oshakati. As we pulled into Okave headquarters, I had already rehearsed my lines. Home, hearth and a girlfriend were waiting in England, but I was here and it would be foolish not to try pushing it a little further for a decent article.

Limping into Captain Ley's office in my diesel, dirt and sweat-stained clothes, face and arms just as filthy and crisscrossed with scratches from battling the bush and a baboon, I asked if I could sign on for another week. Ley surveyed my dishevelled state, put down his pen and leaned back, hands behind his head.

"I think it can probably be arranged," he allowed, trying to keep from laughing outright at my appearance. "Take a seat and I'll go ask the boss."

6

Sound of Guns

Pierre Botha, car commander, Zulu November: "We had our first experience with outsiders in the early '80s when some South African reporters were allowed in. I can still remember Boesman sending me to meet them in the ops room the day they arrived. The snotty attitude of one of them pissed me off and I went back and informed Boesman about my feelings. Their equipment had already been loaded on our cargo vehicle so we tossed it all into another team's Blesbok and deployed without them!

"During the next couple of years we had a few civilians—equipment testers for manufacturers—go into the veld with us. Because we never had any combats when outsiders were with us, we became highly superstitious and shied away from them. When Brigadier Dreyer told us we'd be taking a foreign journalist, we were not impressed and became very negative about the whole thing. We were one of the most successful teams and didn't want to risk a week without a fight. We managed to get out of it at first because he arrived just when we came off deployment and were on our rest week, so he went with ZA. But then he was staying for another week and it was going to be with us.

"Boesman, Thinus and I began to scheme how we were going to get out of it. We decided to tell Brigadier Dreyer that none of us could speak English, so it would be a fruitless exercise. What was the point if we couldn't communicate with this journalist? We thought this would be our fail-safe way out. Imagine our surprise when the Brigadier said he was sending Jim Durand with us as an interpreter!"

The next morning, I rolled out of Oshakati with Group Zulu November. At the last minute, Sergeant Jim Durand had been assigned to ride with me. I immediately felt guilty when he explained that he had already signed out of the unit, but because no one in ZN spoke English, Dreyer wanted someone along who could translate.

Hardly the image of a killer, Durand was almost baby-faced in spite of the beard he sported. A touch over six feet tall, his soft, well-spoken English was at odds with the jarring Afrikaans-English of most of the unit. Outward appearances belied a reputation for aggressiveness and quick thinking under fire, which had made him one of the legends of the unit. Brand had already related a campfire story or two about him.

After seven years of combat operations, Durand was heading back to South Africa with his wife and new baby to take up somewhat quieter police duties. When he laughingly mentioned that guys always seemed to get hurt or killed just when they were ready to leave, I had an immediate sense of guilt. What if something happened to him simply because I wanted a story?

"No, no, it's okay," he assured me. "If I wasn't doing this, I'd be out setting up night ambushes anyway."

Leading Zulu November was taciturn and barrel-chested "Boesman" (Warrant Officer Stephanus Pretorius in real life, but no one called him anything but "Bushman.") Boesman was in his sixth year and led Koevoet's highest-scoring combat group. The previous February the team was leading a follow-up when they hit a 40-man Swapo ambush. In the swirling confusion of the contact, 35 of the insurgents were killed for only five wounded on Boesman's side. As we rolled out of Oshakati, their tally for the first four months of 1986 stood at 47. Commanding the car I'd be riding in was Warrant Officer Lukas Kilino. Big and powerfully built, his eyes seemed to miss nothing.

Boesman's sixth sense took us into an area where ZN's trackers picked up fresh spoor almost immediately. At one point, they figured it no more than two hours old, and gunships were put on standby. Within a minute, Eenhana called back to say that the Alouettes could be overhead within 12 minutes of getting the word to scramble.

Although a contact appeared imminent, this group of insurgents "bomb-shelled," each taking off in a different direction, and "anti-tracked," backing up on their own spoor, staying on hard ground wherever possible and moving from one tuft of tough grass to another; anything and everything to make their tracks more difficult to follow. The trackers admitted these were some old Swapo who knew how to survive.

Before the sun had set, a TB had been established and fires lit. After a ration-pack supper, Kilino sat cross-legged next to Boesman. There was an obvious bond between these two men, black and white, brought about by mutual respect and sharing extreme danger. "Lukas is from Angola," Boesman said haltingly—so he did speak English, I thought—"and started fighting when he was only 14 years old." Recognised by Holden Roberto's anti-Portuguese FNLA guerrilla movement as a natural leader, Kilino was selected to attend officer's school in Kenya, then spent two years in the People's Republic of China, where he was taught the finer points of both insurgency and conventional warfare. He had made 15 parachute jumps, learned to use explosives, and was familiar with Western and East-bloc weapons. The two-year course had been so difficult, he remembered, and the winters so cold that a number of his fellow Angolans had died during the training.

When the Soviet-backed MPLA seized power in Angola, Kilino, by now a senior officer in the Chinese- and CIA-backed FNLA, became a marked man. Evading his erstwhile anti-colonial allies, he made his way south to Namibia and joined South Africa's little-publicized 32 Battalion. After years of deep-penetration operations against communist forces in the country of his birth, he transferred to Koevoet.

He told me about his brother, who also left Angola to join 32 Battalion. He arrived after Kilino moved to Koevoet, believing Lukas had been killed in the aftermath of the revolution. He served five years as a medic with the highly secret unit, yet never heard his brother's name mentioned. Tiring of the two- to three-month-long missions, he eventually transferred to Koevoet. The reunion of the two in Oshakati—each thinking the other dead for the last ten years—was, he told me, like seeing ghosts come alive.

Kilino asked about the United States, and especially the "Negroes" there, curious to know if they served with whites in the army and police. His Chinese political instructors stressed that blacks in America were still slaves and kept in poverty with no political rights. "And you call them 'niggers'—like 'kaffir,'" he observed. I squirmed and tried to explain that such had been the case—and not so long ago—but that things had changed enormously in the last 20 years.

Before going to sleep, Kilino pointed at me and spoke earnestly to Boesman.

"Lukas wants me to tell you that communists are no friends of black Africans. He says the communists think all blacks are stupid and use them only for their own purposes. He wants to make sure you understand that." I motioned I understood. Kilino nodded and without another word went to sleep.[1]

Mornings at a TB started before dawn when the first sleepy risers stirred last night's coals into life, sending sparks into the cold dark. There was the

---

1   Kilino was later promoted to the rank of inspector-lieutenant. A battery of psychological examinations, which every potential officer must take, showed an I.Q. in the genius range.

lonely sound of a cough here and there; the small ruby glow of a first cigarette punctuated the awakening camp. Sweaters were pulled on against the chill and silhouetted figures slowly began to cluster around the fire, palms towards the warmth.

As thin light began to filter through the bush, more figures slipped from brown, dew-covered sleeping bags, some moving to the perimeter to urinate, others washing from mess tins. Before the sun had made its appearance, there was the smell of coffee in the air. Sleeping bags were rolled up and everything loaded into the idling cars. I had just tossed my rucksack to the policemen at the back of the Blesbok when I noticed Boesman at the edge of the camp. Deeply religious and private, he had unwrapped a small Bible from a piece of oilskin and was sitting alone under a tree, reading a passage. I watched until he finished and carefully rewrapped the Word of God. I wondered which passage it had been.

I was sitting cross-legged, scribbling in my notepad, when I heard, *"Parlez vous Francais, m'sieur?"* Zulu November's ops medic, Sgt Manuel Pedro, squatted in front of me and introduced himself. Trained as a nurse by the Portuguese in Angola, he had joined the FNLA, which operated out of Zaire. When the Cubans arrived to support the Marxist MPLA, Pedro, like Kilino, escaped to Namibia and was recruited into 32 Battalion, later transferring to Koevoet. I very much regretted not having better French to understand everything he said.

When the sun was full born on the horizon, we moved out, another long and dusty day ahead of us. On this morning, a full moon still hung in the western sky. The morning followed the pattern of all the others: stopping at kraals and questioning the locals, moving through the bush to the next kraal, everyone scanning the ground for spoor. Breakfast was a midmorning affair, eaten on the move out of ration pack cans.

We were sitting under a maroela tree during a noontime coffee break when "Contact!" burst from the radio. Behind it was the sound of gunfire. Coffee mugs stopped at lips and were slowly lowered as ears strained to pull more from the air. Then came the call for a casevac chopper.

Silent looks passed between the men. One went to stand nearer the car, as though it would force more from the radio. Finally, the story crackled from the speaker. A group had hit an ambush. Three insurgents had been killed, but one car commander was seriously wounded. The impact of the bullet fired at close range had knocked him completely out of the car. Within minutes, a helicopter pilot taking off from Eenhana confirmed that he was airborne and heading towards them. Nothing more was heard.

Flicking what was left of the coffee aside, we climbed into the Casspirs. The mood was camouflaged with thin jokes. Diesels rumbled, clutches were engaged and we moved out. The routine continued. Later, with two hours of daylight left, we turned west towards the Security Branch base at Ohangwena. Durand and I were sitting opposite each other, eyelids heavy and heads nodding to the sway of the car. The interior of the Casspir brightened as we crashed out of the bush onto a grassy pan dominated by a water hole and spotted with a few stunted trees. It was then that Boesman saw them.

"CONTACT!"

I snapped back from wherever I was, my eyes opening wide and meeting Durand's for one of those interminable half seconds. He held my surprised stare for the same split-second before spitting, "Contact!" and swivelling to snatch his R5. The Casspir's engine bellowed and I heard the guns of at least one car already firing. Then our car was veering hard left, the car ahead breaking to the right, all four Casspirs fanning out across the pan. Totally unprepared for the violence of the manoeuvre, I was almost flung from the seat as I fumbled with the switch on my cassette recorder and scrabbled with the other hand for my camera bag.

Around me, the first infusion of adrenaline had dissolved the lethargy of a second earlier. There was a blur of hands grabbing for weapons and the arhythmic ripple of *shhklacks* as bolts came back and fell on chambered rounds. Muzzles were jammed through the spring-loaded gun ports. Only Boesman had a positive target. But with no one else knowing the strength or location of the insurgents, everyone began laying down suppressive fire to all sides.

Pierre Botha, ZN-4: "We were on our way to Ohangwena to rebunker, going through an area where we'd had success in the past when we came to a kraal clearing and Boesman shouted 'Contact!' over the radio. We all raced ahead and got involved in the fight. As usual, it was chaos as no one knew how many insurgents there were. We started firing into the areas of thick bush which normally served as hiding places."

The high-pitched chatters of assault rifles on full automatic mingled with the deep-throated *thudthudlhud-thudthud* of the .50 calibre Brownings; everyone shouting, firing, looking left-right for targets, some standing and firing over the edge of the Casspir, others through the gun ports below the windows. There was the sudden burn of hot brass on my bare legs, and I heard the hollow *whunk!* of a grenade launcher. The tracker to my right jammed the short barrel of his R5 through the gun port just as the 11-ton car bounced hard over a rut. The muzzle came back inside on full automatic, bullets hitting the pigeon plate and spattering those around him with hot splinters.

I jerked my stung legs away and was trampled by the grenadier diving towards the rear of the car for more ammunition. I was bowled over again as he came back through the throng of unsteady legs, everyone trying to hold on and fire from the shaking, twisting Casspir as it careered left and right to present as difficult a target as possible for an RPG or anti-armour rifle grenade.

I was trying to take photos of the chaos inside, the air solid with the firing, shouting, thin smoke, hot brass, bursts of excited Afrikaans and Oshivambo over the radio, engine racing and drive train screaming in protest as the driver jammed up, down and through the gears. I yelled stupidly at Durand, "HOW MANY ARE THERE? WHERE ARE THEY?"

"WHEN YOU DRIVE INTO THEM LIKE THIS THERE'S NOTHING ELSE YOU CAN DO!"

I tried twice to stand to get shots of what was happening outside, only to be slammed back into my seat by one of Kilino's huge hands. Looking through the window, I saw the ground erupting zipper-like under the impact of .50 calibre bullets. I stood again, ducking under Kilino's hand. In the brief moment before he yanked me down, I saw Boesman's car angling away from us, pouring fire into the bush near the water hole. We raced in behind him, turning to hit the suspected position from the opposite side. Above the roar, I heard Durand yelling, "STOP! STOP! UNDER THE BUSH! THERE'S ONE UNDER THE BUSH!"

We shuddered to a stop. The doors hissed open and I followed the trackers, who half-mooned around a clump of low-hanging thicket, their weapons spitting bursts of high-velocity bullets and erupting streams of empty cartridge cases. Durand was next to me, yelling, "THERE'S ONE IN THERE!" and I suddenly wondered what the hell I was doing outside the car. When the men moved forward, I followed them under the branches, expecting a body, but seeing only webbing and leather pouches, a gourd half filled with homemade mohango beer. The firing had stopped, replaced by hard, gasping laughter and the high-pitched giggles of excitement.

Pierre Botha, ZN-4: "The shooting carried on for a couple of minutes before Boesman shouted to cease fire. We had killed two insurgents. More importantly though, we believed our superstitious drought with outsiders had been broken so we started to warm up to this foreign journalist."

"The bodies are over here," Pierre said behind me. I saw the first one lying face up on a pile of dead branches next to the water hole. Further on, at the base of a tree, was the second, face down. The trunk of the tree bore the bright wounds of bullets. One of the Ovambo trackers yanked the body onto its back. He reached inside the camouflage shirt and pulled a checked collar into view. "Civvie clothes, see?" he hissed, contemptuous of the attempted deceit. He cut the leather web harness away and began laying out its contents. Two types of plastic-finned projectiles were placed carefully on the ground.

"Rifle grenades?" I asked

"The fat ones are anti-armour heatstrims," Pierre nodded. "Goes through a Casspir, easy. The thin ones, they're pencilstrims. Anti-personnel." The ribbed extension for launching the grenades had been shot cleanly off the muzzle of one of the AK-47s.

"Hey!"

I looked up at the shout and saw two of the trackers raise their R5s. From the nearest mohango field a waving white shirt was followed by an old man emerging cautiously from the tall stalks. The trackers motioned him forward, and he shuffled on aged legs to the first body, then to the second, staring dumbly.

"What will you do with the bodies?" I asked, watching the timid arrival from the corner of my eye.

"We'll leave them for the locals to bury."

Boesman shouted for everyone to return to the cars. The sun was dropping rapidly, and he wanted to reach Ohangwena before dark. As we walked towards the cars, the tracker ahead of me hawked and spat hard in the face of the body atop the branches. The flies buzzed angrily and quickly resettled. The old man stood nearby, head bowed as though in prayer. I hoped it wasn't his son lying there. (Two days later, another group working the area picked up information that the two had been part of a five-man team. The others had been gathering food a mile away when they heard the firing and escaped—until the end of the week, when they fell to the guns of another Koevoet group.)

That night around the fire at Ohangwena, a full moon hanging in the African sky, Boesman explained that when we came out of the bush, the two insurgents had broken from their hiding place next to the water hole. Had they stayed hidden, they could easily have taken out one or more of the Casspirs, or gone entirely unnoticed.

The tape I'd made brought everyone gathered round to listen, asking that it be rewound and listening again, recognizing each other's voices amid the fury of the firing. Some re-enacted Kilino shoving me down when I tried to stand. Others howled with laughter as they pantomimed the grenadier running over me once, then a second time. In the middle of it all, Lukas caught my eye. He nodded and pointed at me, then raised a huge black fist, thumb up. I ducked my head and actually blushed.

The morning after returning to Oshakati, I was scheduled on a flight back to Pretoria. On the way to Ondangwa Air Force Base, I asked the army lieutenant to make a short detour. It was Wednesday, the beginning of a new week for half of Ops K. Around the long, corrugated stores next to headquarters, teams were loading up for another seven days in the bush. There was Marius Brand, ever the slouching gunslinger, holster tied low on his thigh, and Shivute, Skim, Thys, and Sandsak, Viljoen, Porky and the others whose names I could never remember, just as I had seen them that first day two weeks before. Shaking hands, saying the good-byes, I was struck with the uncanny feeling that some part of my destiny lay here.

As the car pulled away, I turned to look back, watching until they disappeared from view. You crazy bastards, I thought. Go safely.

7

Ovamboland Return

Thys Loedolff, ZA-4: "A week after Jim left, we were at Eenhana when 21D, the base at Ohangwena, was revved in the early hours of the morning. It was still dark when the SADF woke us up and we were moving in 15 minutes. One Casspir had been left at Oshakati with mechanical problems, and by the time we reached Ohangwena one of the remaining three had broken front suspension blades, and another had snapped a centre pin. The centre pin could be repaired in an hour, but we needed to take the spoor while it was still hot. My car was the only one in good shape, so Marius instructed me to continue the follow-up.

"I loaded as many trackers as possible, and found the spoor of 55 terrs. A group that size makes such a clear path that we were able to move at 60kph, and within ten minutes we had crossed into Angola at St Mary's Mission. I knew that if we hit a contact with only one Casspir we'd be in big trouble. I was scared shitless, but didn't dare show fear as it would ruin the team spirit and you would not be accepted as a section leader any more. So I pressed ahead with a lot of worried Ovambos on board.

"Needless to say, I was on the radio the whole time organizing gunships, talking to Evert from Zulu Yankee, who was coming from Eenhana, and Johan Bosch with Zulu Kilo, who was west of us. We were about ten kilometres inside Angola, not far from Namakunde, when Zulu Yankee showed up. Right after that, Zulu Kilo arrived and triggered an ambush that had been laid for us. Johan got stuck in a shona and was drawing serious fire. Just at that moment, the gunships arrived and saved our butts. The pilot in the command chopper was critiquing our formation and battle discipline when I saw an RPG go right through the rotor blades without touching anything.

"We killed 15 Swapo with no losses on our side, and captured lots of AKs, RPGs and even two SAM-7 'Strelas.' It was the only time I ever saw an AK-47 equipped with an infra-red night sight. After it was all over, the choppers landed to refuel from our Blesboks. The pilot whose chopper was almost hit by the RPG had a naturally light complexion, but when he climbed out, he was much whiter than usual.

"If Jim had stayed just a week longer …"

Back in England, my stories about Koevoet sold well and I wondered where to go next. But sitting at my desk overlooking the quiet Hampshire countryside, I couldn't shake the feeling of needing to return. Memories of the place, the unit, continued to haunt me. Every full moon over the South Downs would take me there as I thought of the people I had met and wondered how they were faring. Were they in the bush at that very moment? Were they okay? Had any of them been hurt? The story wasn't complete; the stories I had written were no more than sketches. There was a book to be written about this obscure conflict, and the people—especially the people—and I wanted to be the one to do it.

Writing to Bernie Ley, I asked if I could return. Then I waited. And waited. Fate had cracked open a door to a war that no other foreign journalist had been allowed to see in detail. Not that I had seen all that much of it; more like a quick peek through a door left slightly ajar. Was there a chance of them opening it all the way in spite of their profound distrust of Western journalists?

It was the middle of November, rain and sleet pelting the windows, when the call came from Oshakati. The connection was terrible, snapping and crackling. I pressed the receiver against my ear, jamming a finger in the other.

"Jim, I have some bad news for you," shouted down the line.

My shoulders slumped. I wasn't getting the authorization. They didn't want a foreigner snooping around. Bloody South Africans. What did they have to hide? "What is it?" I shouted back, not wanting to hear the answer.

"Hate to tell you this, pal, but it doesn't look like you're going to have a white Christmas."

"What?"

"I said you're not going to have a white Christmas. It's summer down here, you twit. When are we going to see you?"

"You're not joking?" I stammered. "I can come back?"

"The boss gave the thumbs up today. You asked for six months, right? He said to tell you that's what you got. So get your arse in gear."

A few days before my departure, Sugar Jones, my best girl and blue-blooded English lady, invited me up to London for oysters and Guinness at a place she knew just off Piccadilly Circus, where she tried—as so often before—to understand why I was doing it.

"You will write, just to let me know you're okay?"

"Every chance I get."

There was a long pause. Our attention centred on the barman who was making a production of drawing the dark Guinness into pewter mugs. He placed them on cardboard mats in front of us and turned to open the oysters.

"You could get shot, you know," running her finger around the rim of the mug. "It's hardly worth it."

"Are you kidding? I'd be crazy to throw it away. This is what I've been working towards since I left the States and started kicking around Africa. It's something I've wanted to do ever since I was a kid."

"But there are so many other things to write about that have nothing to do with violence."

"This is what I want."

"Why?"

"Maybe to find out if I can."

Later that night, she switched on the lamp and propped her chin on my chest. I yawned and peered at my watch. "Do you know what time it is?"

"I do wish you weren't going. What if you should be killed? Or worse, crippled? I'm not terribly keen on the idea of bringing flowers and reading to a bedridden ex-lover."

"I shall surely do my very best not to get killed, Sugar."

"But …

"Come on, Jones. It's okay. Everything's going to be fine."

A week in Pretoria allowed me to renew contacts, find a professional photo lab to develop the film I'd be sending back and sort out my travel arrangements to Oshakati. There was no great rush; the rains were still late.

At the end of the week, I caught a South African Airways flight to Windhoek. Seated next to me was a young geology student who would be spending the next few months with a mining company. The conversation came around to the bush war. He had spent almost a year of his national service "up on the border" and had no fond memories of the experience. When I mentioned what I was planning to do there, he stopped me.

"You mean to say," he frowned, "that you're spending six months in the operational area—and you don't *have* to?"

"Journalist," I offered a little self-consciously.

The morning after arriving in Windhoek I boarded a Namibair twin-engined Cessna 310 and talked my way into the co-pilot's seat. There was a brief stop for fuel in the picturesque mining town of Tsumeb, and then we were off again. Over the Etosha Pan, we descended until less than 100 feet separated us from the salt flats flashing beneath the blue and white belly.

"Just in case there's a terr down there with a SAM-7," the pilot said cheerfully.

He eased us even lower as we flew alongside the tarred road I had travelled with Henk seven months earlier. A delicate pull on the controls lifted us over a tall makalani palm. Black and white soldiers patrolling the road waved from their open-topped Buffels and Casspirs.

Thirty minutes later, we banked sharply onto final approach for the long runway at Ondangwa. Ahead of us, a Puma helicopter had just landed and I saw a brace of stretcher-bearers carrying a wounded soldier from the chopper towards the primary trauma centre. As I stepped down to the sun-softened tarmac, Bernie Ley and his wife Marga were there to meet me.

"Welcome back," Bernie said. "How's it?"

"Great," I said, my head turning to follow the stretcher-bearers. I looked back at him and shook hands. "Good to be here."

In four months, I would be walking across the same spot under entirely different circumstances.

Chris Pieterse, operations officer: "This rather short, scrawny Yank pitched up again and I looked at him in amazement. He was festooned with enough cameras and lenses to be on assignment for *National Geographic*. The jacket had so many pockets, that by the time he had gone through all of them to find a replacement film we would be back in base. Nodding and smiling at everybody; being ignored like any rookie. We were not intentionally rude…"

December 9, 1986

Dear Sugar Jones,

A quiet morning in Oshakati. I've been given a room at Onaimwandi, the Z3 investigative centre next to Koevoet's headquarters. It's spartan but functional, with bed, desk, chair and rotating fan, one of a dozen on two sides of the facility that face an aviary and small zoo. Here, injured birds of prey heal before being released, and a couple of small crocodiles sun themselves alongside a concrete pool. In a separate pool, a young otter latches onto my shoelaces every time I walk past. He waits until I kneel and offer a finger, which he takes firmly between his teeth so that I can tow him back and forth through the water.

The temperature has climbed past 80 degrees Fahrenheit, en route to 100+. Your itinerant scribbler pecks away on his scarred and trusty Olivetti in the shade of a crimson-topped flame tree. Oshakati is something out of the Wild West, a Fort Apache set in a modern war zone. Armour-plated cavalry rolls out of the gates and heads into the bush, returning a week later, some of the men carrying wounds, all of them filthy and exhausted. As they return, others, fresh and clean, pass them on their way out.

Yet life seems to function as casually and complacently as anywhere else. People—most of them in uniform—go to work in the morning and come home at quitting time. They laugh and cry, argue and love, worry about their bank balances, tinker with cars, watch videos, drink, have their scandals, go to church, and paddle their kids like people everywhere. Dirt roads cut through the blocks of cheaply-built prefab homes, and bits of jealously tended grass struggle for survival under the few trees.

There are some things that set it apart, however. At various times during the night, "fire plans" go into effect with tower-mounted machine guns shooting into "no-go" areas lit by mortar-fired parachute flares. Conversation barely falters at the coughing sound of a heavy machine gun, and children babble excitedly at the sight of the slowly descending magnesium flares. Sandbagged bunkers squat as naturally in front yards as children's swing sets and everyone knows how to reach the nearest one by the quickest route. The town has been hit twice this year by stand-off mortar and rocket attacks. The house occupied by one Koevoet officer and his family was demolished by a rocket in the first attack. They were given new quarters a mile from the first, and during the second attack, a mortar round landed squarely on top of it. Neither he nor any of his family were injured, having already taken shelter in the nearest bunker. It's rumoured that when he moved to his third house, his neighbours began looking for new quarters themselves. The only casualties in either of the attacks occurred elsewhere on the base, where a mother and unborn child were hit by a sliver of shrapnel. The mother lived.

Got back a couple of days ago from my first week in the veld, crusted with dust and dried sweat. None-too-subtle hints and slurs by my mentors at the very suggestion of a wash in the bush persuaded me to follow suit and return to base looking like a coal miner after a hard day's work underground. There are some drawbacks to following local tradition, I must say. The Ovambos wash every day. Among the whites, however, it's considered bad form to rid oneself of the topsoil whilst in the bush. Very uncool. Very bloody unpleasant as well.

Woke one morning to see a dozen or more trackers examining the ground just outside the TB. They waved me over. "Onjamba!" the senior warrant officer laughed, pointing at prints the size of dinner plates. One of the car commanders walked up behind me. "Elephant," he translated. "They're saying at least 25 passed by last night." No way, I said. "Lots of them around here," he insisted. "You don't see them very often. They can hear the cars for miles, so they keep well out of our way during the day." How come no one heard them? "Nothing moves as quiet as they do." If ever I needed a reminder I was in Africa, there it was.

Depending on whom you talk to, the rains are either early or late, though certainly sporadic, which means the infiltration is still in its seasonal pre-infancy. Radio reports from groups working across Ovamboland told of a Casspir detonating a land mine (the worst injury a ruptured spleen), four "Victor Yankees" captured, another killed, weapons caches discovered—all in all a quiet period. Another month, six weeks, they tell me, and things will really start happening, with February and March being the peak infiltration period. The Summer Games, it's called. In the meantime, I can look forward to weeks of grinding through the bush and eating lots of dirt.

That this war is little understood—or even known about—in the outside world is hardly surprising; it is remote, there are no fixed battles, it involves few but a local population caught tragically in the middle and the sons of South Africa and SWA/Namibia serving here "up on the border." It is a hazy side issue to the big South African picture, and dimly seen as through a mirage.

As far as the international community is concerned, South Africa illegally occupies this country. As far as the South African government is concerned, it is protecting—or preventing—Namibia from becoming another Soviet-dominated country on its border until genuinely free elections can be held. Which means that they're unlikely to allow elections until they can be assured of a pro-Pretoria—or at least tame—government being voted in. Or can no longer afford either the economic drain on their resources or the political price of international condemnation.

Swapo's claim (backed to the hilt by the United Nations, naturally) that it is "the sole and authentic voice of the Namibian people" is no less one-sided and intransigent. While there are obviously Swapo supporters among all the various ethnic groups, the hard fact is that Swapo is an Ovambo-based movement, and representatives of other tribes within the organization constitute a small minority. Disillusioned members who have returned to Namibia continue to tell stories of almost inconceivably brutal treatment at the hands of the predominantly Ovambo hierarchy. (Stories, by the way, which are ignored or vehemently denied by Swapo's supporters in the UN—press included—here and overseas.)

Should elections ever come to pass, it must be borne in mind that 55 percent of Namibia's population is made up of the seven tribes of the Ovambo people. The inescapable conclusion is that Swapo would be voted into power. How much of that would be due to its intimidation of a politically unsophisticated rural people, or to the same people's desire to see "scientific socialism" at work, or to outright tribalism is open to conjecture. Africa watchers, political scientists and sociologists could argue it till the cows come home and likely still be no closer to the truth.

Am only now beginning to appreciate that in terms of combat efficiency, these guys I'm with are probably as good as their reputation. They very much fit the mould and psychological profile of other elite special warfare units: loners, reasonably intelligent, extremely aggressive, and thriving on adrenaline highs. If they're not fighting insurgents, they're getting into punch-ups with the army or amongst themselves. Whatever their rationale for being here—protecting Namibia, South Africa, or simply the lot of a policeman—the fact is that most of them love and need the constant stimulation of combat. All are volunteers, and many extend their service far beyond the two years they're expected to stay with the unit.

I've yet to discover what's behind the perception that Koevoet is manned exclusively by social misfits and psychopaths whose brutality towards the civilian population is reminiscent of Nazi death squads. Aside from being witness to a teenage Ovambo boy cuffed sharply on the ear, I've seen no evidence of physical intimidation. And yes, you're right: I'd have to be naive not to think that my presence keeps them on their best behaviour. And, like you, I've also wondered if the reason I've been allowed to return is because someone saw the possibility of using an outsider to paint them lily white.

Am I being co-opted as "a tool of the South African security forces?" I'd like to say certainly not, but in all honesty, I don't really know. If these people are as Neanderthalic and brutal as Swapo, the anti-apartheid movement, the Council of Churches in Namibia, United Nations and even some South

African newspapers say they are, then I will undoubtedly see it over the next few months. To maintain their effectiveness, they'll not be able to alter tactics or personalities just for me once the infiltration arrives. Their entire raison d'etre is killing "terrs," and their record on that is unmatched in the operational area and one in which they take great pride.

It's slowly starting to penetrate this thick skull of mine that it's all for real, no Hollywood or Pinewood Studio production where after "That's a wrap!" the extras and stuntmen pick themselves up, brush themselves off and start all over again. Of course, etiquette, bravado and a youthful sense of immortality preclude any serious mention of death. Their successes against the opposition, however, that's something else again. Discussion revolves around the latest contacts and how many koppe ("heads" – their slang term for kills) they've tallied since the beginning of the year. In between their week-long trips into the bush, these 18 to 25-ish year-olds drink heavily, play hard and tell the most extraordinary stories with all the aplomb of suburban commuters on the train home.

Although the pieces I wrote on them earlier this year appear to have gone down well, a deep-rooted suspicion of the media means not everyone is happy with my presence. There's no question that my behaviour in the veld is quietly observed and discussed, so it behoves me to keep my mouth shut, look, listen and be as unobtrusive as circumstances allow. Brigadier Dreyer may have approved my presence, but I'm very much on probation with the guys doing the fighting, which makes me more worried about doing something stupid in front of them than being hurt. Curiously, it is the Ovambos who appear the most concerned about showing me the ropes, treating me like some sort of respected, but not very bright, elder. They keep a protective eye on me, you'll be pleased to know.

One of the biggest difficulties is language. Although most of the whites speak English to some degree, very few of the Ovambos have ever had the need for it. As a result, there is a wealth of stories that will remain sadly untapped simply because I can't talk with them directly. Many of these black policemen have seen a hundred times the combat experienced by most of the young SADF conscripts who spend their obligatory year in the operational area. The story I hope to tell will be the poorer for the omission of their experiences.

Permission to stay for as long as six months is unprecedented; no other journalist, whether foreign or South African, has ever spent more than two or three days with these guys. But the good Lord willin' an' the creek don't rise (a genuine American ruralism), I won't need that much time. With luck, the end of March or April should see the project in the can.

I return to the veld tomorrow for a week, am back here for one night, then out again for another week, so it's unlikely you'll have another letter from here until well after Christmas. Lift a cup of good cheer for me. Miss you.

Fifty kilometres south of Oshakati, Jackie and I stood on the berm surrounding the Security Branch base at Okatope. Jackie, dark complexioned, with straight, black hair and the build of a rugby player, was, in the words of one Ops K officer, "certifiable." "Genuine," he added seriously.

"Jackie?" someone else mused. "Man, Jackie's crazy," shaking his head. "Did you hear about that last thing he did on the other side of the cutline?"

No, I said, I hadn't heard, what was it? But he just shook his head again, smiling in the private way people have of conferring special status for being certifiable.

But I never saw that part, only heard about it second- and third-hand; snippets of stories which had already taken their place in a private compendium of Koevoet mythology and folklore. Exploits and derring-do that on the surface were risks for the sake of risk, yet on more sober analysis indicated a natural flair for bush warfare. They enjoyed talking about his craziness in the bush, his practical jokes out of the bush. What no one ever mentioned was his humanity.

For me, Jackie was warm, intelligent, incisive, funny; qualities which overlapped like medieval armour a complex character of infinite contradictions. A doting father with a shy and breathtakingly beautiful young wife (who agonized over his trips into the bush), the respect his men had for him was earned and returned measure for measure.

"This really is their country," he said. "We're only here temporarily to help them. The blacks in my group, they'd be killed if Swapo took over. They've already told me that if that happens they'd go into the bush and fight their own war against them. We have to make sure they don't have to do that."

It had been another long, hot day. Spoor found and lost the day before had been picked up again this morning. The three insurgents being chased knew their anti-tracking, making it slow, hard work for the Ovambo policemen. At one point, the faint tracks completely disappeared near an isolated kraal. As we approached the primitive enclosure, the Ovambo farmer watched us suspiciously from inside. When we pulled up next to it, he lifted two termite-eaten logs from the entrance and stepped out, resignation etched across his deeply creased face. As the trackers began to question him, he shook his head determinedly. Voices were raised, and I watched as he was backed up against the log barricade.

One had begun prodding his chest when four more Casspirs emerged from the bush and stopped in the shade of a maroela tree. Eight armoured cars bristling with machine guns and almost 90 armed men were enough to cow anyone. As one of the trackers raised a hand Jackie climbed over his gun mount and on to the car's bonnet, stepped down to the heavy steel bumper and jumped solidly to the ground. Benjamin, a huge, squint-eyed Ovambo who was Jackie's right-hand man, followed menacingly from his own vehicle to take over the interrogation. The farmer lifted his arm to ward off the threatened blow and continued shaking his head. Benjamin turned, spat and spoke angrily to Jackie in Afrikaans. I left my vantage point in the Casspir and joined them.

"What's he saying?" I finally asked.

"No," Jackie said wearily, "this old guy told Bennie to go ahead and hit him. He said we can hit him all we want to, but he knows we won't kill him. He says if he tells us what we want to know and Swapo hears about it, then they'll come back here and kill him for sure." Jackie and Benjamin returned to their Casspirs. The trackers fanned out around the kraal to try finding the spoor left by the humane freedom fighters the old man had never seen.

The group I was with had worked alongside Jackie's until personality conflicts got in the way and we separated. I was wishing now that I'd accepted his invitation to join him. I found myself sharing his dislike for the man whose car I shared. A sneering, taut little bully whose attitude towards his men was directly opposite to Jackie's, he would prove to be one of the few members of Koevoet whom I could abide neither in nor out of the bush.

"Nothing but a bunch of fucking coons," he sneered, waving a hand towards the men around us, men his life depended on in combat. "I have to work with them, but I don't have to kiss them. Parasites. Make no mistake, I'm no *kaffir boetie*[1] like your friend Jackie."

By the time we broke away from Jackie, the insurgents had made good their escape. Our ears pricked up a few hours later when Jackie's voice came over the radio. They'd found the body of a civilian, apparently killed by the three insurgents. There was no obvious motive other than their suspicion that he might report their presence to the pursuing Koevoet groups. Sometime in

---

1   Afrikaans equivalent of "nigger lover."

the mid afternoon, we heard that the chase had ended in a sharp, abbreviated contact. The bodies of the three Swapo insurgents now lay where they had fallen in the bush.

Soon afterwards, the Jackie's men found a POM-Z antipersonnel mine the insurgents had set alongside a bush trail. The green, pineapple-sectioned bomb had been hidden behind a tree, the almost invisible trip wire stretched across the path. The pin to the detonator had been withdrawn most of the way. The slightest pressure would have set off an almost instantaneous explosion of deadly shrapnel.

One of his car commanders later described how Jackie had squatted, studied it for a moment, then moved around and knelt on the far side of the tree. To Benjamin's disapproval, he reached around the trunk and carefully seated the pin before disarming the device. A slip, and the resulting explosion would have torn away both hands. When I saw Jackie, I asked him why he'd taken the risk, why not just leave the damn thing? He looked at me steadily.

"What happens when one of the PBs comes along and trips it? Can't just leave it there. Jesus. These are people, not animals. We couldn't just drive off and forget about it. They have it bad enough already without us leaving things like that for them." He turned to Benjamin and translated my question. Bennie gave me a flat stare.

Unwilling to meet their eyes, I looked over Jackie's shoulder, feeling chastened and embarrassed. It was another reminder of how little I knew, how much I still had to learn.

The sun casting long shadows, Jackie stood, hands in his pockets and leaning backward in a characteristic pose that identified him from 100 metres away. A head taller and proportionately wider, Benjamin slouched next to him, scowling and squinting in two directions at once.

"This is my area, the south," Jackie said, his eyes on the horizon. "This is where I like to work." Unlike the north-central and eastern areas of Ovambo-land, the bush here was sparse and scattered, the kraals more numerous and closer together. If insurgents were reported, Jackie would be the first on the scene to dig them out. The network of friends he had cultivated among the local population was unique and invaluable. "Most of the Ovambos around here trust me," he said. "If there are any terrs around, I hear about it sooner or later."

I thought it must be damned dangerous; an Ovambo farmer in his remote kraal seemed an easy target for Swapo. Jackie nodded. "That's why no one but me and Bennie know who they are. Most of the local pops are too afraid to say anything. And you really can't blame them. Most of them just wish everyone would go away and leave them alone. Us, the army, Swapo. These are good people here. Genuine. Pretty unsophisticated, no real politics. All they want to do is grow their mohango, raise their cattle and goats, make babies, drink beer. Whatever. They're just caught in the middle with no way out. I feel sorry as hell for them.

"But the gooks come along and tell them they have to give them food and maybe hide them. They can't say no. The terrs have the guns and they don't. Then we come along and tell them they have to tell us where the terrs are or where they've gone. Sure, we try to scare them into telling us sometimes. Poor bastards. The gooks fuck with them, then we come along and fuck with them. We're trying to protect them, but it's a crazy way of doing it.

"Okay, so we intimidate them, maybe push them around a little sometimes. I guess the difference is that we don't threaten to kill them. That's how the terrs get what they want—how some of the locals get forced into helping them. Who are you going to listen to, someone who looks mean and yells a lot or the terr you know is going to use his bayonet if you don't do what he says? I know what I'd do in their place. That civvie today, the one those three terrs killed, he'll make a stronger example to the PBs than I'll ever be able to." He took a long, last pull at his beer before throwing the can aside. I could feel his anger and frustration, a story that was struggling to get out.

"We were working not far from here one day when this woman comes running from her kraal. She was crying and screaming that Swapo had killed her husband. We followed her back to the kraal, and she showed us where he was buried. We had to dig up the body to confirm what had happened and write a report. It wasn't very pretty."

Bennie interrupted to say something in Afrikaans, then stalked off towards the cars, beer in hand. Jackie paused, shifted, and reached down to pull a tough grass stem growing from the berm. He chewed on the end, looking out over the flat, sandy vista punctuated here and there with clumps of bush between the scattered kraals.

"She told us five terrs came to their kraal a couple days before and accused her husband of being an informer. They tied him up, then gathered 15 or 16 people from other kraals to watch. When they had everyone there, they popped his eyes out with the point of a bayonet so they were hanging down on his cheeks. They tied a rope around his waist, held one end, and made him run around in a circle at the other end of it. While he was going around, they made him sing a little ditty they made up for him. The thing he had to sing was: "If you see Swapo, call the security forces, if you see Swapo call the security forces." His wife said the gooks thought it was very funny, because of the eyes bouncing around on his cheeks.

"After they got tired of that, they forced the PBs—they made each one of them stab him with the bayonet on the end of an SKS rifle. After that, they cut his head off, stuck it on a stake, and tied his body to the kraal fence. Just as an example and warning to other informers."

Jackie paused again. Beyond the barbed-wire fence the menacing outlines of the Casspirs stood silhouetted against the darkening sky. The Ovambo constables stood or squatted around cooking fires, their laughter incongruous and somehow indecent after what I had just heard.

Jackie took the grass stem from his mouth, examined it briefly and dropped it. He put his hands in his pockets, leaned back and looked at me. He shook his head. "The funny thing," he said, his arm going up at the beckoning wave from Benjamin, "is that they were wrong. We questioned him a few times, but he never told us anything." Jackie started to move away, then stopped and looked back at me. "You know the only thing he ever told us that was worth repeating?"

I shook my head.

"He said all he really wanted was for everyone to just leave him alone."

8

Birth of a Legend

Wednesday mornings at Okave were always a scene of mild chaos. Dozens of Casspirs, Wolf Turbos and their Blesbok and Strandwolf support vehicles parked in jumbled disarray across the parade ground and between the long, parallel sheds. Twenty-eight *gevegsgroepe*— battle groups—were based here, evenly divided between Alpha Group and Bravo Group, and all beginning with the "Zulu" prefix. When the letters of the alphabet, save Z and R (reserved for the radio repair shop), had been assigned, four more teams were formed using "Zulu 1" as a prefix.

For half the unit, it was the first day of another week's deployment to the bush; for the other half, it was the first day back in base after a week on operations. It wasn't difficult to see which was which.

Unconcealed excitement marked the teams heading out after a week of report writing, vehicle repair and heavy drinking. Men moved between cars and the stores, loading weapons, ammunition, and medical kits. First into the Blesboks and Strandwolfs went drums of diesel and jet fuel, the latter for refuelling the helicopters in the veld. Then came bedding, cases of ration packs, extra ammunition, tools, and spare parts. Cars moved in dust-raising relays to Zulu 12, the garage, to have their fuel and water tanks topped off.

For the returning teams, there was a slower-moving and quiet relief after a week of long, hot days crashing through the bush, eating on the move, wearing a permanent layer of topsoil and sleeping on the ground. Cars were being unloaded and washed, weapons stripped and cleaned, punctured tyres patched. Vehicle damage suffered in combat with Swapo or, more often, with the terrain was assessed, and the cars taken to the garage for repair. Malfunctioning radios would go to the "White House" to have their circuits checked and faults rectified by the electronics wizards.

Inside the storerooms, inventories were being taken to see that all weapons had been returned and, if the group had had a contact, how much fresh ammunition would have to be drawn. These men were looking forward to long, hot showers, real beds and some hard drinking. "Getting ambushed" was the popular term, and an ambush in the Okave Club could often result in heavy casualties. On the mornings after a "serious ambush," more than one sour-mouthed, head-bursting Koevoet cop had wished he were dead.

Next door at Zulu 3, Koevoet's Onaimwandi investigative centre, the deploying group leaders and senior Ovambo NCOs listened to a situation report from one of the unit's operations officers. Intelligence pooled from all the security force units in Sector 10 pinpointed suspected Swapo infiltrations, force strengths, where seen by the local population and last-known directions of movement. Of special note was information that Swapo had received a number of SAM-7 ground-to-air missiles, and were planning to shoot down a "Flossie"—a SAAF C-130 Hercules—as it was coming in to land at Ondangwa. Teams working south of Oshakati should be especially alert to reports of Victor Yankees carrying the weapon. Group leaders jotted down the information in small green notebooks.

If the army had something cooking, an intelligence officer from Koevoet's archrival, 101 Battalion, would be on hand for an additional briefing. Although a Koevoet group would happily chase spoor into an area where 101 was working, by tacit agreement they tended to avoid each other in the bush. Interservice rivalry was not an unknown phenomenon and disagreements had occasionally arisen when a short-tempered Koevoet team leader thought a 101 Battalion Romeo Mike[1] team was trying to poach "his" spoor. Of course, as I was often reminded, it was always the army that started the fights, the bastards.

This long-standing rivalry was not reserved for the bush, nor the outcome guaranteed. One evening in Driehoek guest house, two of the Ops K lads were well into their cups when a strapping lieutenant from 101 Battalion took a seat at the other end of the bar. The two cast hooded eyes in his direction and commented on the unsavoury ancestry of army officers in general and this one in particular. When the lieutenant failed to respond, they were obliged to speak to him directly. His manner was to keep his own counsel and elbows on the bar. This they took as a direct affront, the smaller of the two allowing he was going to teach him some respect. His friend said he would help. The smaller one shook his head. "This is my fight."

"But I want to help."

"No way, man, this one's all mine. I'm going to show the bloody army some manners."

1　NATO phonetic alphabet designator for *Reaksiemag*—Afrikaans for "Reaction Force."

"So what do I have to do—just watch? Come on, man, you had the last one. It's not fair."

"Too bad." He slipped off his stool and swaggered up to the lieutenant, who sat his beer down and held his palms out.

"Look, man, I really don't want to fight, okay?"

"Whatsamatter, afraid? All you army bastards are afraid. No good at killing terrs and can't take care of yourselves in the bar, either. Well, this is it, pal. Come on!"

"Don't just talk to him, hit the son of a bitch!" shouted his friend, who jumped off his stool and strode angrily up behind his partner. "Let me at him," he demanded, reaching over the broad back.

"I told you, this was my fight," the smaller one said, placing the flat of his hand against his partner's chest and giving him a steady look. Turning back with a disarming smile, he unleashed a sudden blow. Unfortunately, he'd picked the SADF's middle-weight boxing champ. The lieutenant neatly side-stepped the roundhouse, dropped his shoulders and with a crushing left-right combination, laid the policeman full-length on the floor.

The standing cop focused a bleary eye on his prostrate partner. "You're right," he said, sitting down and picking up his beer, "it's your fight."

Occasionally, an intelligence officer from the Reconnaissance Commandos[2] would also drop in to pass on information. If the "Recces" were operating south of the cutline, it was designated a no-go area until they had withdrawn. Inasmuch as they wore Swapo uniforms and the whites covered face and arms with heavy black camo cream, an unexpected confrontation could have disastrous results. (A story passed round the campfire told of two Koevoet groups chasing spoor for days, only to have a white Recce, stripped naked and his black makeup scrubbed off, step out of the bush with arms raised. Given that the Recces were the elite of the security forces, the story was related with great relish. Part of the mythology.)

Meteorology was a subject of particular interest. Until the rains began in earnest, the work was slow, boring and exasperating. Without rain, the trees remained bare from the winter leaf fall and there was little groundwater, both of which Swapo needed for its annual infiltration. Leafless trees made them vulnerable to detection from both the ground and air, and a lack of year-round

---

2   South African special forces that, like Britain's SAS, specialise in operating far behind enemy lines. As with Koevoet, most were black. Although they operated primarily in Angola, occasional special missions saw them in Namibia.

water holes limited how far they could travel with only canteens. The rains sometimes arrived in early December, but not this year. The skies remained an unvarying pale blue.

"Fucking weather," someone muttered from the back of the room.

After the briefing they wandered across the parade ground to headquarters, where breakfast was being laid out atop concrete picnic tables on a tree-shaded patio. Plates were piled with pap, sauce, fried eggs, fried fish and tomatoes. Between mouthfuls, those who had just returned from the bush added the minutiae which had been missing from the formal briefing: who in particular among the PBs had good info, suspicions about which kraals were being used by Swapo, hunches where the insurgents were likely to be operating.

But even amongst friends, some information was always held back. The unit was split down the middle. When Alpha Group's 14 teams were in the bush, Bravo Group's 14 teams would be back in base. Neither was prepared to help the other too much for fear of the rivals accumulating more kills at the end of the year. Friendship and unity of purpose went only so far.

By 11 o'clock, the last teams were rolling out of Oshakati. Two hours later, they had fanned out into the bush to begin the search. Typically, two combat groups of four armoured personnel carriers and one supply vehicle each worked together, one group or team—the terms were interchangeable—stopping at a kraal, the second leapfrogging ahead to the next kraal, trackers debussing to question the PBs. Had they seen any Swapo? When did they pass? How many? What weapons? Which direction were they moving?

More often than not, the locals would have seen nothing, since the insurgents avoided most kraals, stopping only at those known to be sympathetic and trustworthy. But even if they had not seen Swapo, the "bush telegraph"— gossip passed back and forth while gathering firewood, fetching water, herding cattle—often provided valuable information.

"We heard that three Swapo passed near here last week, moving south."

"Who told you this?"

"So-and-so," pointing and snapping their fingers in the direction of So-and-so's kraal.

And so it went, long hours of detective work: stopping, questioning, scanning the ground for spoor. Days might be spent following up on the vaguest of information. This was the grinding, boring and exasperating side of the war, but part of what made Koevoet the most successful counterinsurgency unit of the war.

In December, the summer temperatures can reach over 100 degrees Fahrenheit. And it is dry, the rains still a month or more away. Dust billows behind the cars as they work their way through the dense undergrowth, eyes flicking from ground to bush and back again. By late morning, the heat inside the cars is fearsome; sweat beads and trickles down foreheads and cheeks, streaking the layers of dust and dirt. The backs and underarms of shirts turn black with sweat. The only relief is to sit on the rim of the car's open well and hope to catch a hint of breeze, even though the dust raised by the car ahead adds yet another layer to damp arms, legs and faces.

In really thick bush, there is no option but to sit inside to escape the slapping branches and thorns of acacia trees. But then you are subjected to a constant rain of twigs, rotten branches, leaves, bugs—Lord, the bugs! Especially spiders. Spiders of every conceivable colour, size and shape, dozens of them. And even more varieties of ants, and hairy and smooth caterpillars, beetles and hoppers and moths, and sometimes even a snake, which is guaranteed to liven things up considerably (inasmuch as black mambas are occasionally found in trees, not even an unexpected contact could trigger such impressively quick reflexes). The floor of the car gradually disappears under the debris. Bugs brushed from bare arms and legs scurry into cracks and crevices inside the car, some crawling thing inevitably leaving a swelling white lump somewhere on the skin.

By now I was accustomed to the cornucopia of weapons. Atop the cab was the main armament of two light machine guns or, more commonly, a .50 calibre Browning with two of the lighter guns, while a select few favoured one of the ten 20mm cannon in Koevoet's inventory. Some cars, particularly the Wolf Turbos, had an additional .30 calibre Browning in a ball mount through the co-driver's bullet-proof windscreen. Inside, at least ten R5 assault rifles with 50-round magazines were propped against the hull. Somewhere there would be a single-shot 40mm grenade launcher or one of the new six-shot models. In addition to their R5s, some of the trackers packed 9mm Berettas in holsters or shoved behind their web belts. At least one car per group carried a 60mm mortar, its crew adept at firing it while rolling through the bush.

Captured weapons also found their way into the cars. An AK-47 might be seen in a corner. A RPG launcher lay on the floor, warheads and bright green boosters jammed somewhere convenient. A former insurgent now working with Koevoet cradled a Soviet RPD light machine gun, a favourite from his days with Swapo. Taking the concept of maximum firepower seriously, some car commanders included three or four Soviet-made PKM medium machine guns positioned to be fired through the spring-loaded gun ports. The term "bristling" didn't even begin to describe it. Each car was a self-contained, rolling arsenal.

But hardware and firepower were only as good as the people using them. Each man was a volunteer. Almost 90 percent were local Ovambos, the same tribe that constituted an even larger majority of Swapo insurgents. They were not only on intimate terms with the terrain, language and culture of their fellow tribesmen, but had earned a reputation as aggressive and deadly bush fighters.

Tracking skills had been honed since childhood. Born and raised in traditional kraals, their first responsibilities were as *kamachonas*—herd boys—minding their fathers' cattle and goats. These represented the wealth and status of the family; if one strayed into the bush, the lad was responsible for finding it. By the time he reached adolescence, he could pick out, identify and follow the faintest spoor. It was a skill easily adapted to following men.

As a defence against this, new Swapo conscripts were taught anti-tracking—how to hide their traces by keeping to hard ground, stepping from fallen branch to fallen branch or moving through shallow shonas during the rainy season, techniques that had saved many of them. A Koevoet group leader would move heaven and earth to recruit a team of spoorsnyers good enough to spot the traces left by "heavy anti-tracking."

Zulu Foxtrot's team leader, Louis "Botes" Botha, pointed towards a young man who was slowly but steadily picking out the almost invisible trail left by two insurgents. "See that one?" lifting his chin towards the totally absorbed youth. "We were chasing him about four years ago. His anti-tracking was so goddamn good we decided we had to capture him alive. It took a week with our best people trying to stay on his spoor. When we finally got him, it turned out that he'd taught anti-tracking at Swapo's training camp at Lubango. After we showed him that the situation here in South West wasn't what he'd been told by Swapo—I mean, he couldn't believe all the Ovambo businesses and how many had cars, that they could travel and live wherever they wanted—he decided to join us. Takes a terr who's bloody good to throw him off the spoor."

I glanced at the light machine gun balanced over his shoulder. "You're kidding. You've got an ex-Swapo armed and working for you?"

He seemed surprised by the question. "Sure, why not? Oh, some we capture are committed Swapo, but most have a big change of attitude when they see what's really happening on this side of the border. If they decide to work with us, we're happy to take them. They're paid well, given uniforms, medical care. It's a lot better than what they had in Swapo. I guess we have 40 or 50 ex-terrs in Koevoet right now, and not one has deserted and run back to Swapo."

Most of the Ovambo policemen were in their late teens or early twenties and immensely proud of being part of Koevoet. Although many of their fellow tribesmen wore army browns and served with the SWATF 101 Battalion, Koevoet's olive green uniform immediately set these men apart. Each team had its own T-shirt and totem—an elephant, lion, badger or scorpion, a lynx, snake, crocodile or other creature considered dangerous or disagreeable. The T-shirts invariably showed an insurgent being attacked by the adopted totem, the enemy's AK-47 broken in half, just as in simpler days a warrior's spear would have been broken to show defeat.

They revelled in their reputation as swift and efficient killers. The scathing anti-Koevoet propaganda taken from the bodies of the insurgents only reinforced the image they had of themselves. And their swaggering cockiness told the casual observer just how good they believed themselves to be.

The whites came from the South African Police or South West African Police. After volunteering, they were subjected to a selection course under as realistic conditions as possible. It was not unknown for new members to hit contacts during this phase of the training. Once accepted, they were expected to stay with the unit for at least two years. They often stayed longer. At least one team leader had spent eight years with the unit. Another had 14 years of police work on the border, with three of those in Koevoet. Group leaders and car commanders with four to six years in Koevoet were not uncommon.

Although some of the unit's ops medics came from the police, many were from the South African Medical Service, a branch of the SADF, and had volunteered to spend their compulsory year in the operational area with Koevoet. Army background notwithstanding, they wore green and were considered part of Ops K.

Johannes "Sterk Hans" Dreyer was as much a legend as the unit he commanded. A rangy grandfather with a bristling moustache and explosive temper, he was revered by his men. "I was sent up here in 1978 to see what role the police could play against terrorism," said Dreyer, relaxing in his panelled office decorated with Koevoet memorabilia. Drawing on experience gained with the South African Police in Rhodesia, he first envisioned a Selous Scout-type unit, employing local blacks as pseudo-Swapo.[3]

"I learned in Rhodesia that you must use the local population because of their knowledge of the customs, terrain and language. An all white force would really be ineffective in this kind of war." Dreyer approached a senior Ovambo headman and discussed his ideas. The headman was taken with the concept, and at Dreyer's request, recruited 60 men skilled in tracking. "We operated on a shoestring budget back then," Dreyer recalled. "I was allowed to bring four officers with me and recruit two more here. We were given two bakkies and two cars. That we never hit a land mine is a miracle."

Listening to his operators in the field, Dreyer soon backed away from the Selous Scout idea, deciding that highly mobile and heavily armed hunter-killer teams was the best way of dealing with the insurgents. Viewed with much scepticism and not a little suspicion by Higher Up, the first few months of the unit's existence were spent on training, developing tactics and scrounging equipment wherever it could be found or stolen. Those in charge were not ready to spend money on what seemed a harebrained idea.

"Our first major success came during the '79 Swapo infiltration, when 12 terrs managed to reach the white farming area east of the Etosha Game Reserve." Dreyer circled an area on the wall map with his finger. "On one farm here, they killed an old man; on another not far away"—his finger tapped the map an inch from the first spot—"they killed a white grandmother and her two grandchildren, ages two and four. They were all bayoneted.

"The army had moved into the area, but weren't having much luck. I finally convinced them to give us a try." Twenty-three Ovambo trackers and one white were flown to the scene. They picked up the spoor and followed it for the next seven days. In the ensuing contact, two insurgents and the white group leader were killed. "Everyone was amazed that we could follow spoor for that long." said Dreyer smugly. "Except us, that is." Dreyer's vision of using skilled trackers to bring the enemy to bay had worked. "I knew then I had something golden. It wasn't long before we were killing 50 to 80 terrs a month, the equivalent of a Swapo company."

For the first three years, the existence of the South West Africa Police Counter-insurgency Unit was a closely guarded secret. Although its reputation grew rapidly among those charged with stopping the insurgents, no mention of

---

3   Between 1967 and 1975, the South African Police were drawn in to work alongside Rhodesian units during the counterinsurgency war in what is today Zimbabwe.

it appeared in the press or any official document. In spite of its growing success rate, however, Ops K remained the bastard stepchild of the operational area. The men worked mostly on foot with outdated equipment, little support, and even less recognition from police headquarters.

"Of course, we did manage to 'borrow' a few things from the army," one old hand smiled. "Getting past guards, through barbed wire and into army supply depots taught us a few things about infiltration ourselves."

With statistics in hand, then-Colonel Dreyer flew to Pretoria to argue his case. His reception was chilly. "I was pretty aggressive," he admitted, "but I knew what I was talking about and they didn't." Dreyer and his numbers were impressive enough to convince headquarters that the fledgling unit should be expanded. Money and equipment were soon on their way, including three Hippo armoured personnel carriers, the petrol-engined and completely enclosed forerunner of the Casspir.

"Before the Hippos arrived, those were the days when groups of 60 or 80—hell, sometimes even 100—terrs were coming across," one founding member said. "Those were some serious contacts. There were a lot of times when we were completely outnumbered." He described his group of 30 men running for two days to stay ahead of more than 100 pursuing insurgents. "Our radio batteries were flat, so we couldn't call for help, and we'd used up most of our ammunition in the three contacts we'd already been in." They escaped.

"Would you believe when we first got those cars, no one wanted to use them?" said Dreyer. "I actually had to order the group leaders to take them." The first contact involving the Hippos resulted in 18 dead insurgents. "And that was with only two cars. After that, everyone wanted them."

To the horror of the Hippo's designers, the inventive operators set about customizing their new toys. "The Hippo had a closed top," Gene De Kock said. "Not only did it make it too damned hot inside, but cut way down on visibility and fighting capability. Shooting out the gun ports is fine, but there are definitely times when the people in the back need to stand up and shoot. So we just got some cutting torches and opened her up. No problem, but the factory people back in South Africa went ape shit." Interior water tanks were added, as well as extra radio racks and more armour protection for the man standing behind the gun turret.

"We really didn't know much about arming the cars," another early member explained, "or even the best way to use them. There were lots of midnight bull sessions, trying to work out the best tactics. It was all new. There weren't any books on it. No one had ever used APCs in the bush the way we were trying to do. We experimented with all kinds of weapons. Our first gun mounts were homemade things that didn't work too well. We stuck .50 calibre Brownings in them, .30 calibre Brownings, GPMGs, Russian PKMs. Some people even got some captured Russian 14.5mm guns from the army and tried them out. Gene de Kock actually tried two of those 14.5s. Took a big man to swing that turret! Frans Conradie talked someone in the Air Force out of a 20mm gun and mounted that on his car.

"We had one of the 14.5s," he reminisced. "Someone shoved a rag up the barrel to keep leaves and branches out while driving through the bush. He didn't understand the ammunition was high-explosive stuff designed to detonate as soon as it hit something. Man, the first round hit that rag and exploded. Blew off the end of the barrel and peeled back part of what was left like a banana skin. After the contact was over, we got a hacksaw out of the tool box and just sawed it off behind the split. Still worked fine."

After much experimentation and discussion, each *gevegsgroep* was eventually organized into 40 Ovambos, four whites and four diesel-engined Casspir APCs. Added to each team was a Blesbok supply vehicle to carry extra fuel, water, ammunition and food. Koevoet's course was charted.

Living up to his reputation for contrariness, Dreyer began butting heads with the army over defined areas of operation. He wanted—and demanded— unlimited freedom of movement throughout the operational area. Dropping a hot spoor just because it crossed into an army unit's area was unacceptable. As usual, he got his way.

"We've got a good boss," one group leader said proudly, "he lets us go where we want. And if the terrs head back across the border into Angola, we'll chase them as far as they want to go."

Men, tactics, equipment and a maverick in the driver's seat had made Ops K one of the world's most spectacularly successful counterinsurgency units. Nonetheless, all its members insisted that they were still policemen. "We're just stopping criminals and preventing crimes."

Sergeant Jerry Mbwale was 22 years old, a bright, good-looking six-footer with six years in Koevoet. He couldn't really remember the number of contacts he'd been in, just laughing and shaking his head. "A lot, very many," he said.

Jerry was typical of the young Ovambos who made up the bulk of Koevoet's NCOs. A member of Boesman's Zulu November when it was ambushed by the 40-man Swapo detachment, he had been seriously wounded by an RPG during the contact. Shrapnel from the Soviet-made rocket blinded him in one eye and left his chest and shoulders a mass of scar tissue. As a result of his injuries, Jerry was taken off operations and made a special investigator.

Although most of his duties now entailed plain-clothes office work, he was not above dressing in captured camouflage, shouldering an AK or RPG, and with one or two of his operatives, slipping into the bush to visit remote pro-Swapo kraals and cuca shops. Posing as freedom fighters, the information they picked up was often invaluable to Koevoet's counterinsurgency efforts.

When not working, Jerry studied hard to pass his exams so that he might eventually be eligible for a commission. It was difficult not to imagine him as one of Koevoet's first black officers. Although his mother tongue was Oshivambo, his Afrikaans was equally fluent and his English more than passable. Over coffee one morning, he told me a little about himself.

"You know, my father, he doesn't have any qualifications and did not understand why I should go to school. He just sent me to watch the cattle when I was a boy. At that time, I was very stupid and very young and didn't know anything. There was no difference between school and life. I told my father I wanted to be a policeman, but he said it was more important to have cattle than to be a policeman.

"Me, myself, I discussed things with political people who said we must go outside to Angola for better education so that we can bring freedom to Namibia, and that we must take the white people out and bring another white people in we can work with. But I couldn't understand why we should bring in other white people, Cubans and Russians. I saw that Swapo only wanted to take schoolchildren outside to become soldiers, not for education, but I didn't want to go. I discussed with myself that it was better to go to school here and become a policeman than to go outside.

"In 1979 I had to leave school because Swapo took my uncle outside, and he was the one helping me with school and money. I did not understand the politics of Swapo, but I thought this was very bad. They came during the night and just took him away. So, in 1980, I didn't tell my father I was leaving to become a policeman, because I knew he just wanted me to watch the cattle. But when I came to the police I did not know anything. But I could see that Swapo was much worse than the South Africans. I wanted to fight against Swapo. I thought to free my uncle from Angola, but I was very stupid because, perhaps, really he was already killed.

"You know, the black people in Namibia can go where they want, even they can live where they want. They can have good businesses, too, if they work hard. There are many rich black people in Namibia. I think, really, education is not so good, but it comes better, but Swapo want to take the schoolchildren outside to make them soldiers. Swapo, they are telling us this is freedom.

"I, myself, I have nice clothes and a car and a good house, and I am working for more education because for a policeman this is very important. I think, really, anyone can do this in Namibia. You know, these Swapo who work in the bush are just stupid people who make a lot of trouble. They are telling us it is for freedom, but I, myself, I do not believe it."

9
War Stories and Patrols

December 12, 1986

We were five kilometres inside Angola, Zulu Alpha's four Casspirs advancing in a ragged skirmish line through the thick bush. A late-morning sun had turned the interior of the cars into ovens. The black policemen, ignoring the ever-present threat of ambush, rode on the coaming, scanning the ground for spoor. Diesel engines rumbled and branches scraped along the steel flanks. Above the noise, the radio crackled.

"Zulu Alpha, Zulu Mike."

Marius Brand raised his handset and pressed the transmit key. "Koos, Marius. Gaan." Go ahead.

Koos Combrinck, the new group leader of Zulu Mike, spoke briefly. Brand slipped the handset clip through the epaulet on his shirt and leaned down to order the driver to stop. The Casspir coasted to a halt, engine idling. The sweat-soaked driver slipped past Brand's legs to stand next to me and breathe slightly cooler air.

"Zulu Mike's spoorsnyers have fresh info," Brand told me. "Four terrs were in this area last night, heading east."

Otto Shivute stood atop the car and scanned the horizon. He leaned over and touched Brand's shoulder, the other hand pointing off to the left. Just above the trees a kilometre away, a haze of yellow smoke rose from a grenade thrown by Koos to mark his position.

"Maybe we have something," Brand mumbled, massaging the back of his neck. He looked down at the driver and pointed towards the smoke. "Hey! Kom! *Komesho*!" he said irritably in a mixture of Afrikaans and Oshivambo, waving the car forward with the palm of his hand.

The driver wiped the sweat from his face, took another gulp of air and dived back to his seat. He worked the gearshift lever with a gloved hand, let in the clutch, and we lurched forward. Bush and small trees fell under the steel bumper. Alongside us, the driver of the Blesbok disappeared into his cab, pulling the hatch cover over his head. There was a belch of black exhaust, and the supply vehicle tucked in to follow in our flattened wake.

When we found Koos, Zulu Mike's trackers already had the spoor. But the ground was hard, making it difficult follow. We leapfrogged half a klick beyond them—*voorsny*—and Zulu Alpha's trackers leapt out to form an arc of searchers. As soon as they found fresher spoor Brand advised Koos and threw a smoke grenade. Koos recovered his trackers, caught up with us and bulldozed through the bush for another few hundred metres. Zulu Mike's trackers dropped off the sides of the Wolfs and fanned out again, walking sticks tapping faint impressions in the sand. And so it went. But slowly. Very slowly.

We were ploughing through the dense undergrowth when the Casspir clipped a termite-eaten tree, shearing it off at the base. Tinder-dry branches exploded in an avalanche of debris. I saw stars when a limb landed squarely on my head. Sinking to one of the seats, I felt a trickle of blood start down my forehead. Shivute shouted at Brand, who glanced at me, then immediately grabbed the handle of the Browning and swung the muzzle across the bush around us. When Otto told him what had happened, Brand relaxed against the armoured back plate and they both started laughing. "What the hell's so funny?" I grumbled.

"For a second we thought you'd been shot," said Brand as Shivute handed me a wet rag to wipe the blood away. They were still choking on suppressed giggles as Sergeant Pedro Banganga, ZA's medic, sat alongside and gently parted my hair to daub the cut with Betadine. I started to dismiss it as a rough joke, then realised that it was no joke at all. Never mind that I was a non-combatant, somewhere out there were people who would kill me if given the chance. I was white and wearing the uniform of their most hated enemy, which made me as legitimate a target as any of the men around me.

The spoor eventually disappeared in the sun-baked ground.

We RV-ed with Zulu Mike at the next kraal, where the trackers were bargaining for fresh meat. Chickens seemed to be on the menu, until they saw a herd of goats. A price was agreed, I chipped in my share and rands were passed to a delighted Angolan peasant. Three goats were quickly trussed and lifted into the back of the Blesbok. Supper.

"We got robbed on the price, but it's a nice break from rat packs," said Brand.

"How is he going to use South African money?"

"No, he'll go across the cutline some day to buy a few things he can't get here. Or he'll trade them with another Angolan for something. If we had offered him Angolan kwanzas he'd have laughed in our faces. They know rands are worth something, but kwanzas? Completely worthless."

He laughed. "Did you hear about the guys who rustled a couple of cows last year? They decided the boys deserved some fresh meat, so they shot two cows they found in the bush. Didn't pay anyone, didn't bother to find out who they belonged to. That night they had a lekker braai.

"A few days later, an old Ovambo marched into the Brig's office. His donkey—with the heads of those cows tied on it—was out in the car park. He was quite pissed off. He'd done a little detective work himself, talking to the local pops from neighbouring kraals who'd seen what had happened and remembered the group letters from the cars. He wanted payment for his cattle, and he wanted it in rands. The boss called in the two group leaders, gave them serious shit and made them pay twice what those cows were worth. No one's tried that trick again."

An hour before sunset, we made our TB for the night. Bedding and food were unloaded, dried branches dragged in, and fires lit. Tent poles were cut, ponchos stretched over them and pegged down. The throats of the three goats were cut, the carcasses hung from trees and skinned and butchered. Haunches and ribs were hacked off and distributed. Water boiled in fire-blackened kettles and coffee bags were dropped in and allowed to steep. The aroma of sizzling meat wafted across the camp. No Tabasco-boosted, rat-pack potfuck tonight. As we pulled the tough flesh from the ribs with our teeth, I asked Brand about the bad blood between Koevoet and the army.

"I guess it started in the early days of the unit," he explained, licking his fingers. "Because no one was supposed to know we existed, the army got the credit for all our kills in official press releases. Even back then, we were getting a lot more than them. The army tried to bring us under their command, but the boss wouldn't go for it. You can't do what we do and operate according to a book the way the army does. They finally copied our tactics with 101 Battalion, which stole a lot of our best Ovambos by offering higher pay, but they still couldn't get the kills that we do."

"Why not? If they have Casspirs and they're using trackers the same way, what's the difference?"

"For one thing, we use basic police techniques of investigation and follow-up. And we're flexible—the boss knows we understand what's happening on the ground and lets us make the tactical decisions. But the army, they have rules of engagement. If they find spoor that goes across the yati, they have to radio back to their base at Rundu and get permission from a senior officer. And if that guy is worried about making a decision, he'll pass it to Sector 10 headquarters in Oshakati. Once you start going through all that bullshit, you lose tactical control. If you've got spoor, you have to make decisions now-now, not half an hour or an hour from now. Also, the army guys are assigned up here, rather than being volunteers. And usually they're not here more than a year, so just when they're finally getting to know the terrain and getting a little experience, they're sent home. It takes a minimum of two years in the veld before one of our people has the experience to be a group leader, but the army puts lieutenants in those positions that don't have any at all."

"But why do you guys get into so many fights with them?"

"Because we don't like the bastards."

"Right, well, yes … " I coughed politely.

Later, sitting around the campfire with a last cup of sweet, milky coffee in hand, Brand and the others brushed off their favourite stories for an audience of one. I laid out my cameras for their nightly cleaning and sat back to listen.

"We picked up the spoor of about 30 terrs, but most of the cars got stuck in a shona. The trackers were out trying to find the spoor. Only my car was free—and the Blesbok—and I said to the Blesbok driver over the radio, 'Okay, you stay with the trackers, I'll go forward.' Ahead, I saw someone near a kraal. It had to be a terr because all the civvies had run away. I told the driver to go into the kraal, and we were circling around inside and the terr jumped out with an SKS and I got him with my pistol."

"We were trying to get to Elundu before dark. We should have stopped and TB-ed in the bush because it was getting late. There's one place where the terrain along the side is higher than the road, perfect for an ambush, and they were waiting for us. I was driving, and we took three RPGs. Bang, bang, bang! One went through the engine, the other two behind me. One hit Captain Koch, who was sitting behind me. If it hadn't hit his rifle first, it would have killed him for sure. The engine stopped when the RPG hit it, and I just instinctively pushed in the clutch and we kept rolling until we were past the ambush. I had picked up lots of little pieces of shrapnel in the back of my head, neck and shoulders from the RPG that hit the captain. We were still moving, and I reached up and touched the back of my head and felt my whole scalp move. I looked at my hand and there was a big lump of flesh in it, and I put it back really fast. I thought it was part of my head. It was actually part of the captain's arm. They really hammered us."

"You know Louw van Niekerk, the big Afrikaans guy with the scar on his cheek? Well, they had a contact, and this terr surrendered at the end of it. Louw's driver stopped in front of him, and Louw climbed down from behind the guns onto the car's bonnet. As he jumped to the ground, the terr reached down and grabbed his AK and fired while Louw was still in the air. He had his mouth open, and the round went in his mouth and out the side of his cheek. Missed his teeth, jaw, everything, just went through his cheek. The terr didn't get a chance to fire a second round."

"Sakkie—maybe you didn't meet him when you were here, Afrikaans guy—he never saw the terr. They were on a follow-up when a terr jumped up in front of the car. Heatstrim came through the gun mount and caught Sakkie in the chest. Never had a chance."

"I was passing a tree as we were going into the contact, and I caught a glimpse of something behind, and I looked back, and a terr was standing there with an RPG-7. He was too far back, and I was already busy shooting. I looked back again and realised I must get my guns around before he killed me; I didn't even think about my pistol at that time. I yelled at my driver that there's one right behind us, and he turned the Casspir. I looked at my LMG: it's empty. Looked at the .50-cal: there was only a short piece of belt left, maybe 10–12 rounds. I had to keep this gook worried, and I started squeezing off shots, one by one. I got off three or four rounds before I could reach him and then gave him everything I had. It was … exciting."

"I've never had my car shot out, but they've come quite near—hit the tree next to me with an RPG, but never did they shoot my car out. I think there's about three, maybe four, bullet marks on my car that I've been driving for the past two years. That's all. I was lucky, and I believe God looked down on me. There are a lot of times that they lined me up, but I saw them first. And I don't miss at that stage."

The fires slowly died to embers and conversation faltered. From different places inside the perimeter, there was low murmuring and quiet laughter from the Ovambos. Some winged insect, only slightly smaller than a B-17 bomber judging from the sound, droned determinedly across the camp. A black velvet sky dripping with stars draped itself from horizon to horizon. The sudden streak of a shooting star appeared and disappeared so quickly you wondered if it had really been there. The faint, pulsing glow of lightning far, far to the north was a reminder that the rains still had not arrived.

The rains, you wondered, snuggling into the sleeping bag, when will they come? And what happens when they do?

The next day followed the same pattern as the day before: moving through the bush, stopping to question the locals, moving on, stopping, and on and on with no good info or even a trace of spoor. Late that afternoon, Brand turned to me. "I think we'll try setting up an ambush tonight near the yati. Me, Koos and about ten of the trackers. Want to come?"

"Sure," I nodded. Inasmuch as I wouldn't be able to use my cameras, I'd be a useless addition to the enterprise, but the invitation had been tendered and it would be bad manners to refuse.

We stopped at Ohangwena and set up the TB outside the police base. Brand and Koos picked a dozen constables. They loaded extra magazines and packed small rucksacks with the barest essentials. Koos, 22 years old from Roodeport, was another tall and quiet one with an infectious grin and all the easy grace of a natural athlete. He pulled on a camouflage jacket as I began snapping photos of the preparations.

"Don't take my picture with this thing on," Koos said. A few months earlier, Dreyer had changed his men's uniforms from camouflage to a solid olive green to distinguish Koevoet from those serving in the Security Branch police. "We're not supposed to wear them anymore," he explained. "If the Brig saw it, he'd kill me."

We boarded one of Zulu Mike's Wolf Turbos and drove east to be dropped five kilometres south of the border. As the sun slipped towards the horizon Brand gave me a quick briefing.

"Stay behind me and don't talk. If we hit something, get down and stay down until I tell you it's okay. When we get close to the cutline, the boys will play terr-terr and drop into some of the kraals to ask about any other Swaps in the area. Some of the PBs around there are pro-Swapo, but in the dark they won't be able to tell the difference between our people and the gooks. If everything seems quiet, we'll set up about 100 metres south of the cutline. Okay?"

We spread out, detouring widely around any kraals. Just after sunset we were crossing a dirt road when the headlights of a battered pickup truck appeared through the trees. The policemen waited in cover until the bakkie neared us, then stepped into the road. The driver slammed on the brakes and slid to a stop. A cloud of dust rose like fog in the headlights' beams. Silent figures surrounded the bakkie. One constable, assault rifle at the ready, opened the door and motioned the driver out. He was a minister at a nearby church. Brand questioned him as the constables searched the vehicle. When nothing was found to arouse their suspicions, Brand told him to go home. "I'm sorry, Domini," Brand said when he protested, "but it is after curfew and this road is closed."

The angry churchman slammed his door, turned the pickup around and sped into the gathering dark. We were 100 metres beyond the road when the bakkie returned, horn blaring, as the preacher headed for his original destination.

"So much for surprise," Brand hissed.

A rising half-moon, bright enough to throw shadows, rose in the east. In twos and threes, we slipped across a trail, appearing for a brief second in the soft light before disappearing back into darkened cover. An hour later we were winding between close-spaced kraals. Fires inside the enclosures cast orange glows against thatched roofs visible above the crude log palisades. Occasionally, we could hear muffled laughter and conversation.

We froze in the moonlight and crouched as a woman came out of a kraal. She hoisted her dress and squatted to urinate. When she disappeared back inside, we began moving again. Near another kraal a dog began barking. We sank to our haunches. A figure appeared at the entrance and stood silently. We held our breaths. There was a loud belch, followed by a slurred command to the dog. It quieted for a moment, then started barking again as we rose and took the first step. We halted, cursing silently. The figure reappeared. There was a sharp yelp, and both dog and master disappeared.

Close to the yati, Marius and I stopped in the shadow of a makalani palm. The trackers dissolved into the night to play terr-terr, posing as Swapo insurgents. We waited. As the moon rose higher and higher, we shifted to stay in the shadow. An hour later, two of the trackers silently materialized. One whispered close to Brand's ear, his teeth flashing in a shared joke.

Marius smiled, leaned towards me and whispered: "He asked a woman at that kraal over there if it was safe to cross the yati back into Angola. She told him there were no security force people around and that if he walked down that trail, it would take him to the border. She told him many of the freedom fighters used it."

Following the path, we stopped where high ground commanded the approaches from north and south. The team split to the east and west, each half moving 30 to 40 metres up the opposing slopes to where the first thin cover began. The policeman next to me set up his pack mortar and placed half a dozen illumination rounds next to it. I lay on my stomach and faced down the incline, propping my chin on crossed hands and wondering what the hell I was going to do if anything happened. Just stay down and hope an unlucky round doesn't catch you. My head lifted as something large and scaly climbed up one elbow and crept slowly across both arms. It dropped off the other side and continued on its way into the darkness.

Just before midnight, two old men staggered by, black silhouettes in the silver moonlight and drunk as coots. Muzzles tracked them. I ignored the urge for a cigarette and tried to pick out the policemen scattered under nearby bushes, but could see nothing to betray their presence. Pulses of lightning to the north captured my attention for a while. Towering clouds would suddenly appear, lit from inside as the lightning flickered on, then off again, too far away to hear the thunder. As if awakened by the distant glimmers, something chirped sleepily in the calm night, then fell silent again. I stifled a yawn and rested the side of my head in the crook of my arm.

I opened my eyes to the pale light of early dawn. Brand was on the radio, telling Otto that we were ready to be picked up.

"Have a nice sleep?" he asked, turning to pack the radio.

Looking around me, I saw that the others were standing and stretching stiff backs and arms. Koos waved me across to his side, and we walked to the wide strip that separated the two countries. He scanned the tree line on the far side of the yati. "Christ, my back teeth are floating." "Yeah, me, too." And like a couple of kids on a dare, we jogged across to relieve ourselves in Angola.

When the next invitation came, I started to realise that Brand liked working on foot. "We're going to try a silent follow-up on the other side of the cutline," he said a couple of days later. "Ten, maybe 15 klicks is all. You want to come with us?" Which was sort of like saying, You can come along if you're not scared. Which didn't give me any choice at all. I suspected that, like the night ambush, it was a test (on top of the RPG and Bobba the baboon). But it was also a mark of confidence by the trackers. If they had told Marius or Koos they didn't want me there, I would have been out. And I wouldn't have been the first.

"Where's so-and-so?" I had asked on my return.

"Gone," was the brief answer.

"How come? He hadn't been here that long? Did he get hurt?"

"The trackers didn't want to work with him any more.

"Why?"

"We hit a contact and when a terr jumped out of the bush next to his car and opened fire, he ducked inside and froze. After it was over, my senior Ovambo came to me. He and the boys had talked it over, and they didn't want to go on another deployment with him. He told me they couldn't trust him after that."

"What should he have done if he couldn't get his guns around?"

"Used his R5 or pistol. Whatever. But he shouldn't have frozen."

Zulu Alpha and Zulu Mike crossed the cutline and stopped near a known infiltration route that led from the Fapla base at Namakunde to St Mary's Mission south of the yati. With a little luck, Brand said, we might intercept some terrs before they reached the border. Unlike the night ambush attempt, where too many people were a liability, this time there were over 30 of us. Before setting out, Otto gestured towards me and spoke to Brand.

"Otto says the boys want to know where your weapon is." I asked him what the hell they were talking about. "They say you should have a weapon," he translated. "They say if a terr jumps up in front of you maybe they won't see him in time, that he's going to shoot you while you're taking pictures of him. If you're coming along, they want you to be armed."

I knew that many journalists in Vietnam went armed and some had actively participated in combat. When the shooting started, no one was going to ask if you were a non-combatant before squeezing the trigger.

"Why didn't they want me to carry one last night?"

When Brand translated, they laughed. "They say at night all blacks look the same and they didn't want you to shoot one of them by mistake." Otto snapped a magazine into an R5, chambered a round, flicked the safety up and handed it to me. With a look at the determined faces, I hefted the sling over my shoulder as Koos dropped an extra magazine into the cargo pocket on my leg.

"You never know," he smiled, patting my shoulder.

"Stay away from me and Koos," Brand said. "If we hit a contact, the three of us are going to be priority targets. They're told to try to kill any whites they see first. No reason to make it easier for them."

Thanks a lot, I thought. *Terrific.*

For the next two hours, we moved fast through the bush, slowing only when we came upon the occasional kraal. Approaching across open fields of freshly sprouting mohango, the lack of cover made me distinctly uncomfortable. But the feeling of vulnerability was eased when I looked to either side. The silent skirmish line emerging from the bush had a sinister, almost spooky aura about it. I could imagine what the Angolan peasants felt. We'd stop briefly as family members were separated and questioned. There would be a quick conference and then we were moving again, regaining the welcome security of the bush on the other side.

We'd left one kraal ten minutes behind when one of the trackers stopped and beckoned others to him. They motioned me down, and I squatted on my haunches as they examined the ground and then looked ahead. Spoor. One trotted off to find Brand, who soon weaved his way from the left. He dropped to one knee next to the fresh track.

"Fapla—Angolan Army," he said. "See the tread pattern of the boot? Swapo cut them off the soles of their boots. This guy was probably heading to the mission hospital the other side of the cutline. We arrested three of them there a few months ago. Their own medical care is so bad some of them sneak over to our side." His eyes traced across the terrain ahead. "We'll let him go. As fast as he's moving, he's already long gone. Probably saw us." Brand stood and laid the rifle across his shoulder. "If there are any terrs between us and Namakunde, this guy has warned them for sure."

The trackers repositioned themselves to my front and sides and we set off again. For the entire two hours, I juggled the short-barrelled assault rifle from shoulder to shoulder, across the back of my neck, slung under one arm and then the other, wondering what would have to happen before I would use it.

God knew, I wasn't there to kill anyone. My job was to observe, to take photos and notes, to report; yet here I was, armed. Once you had it, you couldn't be a shooter *and* a journalist. My excuse for having it was that Otto had given me no choice if I was to go with them. But I did have the choice, and it had been mine alone: go armed, prepared to use it as they had the right to expect, or stay with the cars until they returned. And without thinking of the consequences, I had taken the first option.

I struggled for two hours with doubts and questions. My acceptance of that weapon had raised a double-edged set of moral and ethical dilemmas that I never was able to resolve totally. The patrol was without incident. In the end, I knew there was only one answer. But I would never really know for sure.

("Hey, man, you ever carry a weapon on one of these trips?" "Are you kidding? That's the last thing I'd ever do.")

10

"I Am Going to My Darling Today"

December 27, 1986

Dear Sugar,
Have been here just over a month now, with most of that time spent in the veld.
It's been exhausting, dirty, and frustrating, with everyone assuring me that it's
still the quiet time, that we're still at least a couple of weeks away from the
beginning of the annual summer infiltration. "It's always like this right now,"
they keep saying. "Don't worry, the terrs will come. Genuine," they add, as
frustrated as I over the inaction. "The rains are late; the terrs will come with
the rains." So it's been lots of days rumbling across the landscape, watching the
trackers questioning the locals at their primitive kraals in the middle of nowhere,
chasing and losing the occasional spoor, but all in all, a fairly undramatic time.
Until three days after Christmas.

Jack Bouwer, team leader, Zulu Tango: "We were getting ready to deploy
when our ops officer, Major Willem Fouche, told me that an American
journalist was going to accompany us. When I shared this unwelcome
information with Ox du Preez, Angus Pursell and Gavin Manning, the
response was, 'How can we trust some foreign journalist who's probably
going to write a lot of kak about Koevoet like everyone else in the press?' For
the next week he was constantly asking questions and doing the bit with his
cameras. We were too scared to go for a shit without being photographed.
Angus and Gavin were English speaking and they eventually started talking
to him. Ox didn't have much English and hardly said a word. By the end
of his time with us, Jim and the whole of ZT, including the Ovambos, were
best friends. In the days and weeks to come we shared quite a few drinks and
stories with him, but he did like to take risks."

Its totem was *Omanda*—the black rhino—and if there was symbolism to be
found it was in Zulu Tango's collection of robust personalities. There was no

question who was team leader. With his powerful build, thick red hair and full beard, 28-year-old Jack Bouwer lacked only a battle axe and drinking horn to complete the picture of a Viking warrior. This was reinforced by an intimidating personality that saw me tread warily around him. His English was good, but at first the four-year Ops K veteran seemed barely to tolerate my presence and volunteered nothing. It wasn't until we'd enjoyed a few beers halfway through the deployment that he started to open up.

Johnny Mwashitinayo, the team's senior black warrant officer, was impressive by any standard and projected the charisma and competence of natural leadership. He and Bouwer were quick to recognise the depth of my ignorance, and Mwashitinayo assigned three of his men to keep close watch on me. Sadly, we had no common language and I regretted not being able to speak with him directly. As Bouwer later said of the man, "Johnny was not only respected by everyone in Zulu Tango, but by all the members of Koevoet. Our daily planning was greatly helped by his knowledge and direct input. He stood out as a leader and whenever we had a shortage of section commanders, he took charge of one of the four Casspirs. I later nominated him to go on a shortened SWAPOL officers' course, which he successfully completed."

Jack's second-in-command was Rhodesian-born Gavin Manning, whose family had immigrated to South Africa 12 years earlier. Tall, slender and every girl's heart throb, he sported a mop of the blondest hair I'd ever seen. Had he exchanged his Koevoet T-shirt and peaked cap for a blue blazer and boater, he would have been the image of a posh Oxbridge undergraduate at the Henley Regatta. The foppish image was deceiving; at 23, Manning was a ruthlessly efficient operator with a quick, analytical brain, equally adept in English and Afrikaans and speaking fluent Oshivambo. In recognition of his reflexes and shooting skills, the trackers had christened him *Okaiimbi* after the African Yellow-billed Kite, known for striking its prey with speed and accuracy. His instinctive distrust of the media mirrored Bouwer's.

Gavin Manning, ZT-2: "When I heard about this journalist coming out to the bush with us, I was dead set against it and voiced that sentiment to Jack openly. But the unit's officers had decreed otherwise. So be it, I thought. However, given he never complained about anything, was naturally inquisitive and seemed prepared to listen to our side of the story, my opinion gradually changed."

Also 23 and from Durban, dark-haired Angus Pursell commanded ZT-4 and had been with Ops K for a little over a year. More reserved than Jack and Gavin, the rapport between him and the men in his car was obvious from my first day with the team. Their name for him was *Ekodi*—the African Hawk Eagle—for the eagle tattoo on his arm. He gave the impression of being solid and dependable.

If anyone deserved a nickname in both languages, it was Chris "Ox" du Preez, though "Main Battle Tank" would have been equally appropriate. A little taller than me but massively built, the 23-year-old plugged the command hatch of his Casspir like a cork in a wine bottle. It wasn't difficult to imagine Ox playing prop on the Springbok rugby team, or indeed wrestling his namesake to the ground in one easy throw. The Ovambos were as much in awe of his size and strength as his eyesight, and dubbed him *Nonshilulu* – Man Who Can See Good in the Bush. But English for this burly Afrikaner from the Northern Transvaal was very much a foreign language.

Aside from Johnny Mwashitinayo, the Ovambos that stood out started with Sergeant Thomas Elumbe Phineas, who alternated as the driver for Bouwer and Manning's cars, both men prizing his quick thinking, aggressive driving skills and courage under fire. Inquisitive and good-humoured, Thomas could open a rat pack tin with a long jack knife faster than anyone I'd ever seen. Some months after I left, he would suffer grievous injuries in an ambush near Miershoop. "I took leave and visited him at 1 Military Hospital in Pretoria," Gavin related during the writing of this book. "He told me that when the heatstrim hit, he felt the shockwave and then his ears were ringing. The next thing he felt was something dangling on his left cheek. He pulled it off and threw it aside as Johnny dragged him from the driver's seat and drove them out of the kill zone. He later realised it was his eye he had thrown away. He came back with a glass eye and worked in ZT's store."

The men tasked with monitoring me were an eclectic trio. Warrant Officer Frans Ananaii was a rarity amongst the Ovambos, an atheist who refused to join the morning prayers. Whilst the others lowered their heads, Ananaii, wearing his signature white sweatband, stood to one side and ostentatiously watched the birds. "An excellent tracker," Manning said of him, "and mean as a junk yard dog." Kapinya, sometimes driver in Pursell's car, was ZT's clown. From morning to dusk, he sported huge sunglasses with thick white frames that looked like reverse-image goggles on his black face. Whether in the car or around the campfire at night, he kept everyone in stitches. I didn't understand a word of what he said, but just looking at his mischievous expressions behind the ridiculous sunglasses was enough to crack me up. Then there was Petrus Hangula, over six feet tall, thin as a rake, and a former Swapo insurgent, who watched everything around him with hooded eyes. After setting up a TB, he would stalk Kapinya with the exaggerated movements of a silent-screen villain, suddenly leap on him and the two would engage in mock Kung Fu battles, to the hilarity and applause of everyone.

By the middle of the deployment I had settled into the team's rhythm, and Jack, Gavin and Angus were starting to relax around me. The team pushed hard, but none of the PBs they questioned provided leads, and the only spoor found soon disappeared with anti-tracking, making everyone scratchy and short-tempered. In his role of court jester, Kapinya lightened the mood with constant banter and jokes about the foreign *shirumbu*—white man—riding with them. I happily played the fool, shrugging or nodding whenever it was obvious I was the subject of his teasing. The shirumbu had become their mascot.

To the frustration of all, solid information and clear spoor remained elusive. Action alongside Zulu Tango was coming, but that was in the weeks ahead. On the fifth day, I started coming down with what I thought was the 'flu: nausea, fever, painful joints and splitting headache. When we pulled into Eenhana, I decided to stay there. It would give me the opportunity to catch up on notes and hang loose should a team scramble the choppers, the pilots saying they could set me down alongside or even right on top of one of the cars if that's what I wanted, "No problem."

Major Grant Brooks, the SAAF officer commanding the air unit, had put his neck on the line by officially-unofficially authorizing me to ride with them; "As long as the pilots don't mind," he added. "It'll be up to them." I thanked him, knowing that if something went wrong he'd be taking the heat. "Just don't do anything silly," Brooks said, wagging a finger at me with mock severity.

Captain Rick Dooley, 15 Squadron, South African Air Force: "Owing to past experience, it was difficult to trust journalists, but I felt he was genuine and worth spending time with, both in and out of the cockpit. It was always good to shoot the breeze in the evenings with him and listen to his banter with the Koevoet teams. He seemed determined to capture and make sense of it all, to provide an honest reflection of what we accomplished and stood for, whilst fighting a war which was at times surreal."

I didn't have long to wait. The next morning, a call came in from an army patrol on the Chandelier Road between Eenhana and Elundu. They had tripped a POM-Z anti-personnel mine and needed an immediate casevac. When we landed, the platoon was spread either side of the road in a protective cordon. With fuel tanks still almost full, the Alouette was close to max weight, so I hopped out, and a Caprivian soldier, blood soaking through thick dressings around calves and feet, took my place. Dooley lifted off, leaving me with the soldiers of 701 Battalion. Being in the veld without the reassuring rumble of Casspirs or Wolf Turbos and the bearded, scarred faces of Koevoet was a new experience and slightly discomfiting.

The SWATF lieutenant explained that they had been searching for a group of insurgents that had fired a heatstrim at a civilian pickup truck. He led me to a slight depression in the sand where at least half a dozen insurgents had lain in wait. Further along, I saw the rifle grenade, broken in half, lying on the side of the road.

"It hit the bakkie," the lieutenant said, "but it didn't go off. Maybe rain got inside it. Or maybe it was a dud. Whatever. Those civvies were very lucky."

("We are not committing atrocities," Jacob Hannai had lectured me in Swapo's London office. "We don't see any situation why we have to go and kill our own mothers, brothers, and sisters, because we are fighting for them.")

As soon as the shaken driver reached Nkongo and reported the attack, the Romeo Mike team rushed to the scene in their Buffel armoured personnel carriers. The Caprivian volunteer hadn't seen the trip wire set by the insurgents; the explosion ripped his feet apart and drove more shrapnel into the calves of a white teenaged conscript alongside him. They weren't the only wounded; I noticed spots of fresh blood seeping through the 20-year-old lieutenant's trousers.

Dooley flew back in to pick up the remaining casualty. With enough fuel burned off, he waved me in. As we lifted off, I saw the young officer, head tucked down and holding on to his bush hat, limping away from the sandstorm generated by the downwash. He wasn't leaving his men.

Barely half an hour after landing there was a second call for a casevac, this time for an SADF *troepie* who had sliced open his leg on something. We landed in a sprouting mohango field and I scrambled out to snap photos as he was carried on a stretcher to the helicopter. The smile on his face spoke volumes. He was delighted to be getting out of the veld. Not all South Africans were natural warriors.

Back at Eenhana, I dosed myself with aspirin and buckled down to work, pounding the keys of the portable typewriter that had seen me through Chad, Sudan, Kenya and Uganda. Feeling like shit, my dedication was short-lived. I found myself wandering more and more frequently to the ops room to ask Van, the radioman, if any of the teams were following spoor. But each time he would raise his eyes, shake his close-cropped head and return to reading a well-worn paperback novel. The lurid cover had a square-jawed, muscular hero firing an AK-47 one-handed, while the other arm encircled the waist of a blonde clutching a ripped safari jacket over luscious, melon-sized breasts. Just like in real life.

I closed the case on the typewriter and settled inside the air-conditioned radio room, thumbing through tattered back issues of *Huisgenoot*, a popular South African magazine. The only calls Van received were routine position reports. I'd watch him move the map pins that marked each group's updated location, then return to the journal.

"How much Afrikaans have you picked up?" Van asked, laying down the book and stretching.

I tossed the magazine aside in frustration; it might as well have been printed in Greek for all I understood. "In the veld I guess I can already understand about a third of what's said," I allowed, shaking the last cigarette out of a crumpled pack and lighting up.

"Genuine?" he asked.

"Sure," I said, "It's pretty easy when about every third word is 'fuck.'"

"Oh. Yeah," he admitted, blushing furiously.

After two days of no calls and feeling guilty about not sharing the heat, dust and tedium of the bush (to hell with the 'flu—if I was going to do this story, understand what was happening, I had to be out there with the rest of them, not sitting in air-conditioned luxury), I decided to join the next team to come in for rebunkering.

An hour before sunset, groups began arriving and setting up TBs outside the walls. Among them were Botes Botha and his team Zulu Foxtrot. Over a beer in the air force compound that night, I singled him out. Still a little unsure of myself and not knowing how individual members of the unit felt about an outsider taking up extra space in their already crowded cars, I talked around it until finally deciding that he was approachable. "Is it okay if I go out with you guys tomorrow, Botes?" I asked.

"Sure, Jim, no problem," he shrugged.

Small, married and 30-ish, Botes was one of the longest-serving members of the security forces in the operational area. Eleven years in the Eastern Caprivi, where he ran police boat patrols along the Zambezi River, preceded his three years with Koevoet. Behind an easy-going nature, Botes was a capable counterinsurgency professional, "a good operator," in the parlance of the unit. But even good operators could make mistakes now and then.

"There used to be a lot more ambushes along the Chandelier Road east of here," Botes reminisced. "We were here at Eenhana one morning, two, maybe three years ago, I guess. A couple of groups had already headed out. It was raining, so we weren't in a hurry to go. I was in the toilet when I heard firing. I thought it was only the army. You know, just practicing near the base or something. Then one of my people ran in and said the groups that just left had hit an ambush and the choppers were being scrambled. We jumped in the cars and got going. We were a couple of klicks down the road when one of my boys saw spoor going off to the side and I yelled at my driver to turn. The cars behind us didn't see us leave the road, so we were by ourselves.

"We were trying to follow the spoor, but the rain was washing it away fast so we knew they were bloody close. I heard one of the gunships overhead, but didn't pay any attention to it. We had gone just a few hundred metres south of the road when I saw a terr standing behind a tree with an RPG. He was aiming at us, but he was already to our side, and I didn't know if I could reach him with the guns. I swung the turret as far as it could go and fired and saw him go down. We drove up to him, and I jumped out. He was still alive, and as the medic was working on him I was trying to get info. You know, how many terrs, which way they had gone, what they were carrying.

"Suddenly, on my car's radio I heard Dave Atkinson, the chopper pilot, yelling, 'Botes! Botes! Behind you! Look behind you!' I turned around and, man, there was a terr not more than 30 metres away coming down on me with a Dragunov sniper rifle. There was nothing I could do. No weapon, no time to get behind anything—I was a dead man. That terr had me. Major Dave just put that chopper on its side, and the flight engineer floored him with his 20mm on the first burst. Guess I was lucky," he said, running his fingers through short, sandy hair. "I still have that Dragunov. Nice scope on it. And accurate. But we don't get many ambushes along there any more," he added a little sadly.

Of Botha's car commanders, Flip Fouche was wiry and red-headed with a quick temper, while Marius Gouws was big, quiet, dark-haired and tending to weight. Both Flip and Gouws had a few years behind them in Koevoet. Herman Grobler was the new guy in Zulu Foxtrot. Well built and athletic, he was, like Flip, a graduate of the police special task force school. Unlike Flip, he had yet to experience his first contact as we pulled out of Eenhana the next morning and headed east.

> **Flip Fouche, car commander, ZF-2:** "Having an outsider with Koevoet was the 'talk of the town'—we discussed it in the field, in the bar, everywhere. I even asked Botes, 'What the fuck is this journalist doing here?' I remember the morning at Eenhana when I first met him. I was pouring my coffee and the next moment I caught movement at my back and it was this outsider taking a picture of me. I have that picture and it shows how pissed off I was by this guy pointing his camera left, right and centre. Right from the beginning I had him down as an arrogant bastard, 'finish en klaar!' Over and out!"

By midmorning, Zulu Charlie reported they had the spoor of five insurgents moving north. Zulu Foxtrot rendezvoused with them half an hour later and took the spoor. ZC, in overall command of the follow-up, pushed ahead on voorsny. (Protocol dictated that the leader of the group that discovered spoor had tactical control of the chase, regardless of rank.)

Not 15 minutes had gone by when Zulu Charlie's trackers scrambled the helicopters; the terrs weren't more than ten minutes in front of them. A third fighting group joined us in the suddenly fast-moving chase that led us and the orbiting gunships across the border and increasingly deeper into Angola. After two hours of steady pursuit, the spoor was lost on hard ground, and the groups fanned out to try finding it again.

With the sun almost directly overhead, the pilots radioed that they needed topping up. A wide, treeless landing zone was selected, Casspirs and Wolf Turbos surrounded it and the two Alouettes touched down. Trackers spread themselves between the cars as drums of kerosene were wrestled off the Blesboks and rolled to the gunships. Each flight engineer opened a panel on the side of his helicopter, slid a coiled hose into a barrel and a battery-powered pump began sucking fuel into the depleted tanks.

Botes was on the radio when his frequency was overridden by static. Puzzled, he waited a moment and tried again. Within seconds, his transmission was blanked out again. He ducked inside his Wolf and switched to another frequency. Again, it was interrupted. "Maybe someone's trying to jam you," I suggested.

Botes tried more frequencies but none was workable. "Shit!" he snapped. "That's not jamming, that's another radio set! There are terrs right here!" He shouted his discovery to the pilots. The fuelling was immediately suspended and the drums muscled away. Turbines whined, blades began turning and the helicopters lifted off, the muzzles of their 20mm guns sweeping the bush. We set off again, searching in ever-widening circles as heads swivelled back and forth for a sight of running insurgents.

We stopped briefly alongside the decaying, pink shells of once-graceful Portuguese villas at Chiede while the trackers swept through the crumbling ruins. A platoon of grey-green lizards darted ahead of us into the safety of shadowed rubble, annoyed at the unexpected intrusion. Long-untended bougainvillea straggled over the bullet-pocked stucco. Sun-blistered walls were daubed with the fading slogans of three liberation movements—Unita, Fapla and Swapo. I wondered where the people who lived here before independence were now. One of the groups working voorsny radioed that they had picked up the spoor again. The trackers piled back into the car and we raced on, leaving the villas at Chiede to the sun and silence and faraway memories.

The insurgents continued fleeing north until their anti-tracking techniques saved them from the chaotic manhunt going on around them. The three Koevoet groups turned south and headed towards the border. Shortly before reaching the cutline, we came across an old man driving a pair of heavily laden donkeys. I snapped a photo of his animals, each carrying two large sacks of mealie meal stamped Produce of South West Africa. Botes smiled at my surprise.

"No, a lot of them cross the border to buy things. Haven't you noticed there aren't any cuca shops on this side? They'd have to go a long way north to buy anything, and even then there's not much available according to guys like this one. It's a lot easier for them to get what they need in South West. They're supposed to cross at Oshikango and show their papers, but most of them just cross wherever they feel like it. The only reason we even bother to stop and talk with them is that we usually get a lot of good info. The terrs treat them like shit because they can get away with it. And if they complain to Fapla, well, Swapo uses Fapla bases all the time, so they're not going to do anything about it. The civvies up here have it a lot worse than the ones on the other side. You don't find too many north of the yati that are pro-Swapo, I can promise you.

"No," he said, watching as the old fellow laid a switch on the rumps of his donkeys and continued unmolested into the bush, "we'll stop and talk to them about the Swaps, but we don't bother them about crossing the cutline. They've got to make a living some way."

We TB-ed that night outside the Ohangwena Security Branch base. Old Tom, Zulu Foxtrot's senior Ovambo warrant officer, sat cross-legged side by side with Botes next to the campfire and analysed what had gone wrong with the day's follow-up. His finger drew diagrams in the sand, showing where we'd been when the radio was blanked out, and then the search pattern. As one of the original 60 Ovambos recruited by Koevoet, Tom had seen everything in this war. Botes listened attentively, nodding and asking questions as Tom made his points. Tom finally brushed his hands off against his legs, stood and walked off to check on the men.

"What was all that about?" I asked.

"No, Tom reckons we lost them because Neil—Zulu Charlie's group leader—was just too uncoordinated. He's sure we went right by them, probably within a few feet. At one point we were only five minutes behind, too close for them to have gotten away. I think he's right. That old man knows what he's talking about. Did you hear what he did last week?"

I shook my head.

"We were on a follow-up. The bush was really thick, so we were moving slow. Tom was in front with the spoorsnyers when he looked up and saw two terrs. One of them had an RPG on his shoulder, lining up on the nearest car. Tom had left his R5 in the car—all he had was his walking stick—and there wasn't time to pull his pistol. The other terr was just moving some bush out of the way to give his pal a clear shot. Tom raised the stick over his head, screamed and charged them. Surprised them just long enough for the trackers behind Tom to kill them before they could shoot. Genuine."

Early next morning, Botes switched areas and before the dew had dried Zulu Foxtrot learned that five Swapo, armed and uniformed, had stopped the night before at a nearby cuca shop. No one knew which way they had gone, only that they had been drinking there until midnight. Although the information was solid, the ground was hard and blanketed with the sharp prints of cattle hooves. Flip suspected the insurgents had friends or relatives in the area that had intentionally driven their herds over the spoor.

We stopped near the collection of traditional huts and tin shanties of the nondescript village. Joints aching and feverish from malaria rather than 'flu, and bored at the prospect of another long and inconclusive day, I stood on the seats and leaned against the coaming. There was nothing about the village that made it any different from a dozen others along the length of the Oom Willie se Pad. A few elderly men sat in the sun, puffing on pipes filled with home-grown tobacco. Women passed to and fro with bundles of firewood or water buckets balanced on their heads. Half-naked children played in the dirt. All seemed oblivious to our presence.

Botes and the trackers got out of the car, walked along the edge of the dirt road, and then returned. Flip, Herman Grobler and Marius Gouws moved their Wolfs slowly to the southeast. Flip joined the trackers on the ground. Just to our east was a patch of scattered mopani bush about the size of a football field and surrounded by freshly ploughed mohango fields. The morning air was still cool, the sky streaked with high, wispy mares' tails, the only sound the low rumble of idling diesel engines.

Flip Fouche, ZF-2: "Daniel Taiko, Haifeni Wilibard, another Haifeni whose surname I don't remember, and I were trying find any spoor made by terrs. It was really difficult because of all the locals' spoor, but a sixth sense told us to keep going. If there was any, it would split away sooner or later. After about two kilometres we found what we were looking for. Spoor that might be from terrs broke away into low mopani bushes, but it was difficult to follow because of anti-tracking. I figured it was at least a day old and that they were long gone, so I wasn't armed. The only one of us that had a gun was Daniel. The other cars had moved up and we were in the middle of them when I saw Daniel suddenly give the sign to put the gunships on standby. I was heading back to my car to make the call when … "

It was then that Taiko saw a crouched figure focused on the approaching cars and trackers. He was backing deeper into the low bush, a heatstrim anti-armour grenade on the end of his AKM assault rifle. With a range of 400 metres, it could burn through six inches of steel before spraying the inside of whatever it struck with white-hot shrapnel; the quarter-inch skin of the Wolf Turbos offered no protection. As the figure ducked into thickening cover, Taiko brought up his R5 and opened fire.

I looked up at the sound of shots and saw a tracer spinning crazily through the air. Red smoke spewed from the grenade Taiko had thrown to mark his position. I looked at Botes confusedly. What the hell …? He and the radio both yelled "CONTACT!" and I stumbled backward as the Wolf bellowed and lurched forward. I pulled myself up in the open well, Y-legged across the seats. Behind me, two constables were leaning over the side, looking for targets.

We cut across the northern edge of the bush, then swung hard left. I raised a camera, trying to keep my balance as the stiffly sprung 16-tonne car took the choppy ground with knee-buckling shudders. Thirty metres to the left a figure in dark camouflage ran through the mopani, geysers of sand erupting around him. I jerked the camera up and panned with my longest lens, trying to keep him in the viewfinder as we moved in opposite directions.

> **Flip Fouche:** "We were on the ground, everyone was shooting and all we wanted to do is to get out of the line of fire. Daniel, the two Haifenis and I managed to take cover behind a huge maroela tree about 30 metres away. Just then the driver of the Strandwolf saw what was happening. He raced up and stopped between us and the firing. I ran to it and jumped into the front, then opened the hatch and climbed out with the car's radio. I was kneeling on top with a complete view of the contact scene. I immediately saw two terrs right in front of Botes and warned him over the radio."

A 15-foot anthill was coming up on our left. As we neared it Botes saw one of the insurgents kneeling at its base, firing at us. Botes swung the machine gun mount, but we'd gone too far to traverse the guns enough to hit him, and the trackers were yelling "KOLOMOSHO! KOLOMOSHO! KOLOMOSHO!" (LEFT! LEFT! LEFT!). And then "KO OSHIVANDA! KO OSHIVANDA!" (NEXT TO THE ANTHILL!) The driver took us sharply around the anthill in a wrenching U-turn, Botes and the two constables firing. Branches were scythed off by the streams of bullets and bits of the anthill exploded into dust.

A bullet ricocheted off the opposite side of the car and whined away. Another hidden insurgent barely 25 metres away, was firing at us, the sound of his AK-47 masked by the closer roar of machine guns and R5s. That he managed to miss as we passed him, and continued to miss as we pulled away, was sheer good fortune.

Behind us, Gouws was racing north in pursuit of the one I'd seen running. This was the same insurgent Taiko had fired at. Closing rapidly from behind, Marius couldn't hit him from the bouncing vehicle. The insurgent looked over his shoulder, then started to swing around to bring the heatstrim to bear on the

Wolf. He was too slow; the car hit him, knocking the body forward and rolling over it with barely a bump.

Neliwa, the Ovambo manning the guns on Herman's car, now saw a third insurgent. I looked over my shoulder to see the big Wolf Turbo racing in at right angles to our path, the twin .30 calibre machine guns raising a cloud of dust just ahead of it. I twisted around and clicked off one frame, not realizing that he had just killed the one firing at Botes and me.

Then they were yelling, "KOLOMOSHO! KOLOMOSHO! KOLOMOSHO!" again, and "HUMBA NATANGO!" (SHOOT AGAIN!). We heeled over in another U-turn, Botes still raking the bush around the anthill. I was braced against the side of the car, pointing the wide angle where he was aiming, frame after frame clicking through the camera, when the Wolf hit a hidden tree stump, snapping the right front suspension with a loud crack and slamming me forward. Then Botes was yelling "STOP! STOP!" and for a moment there was silence before the air was split with shouts and whistles.

I jumped out and followed two constables into the mopani. Something wet touched my arm and I looked down to see leafy branches sprayed with blood. Beneath my feet, a trail of it led towards the anthill, where a body lay, still alive, but unconscious and dying. This was no Hollywood death scene. A fist-sized hole gaped on the side of his head; splintered white bone protruded from the left arm, and one leg below the knee lay at right angles, shot almost completely off. His other arm moved slowly, and involuntary mewing sounds came from his throat as the trackers dragged him clear of his hiding place, cut off the webbing and looked through his Libyan uniform for papers. A small notepad pulled from a hip pocket carried two fresh bullet holes. As I walked away, two closely spaced shots broke through the excited voices.

The man hit by Gouws's car lay 30 metres to the north, a flattened heatstrim on the end of his assault rifle. My eyes went from the weapon to the body; the same tyre had gone over his head. I raised a camera, then lowered it, recording the scene only in my mind. At the south-eastern corner, the third insurgent was sprawled face down, two Ovambo policemen stripping the body of equipment. Neliwa rolled the body over and spoke to Botes. He pointed at the body, then stood and scribed imaginary lines through the air from where the body lay towards where we had made our first U-turn around the anthill. Botes turned to me.

"Did you see any tracers?" I hadn't. "Neliwa said he didn't know there was a third terr till he saw this guy's tracers going by us. I'd say from about 20 metres."

Among the documents found was a tattered pamphlet, its cover bearing a photo of Swapo President Sam Nujoma. An article by Nujoma attacked the "murder squads" of Koevoet, 101 Battalion, and the Portuguese-speaking 32 Battalion and eulogized "the many comrades who have sacrificed." There were long, creative tallies of racist bases destroyed, South African soldiers killed and aircraft shot down. Once again, I was reminded of Jacob Hannai's fairy tales in London, seven months earlier. Whether wishful thinking or confidence boosting for the benefit of simple peasant guerrillas like these, none of it was true. The article finished by promising that this was "the year of final victory over the racist South African regime in Namibia."

Botes translated sections of it to the Ovambo policemen. There were hoots of derision and laughter. "Sam's been promising for years that a military victory was right around the corner," Botes explained. He pointed at one of the bodies. "And he keeps convincing youngsters like these that he's right."

Botes laid the pamphlet aside and sorted through the rest of the papers. One had a crudely drawn picture of the army base at Okankolo, stick men with guns representing troops. Childishly sketched vehicles suggested Casspirs entering and leaving the base. These three had obviously been returning from a reconnaissance mission. Their ages and the fact that the leader had stopped where there was no chance of escape testified to their lack of experience and training.

Botes thumbed through the damaged notepad, stopped on one page and read it slowly. He shook his head. "Read this."

> it is good to have this opportunity
> to ratty to you
> because of love to you darling.
> Please tell me if you love me
> baby. But to me I love you and
> I love. Please darling don't forget
> my lovest to you darling.
> I don't have many to ratty
> to you Good-bye darling.

I turned the page.

I love you darling
I love you forever.
Kiss me baby.
I am very happy of you.
I will not forget you baby.
Sex is good to you and me.
I am going to my darling to day
I will cam to slipp to you.
Yes or not daling?
I will not forget my love to you darling.
From Nakale Ya Nakale

I closed the stained pages and handed them back to Botes.

"Poor bastard."

"Yeah."

"Didn't know what he was getting into."

"No. He didn't."

"Should've stayed home and married his girlfriend."

Bodies tied with strips of bark to a bumper and spare tyres, we drove back to the Oom Willie se Pad and stopped at the village of Ondobe. The investigative centre had radioed to say they wanted to collect them for possible identification. While we waited, Herman went into the cuca shop and bought a dozen beers for his first contact. Willem, one of Zulu Foxtrot's senior Ovambos, joined us. The Soviet-made compass he had taken from one of the dead was a rare find. Gouws tried to bargain for it, but Willem only smiled and slipped the thin strap around his neck. Gouws winked at me and rubbed his thumb and forefinger together: he'd eventually get the compass, but it was going to cost him. The other black warrant officers climbed in and the beers went from mouth to mouth as the contact was relived.

Jokes were made about Flip having to take cover behind a tree during the first part of the contact. But everyone knew he'd climbed on top of the Strandwolf while bullets were flying everywhere. Had he not warned Botes about the two insurgents, or if Taiko hadn't spotted the first one, some of Zulu Foxtrot's men might now be on casevac choppers racing for the primary trauma centre at Ondangwa. Beers tilted gratefully towards both men.

Taiko lifted his chin in my direction. "Daniel said the boys are talking about the foreign shirumbu who was standing up taking pictures," Botes translated. "They think you should stay down when you take your pictures. So do I."

"I can't get the snaps if I can't see what's happening," I protested. "Besides, you're even more exposed up there behind those guns."

"Yeah, and that's why we take more injuries, man for man, than the Ovambos. But I'm up there because it's my job, and I know what I'm doing. That's what I get paid for. You're a big boy, so I'm not going to tell you what to do, but you get killed and I'm going to have a lot of paperwork to fill in." I said something stupid about everything being a calculated risk. Botes shrugged and let it pass.

> **Flip Fouche:** "After two or three days, this journalist was still standing and taking all the shit from the heat, bundu-bashing in the Wolf, even when he had malaria coming on, and not complaining. I started to think he might be okay. Maybe."

I made my way through the tangle of black and white legs inside the car and climbed down. The Wolf with the three bodies tied to the outside was parked under a large tree next to the road. Ovambo civilians passed with hardly a glance at the grisly scene. Five metres from where a steady drip of blood spattered the ground two women sat under the tree drinking Cokes.

At some point a passing Ovambo clergyman snapped a photo of the bodies lashed to Wolf. It was sent to South Africa and splashed across a number of newspapers. Scathing editorials would attack Koevoet for not respecting the dead, for its callousness in exhibiting the corpses. None would mention the atrocities committed by Swapo against unarmed civilians who refused to support the liberation movement.

When the car from Zulu Three arrived, the bodies were transferred and it headed back to Onaimwandi. Word came over the radio that the contact had brought the total of Swapo killed or captured by Koevoet to 399 for the year.

The insignificant patch of mopani bush was silent now save for the sound of bloated flies around thickening pools, while columns of ants marched to and from unexpected feasts on things more solid. Crimson spray splashed over pale leaves had turned black under the sun. Soon the only tangible reminders of where it had come from would be Kalashnikovs, spoils of war, thrown carelessly on the floor of one of the cars. On the third day of Christmas.

11

Feeling Sorry for the Poor Bastards

We worked slowly eastward the rest of the day. As the adrenaline wore off, the sweats and fever and dull ache of the malaria returned. Herman handed me a handful of anti-malarial chloroquine tablets, promising the shock of them would make me feel worse for a while, but would knock the malaria back. He was right. Before long, I felt much worse. We pulled into Eenhana base late that afternoon, and I decided to stay there the next day. I did, and then I didn't.

December 30, 1986

Botes and his group had been gone for an hour. I was sitting in the shaded air force compound trying to catch up on my notes again and feeling very rough. Roelf Maritz, the operations officer who'd been unimpressed with my press card my first day with Koevoet, walked over from the radio room. Smirking at my haggard appearance, he made a show of holding up an anti-malarial tablet and washing it down. True to form, I'd been following the example of my mentors by foregoing the bitter pills; screws up your tan, they said.

> **Captain Roelf Maritz, Alpha Group operations officer:** "Was I initially pleased with the idea of having a foreigner go out with the teams? Hell no. I was very negative and outspoken about my feelings as I trusted no media people, and here we were told that we had to take this journalist with us. Ridiculous! I thought the top brass must have gone bonkers and at first told the guys to be very careful when he was around. By now, however, I'd gotten to know him a little better and decided he might be okay."

"Looks like we might have a little activity already," Maritz said brightly. "Zulu Hotel's got good info on a couple of terrs just up the road."

The pilots and flight engineers had dragged themselves from under their mosquito nets in the sandbagged sleeping quarters. Hair tousled and dressed in loose fitting flight suits, they sat or stood around the table, working on cups of milky tea or instant coffee.

"Zulu Hotel just called," Maritz told them, speaking English for my benefit. "They've picked up spoor not too far from here." He jabbed his mug towards the west, coffee slopping over the rim. He placed it on the table and wiped his hands. "Jasper said the PBs put them on to two terrs. He reckons they're about 30 minutes behind them and moving this way."

A few minutes later, Zulu Hotel called again to say they were less than five kilometres from Eenhana and following two insurgents dressed in civilian clothes. The chopper pilots moved quickly into their ops room to slip on shoulder holsters and plot the reported grid references. Flight engineers were already trotting out to prepare the helicopters for take off.

The pilots emerged from the tent and once more took up their positions around the table. The topic of conversation was unvarying. Like every military pilot I'd ever met, they ate, drank and breathed flying. Although all of them were proficient in Afrikaans, a necessary asset when working with Koevoet, English seemed the language of choice. It had become obvious that the chopper pilots and policemen had huge professional respect for each other. Working with Ops K guaranteed action for the gunship crews, while the men in the Casspirs depended on them for air support and casevacs. There were regular sessions devoted to working out SOPs and tactics.

Gavin Manning, ZT-2: "The lack of easily identifiable landmarks in the very flat topography of Ovamboland could be a real problem for the pilots. Making regular tight manoeuvres over a featureless terrain, it was easy for them to become disorientated, just as it was for us on the ground when we had to change direction in the middle of the bush. Telling the gunship that the spoor had changed, say, from going NE to NNW meant he'd have to take his eyes off the ground and read his compass, momentarily losing sight of trackers and cars.

"What we finally hit on was using the standard clock code based on tree shadows. In the morning, the shadows lay to the west, while after midday, they fell to the east, but for our purposes the direction of the shadow would always be 12 o'clock. If the spoor was parallel to the line of shadows, we could tell the gunships that it was running at 12 o'clock. If it turned 90 degrees to the right, it was now running at 3 o'clock. A 90-degree left turn was 9 o'clock, while a reverse direction was 6 o'clock. The same message was heard by car commanders and everyone was immediately orientated.

"With two gunships orbiting over us, the 'double-D' pattern worked very well. If the straight side of the D was the direction of the spoor, one Alo would cover the left side, the other the right. When one was turning over the trackers, the other was at the farthermost point ahead of them, which was a distance based on the trackers' estimate of the lead the terrs had on us.

"When the terrs saw the chopper moving towards them, they'd dive for cover and stay hidden until it passed. The mark they made in the sand was very distinctive, and when the spoorsnyers found one they knew the gooks were under the gunships' patterns and became even more motivated. Depending on whether it was a running or anti-tracking spoor, we'd gain 5-20 metres each time. By altering the gunships' pattern and then noting any changes in the spoor behaviour, we'd know how far ahead to send the voorsny cars. The arrival of the choppers invariably resulted in a running spoor, which almost always ended badly for the enemy. It was for good reason that the Ovambo word for Koevoet was *Makakunya*—'Those who let blood.'"

Thirty minutes later, Zulu Hotel called for the gunships, and I jogged with the crews along the path that led over the berm, across a short bridge spanning a drainage ditch, and onto the hot tarmac where the choppers were spotted. A camouflage-painted C-47 transport, engines running, held its position, waiting for our departure. The pilot showed me where to sit, strapped himself in and started the engine. As soon as the instruments were in the green, the Alouettes taxied on to the runway, and after a short takeoff roll, we lifted into the hot, thin air. The flight engineer grasped the handlebar and chain attached to the breech block of the 20mm gun and drew it back against the heavy spring. He carefully eased it forward to chamber a yellow-nosed, high-explosive shell.

We were still within sight of Eenhana when the pilot tapped my shoulder and pointed ahead and to the left. Smoke from a white phosphorus grenade was billowing out of the bush not more than a couple of kilometres away. Zulu Hotel's team leader radioed that they were chasing two suspects that had been hiding in the area for some weeks. The PBs finally had enough of them when they bayoneted an old man after accusing him of passing information to the security forces.

The helicopters passed over the Casspirs and set up wide orbits ahead of the trackers. Within minutes, we spotted two figures in civilian clothes a few hundred metres ahead of Zulu Hotel's spoorsnyers. On the next orbit, they had covered far more distance than a walking pace could have taken them.

The pilot tightened up his bank and passed over the pair at 200 feet. Neither raised his head.

"What would you do if a chopper was flying low around you, eh?" he asked over the intercom. "Don't you think you'd probably look up at it? I think we might have a couple of terrs here."

The flight engineer swung the muzzle of the cannon and began tracking them. We banked and flew around again, circling not more than 100 feet overhead. Again, neither lifted his head. The pilot radioed that he had two civilians in sight. The team leader asked what they were wearing. The red shirt of one stood out brightly.

"Kill 'em!"

Negative, the pilots answered, we're not taking fire, and we don't see weapons.

"Kill 'em! They're the ones!" he repeated. "The PBs told us one of them has a red shirt!"

Again the pilots refused and continued to circle tightly over the pair. Minutes later, red smoke marked a spot below us. Contact! On the next pass I saw two bodies face down next to a Casspir, the red shirt of one clearly visible. Three or four trackers stood over them, weapons pointed down. Suddenly, dust rose around the prone figures. Then we had flown past the scene and I lost sight of them. Had I just witnessed an execution?

"They got 'em!" I heard in the earphones. I looked at the pilot. He was holding up two fingers.

I motioned that I wanted to join the cars. He nodded, came around in a wide orbit and set the chopper down next to a kraal a few hundred metres from the contact point. I jumped out and ran low under the whirling blades. Behind me, the chopper lifted off in a thick swirl of red dust. A Casspir nosed its way out of the bush. Tony da Costa, one of the car commanders, stood up behind his gun mount and waved me forward. I ran to the open rear doors.

"Come on," Tony yelled over the sound of cars and choppers, "they've already admitted they're Swaps. They're going to show us where they've hidden their AKs!"

What did he say? Did they get the information before they killed them?

"They said they were carrying a pistol and a grenade, but threw them away when they knew we were behind them. Come on. Let's go!"

Climbing into the car, I was surprised to see a prisoner. He was stripped to his shorts, wrists tied behind him with strips of bark. Rivers of sweat ran down his face and his chest still heaved from the chase. He looked terrified. I wondered if they had killed the other to make this one talk.

We bumped and crashed through the dense bush for a kilometre or so to the Oom Willie se Pad and stopped to wait for the other cars. The faces of the trackers were sullen as the prisoner was shoved out the door. He sprawled face down in the sand and was immediately jerked to his feet and knocked down once more. They spat and screamed abuse at him. Many had family and friends who had been wounded or killed by Swapo.

The other three Casspirs and the Blesbok rumbled out of the bush. The second prisoner, as alive and frightened as the first, was dragged roughly from a car. The constables ripped off his shirt before punching him to the ground. A senior NCO, who had once had both shoulders broken when his car struck a Swapo-laid land mine, threw the first prisoner down and jammed the muzzle of his rifle behind his head. The safety catch came down with an audible click.

Oh, shit, I thought, lowering the camera, *I really don't want to see this.*

Tony bulled his way through the circle of tormenters, shaking his head angrily. The NCO grinned and drew the bolt back on the R5 to show an empty chamber. I took his photo.

Stripped to their underwear, the prisoners led us 15 kilometres through the bush to where they'd buried their equipment. The first few times that they pointed to a spot and began digging, nothing appeared. Each failure earned kicks and punches. Walking sticks were laid across bare backs, raising narrow welts. Jasper Genis, Zulu Hotel's group leader, was a loner even by Koevoet standards. Whenever we stopped, the olive-complexioned 24 year-old would stand to one side, seemingly detached, but watching carefully as the men searched for the hidden caches. His rare smiles had no warmth in them.

Eventually, two AK-47s, ammunition, POM-Z anti-personnel mines and mouldy sets of Libyan uniforms with Cuban belt buckles were uncovered. The two stood trembling and sweating in anticipation of being shot. Instead, they were manhandled back into the cars, and we returned to Eenhana. I was dropped off, and Zulu Hotel headed to Oshakati with Maritz and the prisoners. Intelligence officers were waiting to find out about the coming infiltration. Interrogations usually took place immediately after an arrest.

Gavin Manning, ZT-2: "If we had a prisoner, he'd be handed to the group leader so he and his senior Ovambo could start interrogating him. It was urgent that they got as much intelligence as quickly as possible. Once the terrs had regrouped at their predetermined emergency RV—it might be 24 to 48 hours later—and realised that one or more of their number was missing, all signals and emergency RVs would be changed. These signals included things that identified them to sympathetic PBs as genuine Swapo/PLAN combatants, rather than our own Recces operating as pseudo-terrs, and could be as seemingly insignificant as which shoulder or hip their weapons or canteens were on, even the food they'd accept from a local kraal headman. The group leader would have lots on his plate at this stage, interrogating the capture and keeping Zulu 2 up to date with the latest developments, as well as planning and coordinating any spur-of-the-moment actions needed as result of what was learned from the fresh capture.

"It was at times like this that having a good 2iC to coordinate everything was vital. If the capture had info about other terrs, the rest of us moved in the direction he indicated, stopping at nearby kraals to question the PBs or kamachonas about any Swapo in the area. Although fresh spoor was often picked up this way, there was another important reason. By staying slightly ahead of the main body we were also making sure the prisoner wasn't leading everyone into a pre-planned ambush. We picked up fresh spoor on more than one occasion by getting the emergency RV and doing a 360 around it to pick up spoor left by the prisoner's comrades.

"If we had casevacs, it was also vital that progress reports were fed back to the group leaders from Zulu 2 or Zulu itself, regarding their condition. This was in turn immediately passed on to the trackers. Hearing their Buddies were going to make it was a great morale booster and you could literally see their efforts redouble on the spot. They always wanted to know if a casevac was going to end up in 1 Military Hospital in Pretoria. That was sort of a badge of honour, an Ops K Purple Heart."

An hour after Zulu Hotel left, another team scrambled the gunships. I joined Maritz's replacement, Captain Klaus Koch, who had recently returned from Pretoria and the latest in a series of operations to rebuild his RPG-damaged arm. The stiff brace he wore from hand to the middle of his forearm didn't conceal the mass of shiny scar tissue and skin grafts. We soon picked out four Casspirs and a Blesbok. Trackers had fanned out ahead of them, bush hats reversed to display the fluorescent red or yellow patch.

On the second pass I saw a figure dodging desperately through the bush and soft sand, a rucksack and RPG slung over his back. The flight engineer aimed through the reflector sight and squeezed off a burst, cursing when the weapon jammed after only a few rounds. As he worked to clear the stoppage, I saw a Casspir closing rapidly, a haze of thin smoke spilling from the machine guns. I brought the camera to my eye, but it was too late—we'd flown past the scene. Leaning over the flight engineer's shoulder, I tried to follow the unfolding drama as the pilot banked to the left, holding the turn. When we were on the far side of the orbit, I saw a cloud of dust and leaves hanging in the air.

I heard the click in my earphones. "They said a heatstrim or mine he was carrying exploded and set off everything else he had!"

We diverted to another group chasing a second insurgent who had split away from the one atomised by his own explosives. When it appeared the spoor was just minutes old, the chopper set me down and Neil, Zulu Charlie's group leader, took my place in the Alouette, hoping to spot the insurgent from the air. As it was, this one not only knew his anti-tracking, but could also run. He was eventually afforded grudging admiration by the trackers and car commanders, all of whom were exhausted after chasing him most of the day. We returned at sunset to Eenhana.

The next morning coincided with the end of the week's deployment and the last day of 1986, and I hopped a ride with another group back to Oshakati. Dropping everything on my bed, I grabbed a towel and soap and headed for the showers. Chris Pieterse intercepted me.

"Zulu Hotel's taking those two terrs back up, far, far, to lift a few caches they admitted knowing about. Couple days' trip at most. Interested?"

Hellfire and damnation, I thought, *no New Year's celebrations for you tonight.* I grabbed a fresh stock of film and ran out with everything I'd just come in with, including a week's dirt and dried sweat. The two blindfolded prisoners were led in leg irons from their cells and shoved into a Casspir. Swollen faces indicated rough treatment at the hands of their Ovambo interrogators. There was a quick stop to pick up four scrubbed and starched army sappers, and off we went, retracing the trip I'd just made from Eenhana, then across the yati into Angola.

Following their directions, we were 40 kilometres north of the cutline when the prisoners found the maroela tree into which they'd carved a stick man holding a bow and arrow. This was the equivalent of an "X-marks-the-spot" on a treasure map. We stopped. Leg irons were removed and hands tied in front before they were taken from the Casspir. "Show us," Jasper ordered.

Zulu Hotel's ice-cold leader had a very personal reason for finding enemy caches. Prior to my first introduction to Koevoet, a rear wheel of his Casspir had detonated a stack of four Yugoslavian TMA-3 "cheese" mines. Although the blast did not penetrate the hull, two men at the back were killed instantly and the car thrown almost 20 metres, landing upside down. Jasper and the rest of the team sailed a similar distance, but all hit the ground relatively unscathed.

Now eager to please, one of the prisoners stood with his back to the tree and counted his paces to where the first trove of explosives was dug up. There was more in the area, they said, trying to remember the other landmarks. The sappers followed with their mine detector, sweeping each area pointed to. It was the first time I'd seen Koevoet defer to the army. Because of the possibility of anti-lift devices, Jasper, Tony and the trackers kept their distance when their cousins in brown began digging.

When the prisoners claimed to have forgotten the exact locations of their caches, memories were sharpened with cuffs and shouts. As we moved from one remote spot to another, a pile of East bloc munitions slowly grew in the back of the Blesbok. By the end of the day, dozens of mortar rounds, blocks of TNT, rocket-propelled grenades and cheese mines had been dug out of the soft sand. One cache had already been lifted by Swapo; steel bands that had wrapped wooden ammunition boxes lay rusting on the shadow-dappled ground.

We were almost 60 kilometres inside Angola when we stopped to set up a TB. Taking my duffel bag from a pile behind the Blesbok, I noticed the sappers casting disapproving eyes at the many cooking fires being started. They looked painfully innocent in comparison to the blacks and whites of Zulu Hotel. Each shout and burst of laughter among the policemen as they unloaded boxes of equipment, chopped firewood, cut tent poles and rattled coffee cups brought frowns that said clearly, "This is *not* the way we do it in the Defence Force." Craig Rucastle, 18 years old, from Kimberley, was one of them.

Sapper Craig Rucastle, 25 Field Squadron: "I guess we were still really green at that stage. We'd just returned from our first 'mine hunt' near Nehone where one of our Buffels detonated a mine that resulted in a few guys being casevacked. We had heard stories about Koevoet, so when the opportunity to spend time with them presented itself, we were both excited and scared. When I saw the Swapo prisoners shackled to a tree that night, it was the first time I witnessed fear on someone's face. As those days unfolded, it really brought home the true nature of what was going on in the bush."

I was stretching my poncho between two saplings when the lieutenant walked over. "You're an American journalist?" he asked doubtfully, surveying my grubby bush clothes and filthy face and arms. No journalist *he'd* ever seen looked like I did.

"Yeah," I nodded, holding out a grimy hand and introducing myself.

He shook it, wiped his palm unconsciously on his trousers and looked incredulously around the noisy, bustling camp. "How long have you been with Koevoet?"

"Only about a month."

He nodded and pressed his lips together. "Uh, do they always operate like this?"

"I guess so. I don't know, really. What do you mean?"

"Ah … well, is a TB usually this noisy?"

"Oh, sure. Sometimes even louder."

"And the, uh, the fires?" he chuckled unconvincingly. "They usually build fires? Just like these?"

"Yeah, sure. Why?"

He didn't answer, just nodded some more, the up and down eventually shifting to back and forth as his eyes took in the scene. He opened his mouth to say something, then closed it. He cleared his throat and started again. "When do they put out pickets?"

"Put out what?"

"Pickets," he repeated weakly. "Guards."

"Oh, I don't think they bother too much with that," I said, trying to be helpful. "But you don't have to worry," I added reassuringly. "The Swaps can't hit shit anyway.

He stared at me for a long moment. "Bloody hell," he finally breathed, then, "Excuse me," and marched grim-faced back to his men, steering a wide course around Tony, who was furiously pegging down the sides of his bivi and swearing obscenely about missing Koevoet's New Year's party.

When I next looked, the four sappers had arranged their equipment boxes in a circle and were laying out fields of fire and positioning their weapons. The lieutenant held a notepad and ticked off items as he told his men who would be following whom as pickets through the night. Later, I noticed them clustered inside their mini-fort, dipping spoons into cold ration-pack tins as disbelieving eyes followed the outrageous scenes around them.

That night, sitting around a camp-fire with the two manacled insurgents, I asked Jasper if I could question them. I knew I'd have to weigh the fact that the two were still convinced that they were going to be shot and would likely say whatever they thought their captors wanted to hear.

Petrus Hatutale, 27 years old, had crossed into Angola in 1978, having heard that joining the liberation movement would give him an education. He was taken immediately to Lubango Camp in central Angola, where those who had left Namibia for promised education were given courses in weapons training and political indoctrination. The Cuban instructors told his group that Namibia must first be freed from the racist regime of South Africa at all costs. Everyone would then be equal. When Namibia was free, they would have all the education they wanted. But until then, they would have to fight. To refuse the honour of participating in the armed struggle was to be branded an enemy of the people.

For all the talk of equality, Hatutale recalled, the Cuban and Soviet instructors lived in comfortable homes around the camp and had plenty of food, while the Namibian trainees slept in dugouts on beds made of branches covered with grass and often went hungry. The Swapo cadres also enjoyed *droit de seigneur* with the female "comrades" who had escaped from South African oppression.

Since joining Swapo, he had made five infiltrations into Namibia. Another two had been aborted when his group had been ambushed before reaching the border. He pointed proudly to a bullet scar on his shoulder and lifted his head to show another under his jaw. He wasn't sure which enemy units they were, but he thought Unita[1] or 32 Battalion. After his second wound, he thought of quitting, but anyone who refused to fight was taken away and never heard of again.

He was eventually promoted to logistics commander of Echo Detachment, then reduced back to the ranks two months later. "I could not remember where I had buried a big weapons cache," he said sadly. "The detachment commander was very angry."

In 1983, he and five others were sent into Ovamboland to ambush "soft targets," civilian cars and pickup trucks owned by Ovambos. Their spoor was discovered by a Koevoet team and Hatutale lost four of his comrades in a contact near Okatope.

---

1   União Nacional para la Independencia Total de Angola—National Union for the Total Independence of Angola—which was supported by South Africa and the United States.

"I was not told why to kill civilians, just to kill them, because it would help to bring freedom to Namibia."

His previous infiltration had been as part of a four-man assassination squad. The orders from Shekudike, the commander of Echo Detachment, were to kill an old man named Eliaser Wangushu, who lived near Eenhana and was suspected of passing information to the security forces over a hidden radio. Hatutale had been chosen to lead the squad because he had grown up near Eenhana and knew the old man. Wangushu's nickname, he remembered from his childhood, was Fandi.

"We went to his kraal one night," Hatutale told us, "and questioned him about the radio and helping the security forces. He said he had never done such a thing."

"Did they find a radio?"

"No."

What happened then?

"I told Denga kaGerman—he called himself that because he was trained in East Germany—and one other to take Fandi away and stab him with the bayonet so there would be no noise."

"There's no way I can prove it," Tony interjected, "but the odds are that he did it himself. He'd have gotten a big pat on the shoulder from his detachment commander for handling it personally. Killing a suspected informer, especially one he had known before joining Swapo, would have shown his commitment to the liberation struggle. But you can be sure he's not going to admit it now."

"Ask him what Fandi's wife said when her husband was taken away," I said.

"She said he didn't have a radio, but that he was not a big supporter of Swapo, so she understood why we must kill him. When Denga kaGerman took him away, she gave us food."

How did he feel about ordering the death of an old man he had known since he was a boy? Hatutale shrugged; it was forbidden to question orders.

The other prisoner, Martin Haungula, accepted a cigarette with his right hand, touching the forearm with his left fingers as good Ovambo manners required. He could speak fluent Afrikaans from having worked on the railroads in Namibia.

Yes, he also had been recruited by Swapo ten years earlier with promises of education and money, but the only training he had received was at Lubango Camp, where he was taught to use Soviet weapons. He was not happy there, but he was not allowed to leave. What did the political commissars tell him about why he was fighting? I asked.

"To make Namibia free so that everyone will have good education and a nice house and a car."

When asked if he had ever kidnapped children, he shook his head. He had never been ordered to do it, but others he knew in PLAN had carried out abductions. What did they do if the ones they were taking to Angola didn't want to go?

Tony listened to the answer and turned to me. "He says that whoever makes the most noise about refusing to go—whoever's the most difficult one— is beaten up. He says that usually convinces the others. Sometimes, he says, it is necessary to kill the one who refuses the loudest because the others won't go if that one is allowed to stay. Usually it's not necessary, he says, and sometimes they go without anyone making any problems at all."

This was only his third infiltration into Namibia. He had contracted tuberculosis at Lubango and couldn't run very far, so most of his time in Swapo had been spent far to the north in Angola, guarding roads against Unita.

"For someone with tuberculosis you were running pretty fast when we caught you," said Tony.

"I was very nervous," Haungula said seriously, to the laughter of everyone.

Did his political instructors explain the system of scientific socialism that Swapo planned for Namibia? Martin Haungula had never heard of it. Did he know that Swapo claimed to have discovered and arrested 100 South African spies in its senior ranks, or that Andreas Shipanga, once Swapo's minister of information, was now a senior member in the Namibian Government, or that Swapo vice president Misheke Muyongo had returned to Namibia last year?

Not only had he never heard the names, he said, but "As simple soldiers, we would never be told such things."

Had he ever thought about leaving Swapo?

"Yes, but we were told that even if we surrender, the South Africans will torture us to death and that if we try to return secretly to our kraals to live quietly, Swapo will surely find us and kill us."

"You almost have to feel sorry for the poor bastards," Tony said. "They can't tell Swapo they want to stop fighting, because they'll be executed. They're afraid to give themselves up to us, because they believe we'll kill them. Some of the Swaps have actually committed suicide when they thought they might be captured and tortured to death. A lot of the ones we capture are just like these two, forced to go on fighting until we kill them or, if they're lucky, arrest them. You really almost have to feel sorry for them."

Yeah, I guess you do *have to feel sorry for them,* I thought, as I crawled into my sleeping bag on that New Year's Eve in 1986, and dropped off to sleep long before 1987 arrived. *You really do.*

Out of sight far to the north, towering thunderstorms battered Angola, the heavy downpours soaking parched earth and filling dry streambeds. Lightning pulsed and shimmered on the horizon, edging slowly southward as we slept.

12

The Most Ruthless
Killing Machine

On our return to Oshakati, a quick peek at the situation board in the ops room showed everything blessedly quiet, but from the pained expressions and faltering steps of the men who'd seen in the New Year, it was obvious they'd hit some serious ambushes and taken heavy casualties in the Okave Club.

Half an hour under a steaming shower finally left me feeling reasonably clean and human again. I kicked the dirt- and sweat-stiffened bush clothes into a corner, pulled on shorts and T-shirt, slipped my feet into a pair of flip-flops and wandered down the street to Bernie Ley's house. I accepted a beer and dropped thankfully into a soft armchair.

"So how's it going," he asked after we'd Happy New Year-ed each other. "Reckon you're getting the stories and pictures you wanted?"

Closing my eyes, I took a long swallow of the ice-cold brew and sighed contentedly. Pure heaven. "I think so, but you never really have enough, I guess.

"Is it what you expected?"

"I don't think I really knew what to expect," I admitted, kicking off the flip-flops and wriggling my toes. The thick shag carpet under my feet felt splendidly luxurious. "When I left last year, I thought I was the world's expert on this war. The only thing those two weeks gave me was a little background to build on. The mistake I made was seeing the war as the story. The real story is the people: what they think, why they're here, how they handle the whole thing."

"How do they strike you so far?"

"Tough, competitive, reasonably bright; not many dummies among them. And, for the most part—ego aside—they're here because they love the action. Adrenaline junkies, pure and simple. They get off on the high that combat gives them. But I suspect that in the end, when this thing is all over, a lot of them are going to be very bitter."

"Why's that?"

"I remember a drunken conversation with an old friend a few years ago. He'd spent 20 years in Special Forces, three Vietnam tours, some covert ops in South America. I remember him saying, 'We're society's crowbar. They never want to acknowledge the dirty jobs they give us, but when the job is done, they never throw us away; they just slip us back in the toolbox until the next time. And there will always be a next time.' He'd seen a lot of shit, killed people, seen friends die. And when he came home to the society he'd done it for, you know what?—he was an embarrassment to it. I sometimes wonder if these guys here aren't going to have the same thing happen.

"Society gives them the opportunity to go off and do what they want. It says, 'Okay, there's the bad guys and here's the equipment and here are the rules; do what you have to do within these rules to stop them.' And they're so red hot to go off and live at kill-or-be-killed that they accept the terms. No one explains what happens when it's all over and they have to come back to the real world. Where they're suddenly expected to live like the guy next door, rather than part of 'the most ruthless killing machine in the world.'"

"Where did you hear that phrase?"

"I did a bit of reading up on this bunch before coming back. You haven't exactly had a positive press. I'm a little confused."

"About what?"

"Kopgeld—head money—for one thing. They get a bounty for each kill?"

"Absolutely. A thousand rand for a kill, 2,000 for a prisoner. And there's a scale for weapons that goes from 250 rand for an AK-47, up to 10,000 for a SAM-7. Which goes only to the trackers, by the way. Not much when you divide it between 40 to 45 men." Boris, the Leys' Alsatian appeared and Bernie leaned over to scratch his ears. "So what else is bothering you?"

"Most of what I've read paints a pretty nasty picture. You name it, they've done it. Okay, they're no bunch of choirboys, but they don't fit the image of cold-blooded psychopaths, either."

"What's your point?"

"Look, where there's smoke, there's got to be at least a little fire somewhere. Only I haven't seen it. What'd you do, hide all the bad ones before I got here? Ship 'em back to South Africa?"

"How long have you been here now?"

"Counting my first trip, I guess about six weeks, maybe a little more."

"And? Seen anyone beaten or tortured? Civvie bodies left in the dust? Rapes?"

"Having a journalist around can do wonders for people's manners."

"Sure, but you've gotten to know some of them. You think they're all closet baby killers just waiting for you to leave so they can get back to what they really enjoy?"

"Where do all the atrocity stories come from?"

"No, I can tell you that some of them did happen. I'll also tell you that most were the products of overly imaginative journalists who've never been here. Or journalists whose sympathies lie with Swapo. Not all, but some."

"When I interviewed the Swapo guy in London, he got pretty excited when he started talking about Koevoet. Just hold on," I said as Ley started smirking. "Most of what he told me was bullshit. They haven't destroyed Oshakati or any other place. And unless the army is awfully clever at hiding them, there sure as hell aren't '100,000 racist troops' around here. But he was pretty definite about a massacre he claimed Koevoet committed at a place called Oshikuku."

"How much Afrikaans can you read?"

"Are you kidding?"

"Never mind; I've got a copy of the official inquiry back at the office. Get yourself another beer, and I'll be back just now.

Twenty minutes later, I heard his car pull into the driveway. Ley padded barefoot through the door, carrying a thick brown folder.

"I told the general that you'd probably want to know about some of this," he said, dropping it in my lap and heading for the refrigerator. I heard the door open as he raised his voice from the kitchen. "In case you're interested, he said to give you whatever you asked for."

He returned and stretched out on the couch. "Got a cigarette?" I tossed the pack over. "Thanks. I'm supposed to be quitting, but once in a while … ," he paused to light a Chesterfield. "Okay, let me give you a little background. Your pal in London told you that an entire village was wiped out, right?"

"Something like that."

"Well, that's the story put out by Swapo. The truth is that in March '82, ten Ovambos were dragged from their beds and shot. Not an entire village, but bad enough. Three survived, which was fortunate for us, I guess, but seven innocent civilians died that night. That happened; that's a fact, and maybe the only one everyone agrees on.

"Swapo claimed that we did it, and one of our esteemed newspaper editors jumped on it. The official magistrate's inquiry determined that there was no evidence to implicate Koevoet or any other security force unit. Some people said it was all a cover-up. But I'll tell you officially and unofficially that our people had nothing to do with it." He stubbed out the cigarette and pointed to the report in my hands. "Have a look at the first page and tell me how much you can understand."

I opened the cover and struggled through the first few lines before giving up and shaking my head.

He put his hand out and I passed it over. "This is an eyewitness account from one of the survivors. You can make of it what you want." He shifted to a more comfortable position. "This is the official statement of one Jolidye Nauyoma, a 22 year-old Ovambo from the Oshipanda ward—area—of the Kwambi tribal district. The Kwambi are one of the Ovambo sub tribes. Anyway, he starts off by saying that he and the others in the kraal went to sleep on the night of March 9, 1982, at about 10 p.m. Then he says, and I'm translating directly from the statement: 'At about 2 a.m., I woke up. I saw that there were two strange black men in the room. There was a full moon and I noticed that the two men were wearing camouflage clothes and each of them had a rifle. With me in the room were the other people who slept there, Benedikus Nepolo and Shivute Kengaye. We were all forced with a bayonet to leave the room.

"'We left the room, and the strangers made us stand against the outside of the kraal wall. I noticed two more strange black men who were wearing camouflage clothes and carrying the same rifles as the others. I and the other people from the kraal were forced to stand against the kraal wall.'"

He paused in the translation. "The nine people he names ranged from 8 to 61 years old. Four of them were 13 or younger. Anyway, he goes on to say, 'I noticed that a fifth man appeared who was dressed in camouflage and had a gun like the others. Then three of the men started shooting at us. I fell on the ground with the others. I was not shot, but at first I thought I was.

"'After the strangers shot at us, I heard them shooting and breaking windows of a lorry near the kraal. I lay still on the ground for about an hour. I stood up and saw that the woman, Penehafo Angula, and her eight-year-old son Erasmus, also stood up. I and Penehafo and her son went to another kraal nearby. In the morning, Penehafo and her son were taken to the Oshikuku Hospital, and I saw they had bullet wounds.

"'I went to the kraal where the shooting took place and saw that all the other people from the kraal were still lying on the ground where the strange men shot at us. They were all dead.'"

He closed the folder and tossed it on the coffee table. "There are other statements in there from people in neighbouring kraals who were woken up by the five gentlemen in question. Seems they were looking for that particular kraal. All five wore Swapo uniforms, or at least they weren't wearing the camouflage uniforms we used to have, and all five carried AK-47s, and spoke the Kwanyama dialect. Of course, that doesn't mean anything; we've got lots of AKs and captured uniforms and most of our Ovambos are Kwanyamas. If you want to believe Swapo, it was a cold-blooded Koevoet plan to discredit them, just like they say we plant land mines to blow up civvies so we can say they did it. Believe what you want, but I'm telling you that it wasn't us."

"Why would they go to that kraal and blow away ten people? That's not what you might call a positive hearts-and-minds approach."

"It's an excellent hearts and minds, whichever way you look at it. Genuine. If they can convince the PBs that we did it, it makes them more sympathetic to Swapo. On the other hand, if the local pops know it was Swapo—and I think those five went in there to kill someone they suspected of being an informer and didn't want any witnesses—then there aren't going to be many people prepared to give us info. Put yourself in their shoes: 'Man, if I talk to the police the terrs are going to kill me and my whole family.' The same thing happened in Kenya during the Mau-Mau, in Rhodesia, Angola, Mozambique, and it's happening in South Africa against pro-government blacks. In fact it's happened in every African country where Russian-backed 'liberation movements' have operated. Believe me, it works."

"Why couldn't it work just as well from your side? If you turn that reasoning around, couldn't it be just as effective an operation?"

"Because people talk. Someone would have spilled it by now. Another reason—something people are too quick to overlook—is that we still suffer from that old Calvinist thinking. We just can't seem to lay the Bible down when the situation calls for it and pick it up again when the dust settles. If we could, blacks would probably be in a minority in South Africa today; we'd have exterminated them like you did to your American Red Indians. Don't get me wrong: we'll go in and floor someone who tries to hurt us, but, and I'd say unfortunately, the old idea of an eye for an eye usually gets in the way of a no-holds-barred approach to the problem."

"So what else has given Koevoet such a bad name?"

"I guess the most publicized incident was when two of our special constables, Jonas Paulus and Paulus Mateus, went on a private spree one night. They were off duty, got drunk and killed one person, raped two women and stole everything they could lay their hands on. No question about it. We arrested both of them ourselves and turned them over to the regular police. They were tried, convicted and sentenced; one was executed, the other got 12 years.

"And, yeah, we've had other incidents of murder, and most, but not all, were off duty. In each case, the people involved were arrested, tried and, if the evidence supported the charges, convicted. There are eight ex-Koevoet members serving sentences for murder and one other being tried for murder. You might compare that with Vietnam. With the exception of your famous Lieutenant Calley, I don't remember ever reading about GIs being convicted of murdering civilians there, though dozens have admitted doing so since, and quite often with the approval of their officers.

"Make no mistake, we've had some very bad boys in this unit, white and black. But that situation is hardly unique to us. There's probably not an elite force anywhere in the world which has seen extensive combat that hasn't been accused of atrocities. How many of the accusations are based on truth and how many are propaganda from the other side is the big question. During the First World War, the British accused the Germans of raping nuns and killing babies with pitchforks. None of those accusations was ever proved, but people still remember them."

"Okay, but I'm talking about Koevoet," I interrupted.

"Look, nothing justifies murder or beatings. In a perfect world, nothing even justifies threats. But the world isn't perfect and neither are people; you're going to find bad apples everywhere. We do our best to weed those out, but we're not perfect, either. What pisses me off is that it's happened in every war in history, it's happening right now in other places in Africa, but when one of our people does something, suddenly it's worse because we're South Africans.

"You want to talk about atrocities? The very worst we've been accused of doesn't touch what they've done to their own people. And I can guarantee that Swapo will never put any of its 'freedom fighters' on trial for atrocities against the civilian population. I'm not saying that justifies any kind of brutality on our part. But you can't fight terrorism by the Queensberry Rules. It's easy to be idealistic, but try it after seeing what the terrs do to someone they think has given us info; try it right after you've seen what's left of a black kid who's stepped on a land mine meant for his policeman father.

"I really love those people who say: Well, Swapo atrocities, that's to be expected; they're *freedom* fighters, for Christ's sake, so it's okay. But you guys—Koevoet—don't you touch a hair on a suspected terr's head to protect the innocent. Those fucking people won't lose a minute's sleep over a civvie the terrs kill, and certainly not over the death of one of our people, but watch them heat up their typewriters if they suspect one of our boys got out of hand!"

"I hear what you're saying, but those people…"

"Never see the blood, or a leg blown off, or hear the screams."

"Okay, you're right. Most of them never see what they write about. It's easy to be judgmental when you never come face-to-face with it, I guess. And maybe I'm being idealistic too, but I just can't imagine seeing or experiencing anything that would make me lose a basic sense of humanity."

He rose and selected a tape, dropped it in and pressed the play button. As Vivaldi filled the room, he raised his beer. "And I hope you never do," he said quietly, "because it's something you'll never forget."

There was a knock on my door. I opened it to find Jerry Mbwale and two more black NCOs. There were polite enquiries about the malaria and relief that it was over, how I liked Namibia, until Jerry came to the point. "Some of us want you to meet our grandfather," he said shyly. "Perhaps not our grandfather like a white man's, but someone good." I said I'd be honoured. They picked me up the next day and on the way, Barnabas the official interpreter gave me a few pointers on Ovambo manners.

Elenga Tyu Kwanyama Gabriel Kautuima was, as his title said, hereditary chief of the Kwanyama, largest of the Ovambo tribes. A spare old man of great dignity he greeted us courteously as we ducked under the low eave of the thatched roof. We shook hands in the African way, and he motioned us to sit on the upturned logs around the edge of the hut. By tradition, we sat first; to look down upon such a respected elder would be impolite. Chief Kautuima spoke English, but out of courtesy to his counsellors and the serious young men who were his guards, he politely asked that he speak in Oshivambo.

"Tate'Nkulu," (Grandfather), said Barnabas, pointing at me, "this man is from America and asks that you tell him of Ovambo and Namibia."

Elenga Tyu Kwanyama Kautuima, paramount chief of quarter of the population of Namibia, regarded me seriously for a moment. "We hear many things from the outside world. We hear over the radio that the United Nations says Swapo is the only voice of Namibia. But I tell you the Namibians did not send them to the United Nations. They went of their own accord.

"Perhaps some Ovambo person sent these people with a piece of paper saying they came from the people of Namibia. Perhaps it was the kings and headmen of some other place who sent people with a piece of paper. But I am chief headman of the Kwanyama, and I know the Ovambo nation never sent anyone as a representative to the United Nations with such a piece of paper.

"The United Nations see only one side, and they do with us as they please, but I do not know what to say about this. The United Nations would take things away from Namibia. If they take petrol away, for example, they are not against the whites, they are against the blacks. If we can find no petrol, how can we go to the markets, which are far, and make our business. These people who say you should not bring this and this to us—these people are working against us."

He stood and took the tail of a Soviet mortar round from where it was hanging on a roof pole. "If the man who bombarded me with this was a representative of the Ovambo nation, why did he come in the middle of the night and attack my kraal where the children sleep? Is this a man who represents the Ovambo nation? Even on the path to my house, Swapo has planted six land mines and two have killed my people.

"There was a big water tank and water pump to supply water to the hospital. In the night, they bombarded the tank and water pump. The patients were left without water. Only the patients suffered. Those who made the bombardment had their own brothers and sisters in the hospital. Is this the way to treat your own people? Perhaps the reason for planting these mines and bombarding me is because I am a headman and against them and have guards. But the people in the hospital are defenceless.

"We want peace, to sit around the table and talk. But Swapo is against this. They say to the United Nations that all they do is for the freedom of Namibia, but if you see what they do to their own people, you know this is not true. Swapo say they want to free the people, but how will they free the corpses of those they have killed?

"Just as you yourself came to see, I would like the people of the United Nations to come and see for themselves. Perhaps because they have good bread and an easy life, they do not want to leave America and see for themselves. But if I sent a representative to America to speak for me, no one would listen.

"Just as I provide food for my own home, so Namibia—not those from outside—must provide the solutions for the people of Namibia. You can go and write of what I say, but I think it will make no difference. Things will not change. We want freedom, but not the 'freedom' spelled out for us by Swapo and the United Nations. The United Nations should have brought freedom to Angola and Mozambique, which they recognize, but there is death and poverty, not freedom.

"The United Nations started long ago and made many resolutions that came to nothing. And this Resolution 435 will also be thrown away like other resolutions have been thrown away long ago. All these resolutions will get older and older ... and mean nothing in the end.

"This I wanted to say to you."

Sadly, Chief Kautuima's observation that, "The United Nations see only one side, and they do with us as they please," would prove accurate.[1]

---

1   In 2007, NamRights, a non-profit, non-partisan human rights monitoring and advocacy organization, revealed that the Oshikuku murders had been carried out by members of Swapo. The report can be found here: www.nshr.org.na/index.php?module=News&func=display&sid=711

13

Harbinger of War

Oshakati

South West Africa/Namibia

January 1987

It's raining. For days now, the skies to the north have been grey and threatening, the grey moving a little farther south each day. And last night the first of it finally arrived, rain heralded by sudden wind and the distant drums of muted thunder. Tonight again, harder: glistening, thrashing trees caught in the blue-white—fst!— of lightning, the sudden crack! *shaking the air, the rumbling aftermath drowned by the roaring downpour.*

There's been frustration, tenseness, here, waiting for the real rains, the harbinger of war. And now they've come, carrying with them the sounds of destruction.

After six weeks on ops the days had begun to take on a sameness, one blurring into another. You awoke under the wet bivi before dawn to unzip the clammy sleeping bag and dress by feel, swearing silently if you'd forgotten to draw socks and canvas boots well inside the make-shift tent and found them soaked with the night's rain. You crawled out, brushing sand from your hands and stumbling over tent pegs in the dark. *Goddammit*, as you tripped over something else you didn't remember being there and barked a shin, leaning down to rub it. Regaining your balance, you stood, imprisoned by the black vegetation that spread outward to a hidden horizon.

Here and there inside the perimeter others were beginning to move. A brief, racking cough broke the thick silence. Orange glows flickered as fuel tablets were lit, and piles of damp twigs grudgingly took fire. You sleepily took in the familiar scene, yawning and forgetting that only weeks before it would have been beyond imagining. This was your world now—closer to the bone than anything you'd ever encountered.

Going down on one knee, you reached under the edge of the pup tent, patting the sand in search of the roll, then stood and tried to remember the layout of the new camp from the afternoon before. Making your way through the wet bush outside the perimeter, you bumped into one of the Ovambos returning.

"Goeie môre, meneer."

"'Môre, tati."

By the time you returned, more men were moving around the camp. Water was drawn from the spigot at the back of a Casspir and the blackened kettle balanced atop a struggling fire. There was the squeak of a tin provision box opening and the hollow clatter of enamelled mugs before the top squeaked shut again. Sleepy sighs were the extent of the conversation as you untied the poncho stretched between two trees and rolled up the sleeping bag, shoving it all into a diesel-stained duffel bag. As the sky lightened imperceptibly, the armoured cars slowly took form around the camp, bulking silently like scarred war horses patiently awaiting battle.

Someone set the stained collection of chipped mugs in the sand. A piece of cardboard torn from a ration pack was wrapped around the handle of the kettle and the mugs filled with scalding coffee. They were passed from hand to hand and slowly sipped as sleep drained from exhausted bodies. A toe was pushed into the formless lump of someone still in his sleeping bag. There was another persistent jab, and a tired voice growled a muffled oath. The cocoon stirred. The stubbled and dirt-streaked face of a 21-year-old emerged to the quiet laughter of the coffee drinkers. A filthy arm worked its way out of the bag and took an offered cup, drawing it unsteadily towards sun-blistered lips.

The group leader stepped away and climbed into his Casspir. Switching on the radios, he sipped his coffee and keyed the microphone.

"Zulu 2, Zulu 2, Zulu Quebec."

Van, the radio operator in the ops room at Eenhana answered immediately. "Zulu Quebec, Zulu 2. Morning, Toit. How's it?"

Toit told him in which direction we'd be moving and in return Van passed on the latest intelligence about insurgent activity. As Toit jotted down the information, fires were scattered and killed while bedding and stores were thrown into the back of the Blesbok. Guns were checked and sprayed with lubricant, ammunition belts examined. Finally, a loose parade was formed. Bush hats were removed at a barked command and heads lowered as the senior Ovambo warrant officer, David Absalom Aviva, led the group in prayer. On the back of a T-shirt worn by one of the most devout black constables, chin tucked down in close communion with his Maker, were the words *Kill Them All*. Another crisp command and hats were returned to heads, the parade formation dissolving as men moved to their cars. The sun hadn't yet reached the treetops when Toit's car belched dark smoke and bucked forward, the others dropping in behind him. Another day had begun.

Less than five miles away, other men had also awakened. Of the seven, only two had undertaken previous infiltrations. Both were skilled anti-trackers, as evidenced by their continued survival. The others, in their teens and early twenties, were fresh from the Cuban training camps in Angola. Their group of 40 had been at the Angolan army base at Namakunde for the last two weeks, waiting for the rains to begin.

The group, part of Swapo's "Far East Detachment," had received its orders and set out the day before, separating into smaller units of five to ten men each before slipping across the yati. As they split off from the others, the two veterans began badgering the unblooded boys about using the anti-tracking techniques they'd been taught. Better and safer not to leave spoor the racist South Africans and their black lackeys might see, than have to anti-track to escape. Further, they must never again approach any kraals other than those already known to the two older men. For the youngsters, the warnings from the veterans did little to quell their excitement. Why should they be concerned? Hadn't their Cuban instructors told them that the South African soldiers and their few Ovambo puppets were no match for them? Not even the black traitors and white racists of Koevoet stood a chance against them.

The scolding two had received for taking a goat was accepted with good humour. What had been wrong? As soon as the farmer had realised who they were, he had made no attempt to stop them. As an oppressed Namibian, surely he must support their fight against the Boers. It was for him and others like him that the struggle went on. No, he would not inform on them, they confidently told the two older men.

The ashes of last night's fire were carefully scattered. The men stripped the last bits of cold undercooked flesh from the blackened remains and tossed the bones into the bush. Wiping hands on damp trousers, they buckled on their uncomfortable web gear. The leader waved his men forward, and the group began making its way through the wet undergrowth. The stiffness they felt from sleeping on the wet ground would soon be worked out as they continued their infiltration deeper into Namibia.

I had deployed two days before with Zulu Quebec and its regular bush partner, Zulu Uniform. Sergeant François du Toit, ZQ's group leader, came across at first meeting as quietly self assured. Six foot, blond and muscular, his outward calm was deceptive. Under the surface, this 25 year-old was an unpredictable and dangerous man with a hair-trigger temper and lightning-fast fists. Toit's opposite number in Zulu Uniform was Warrant Officer Attie Hattingh, who ranked among the best of the team leaders. Shorter, dark-haired and well-built, his masculine good looks were complemented by a quick intellect and infectious laugh. Attie's younger brother Adriaan commanded one of Zulu Uniform's four Casspirs. Though quieter, Adriaan was otherwise almost a carbon copy of his older brother. In a private moment, Attie confided how much he hated sending Adriaan sweeping ahead on voorsny during a follow-up, knowing that he would invariably be a first target for the desperate insurgents. When I pressed him about it, Attie paused for a moment to look across the camp at Adriaan. "We both understand the risks," he said quietly. "This is where we belong."

François du Toit, team leader, Zulu Quebec: "When I heard about this journalist in town, I expected a pushy, arrogant guy. Then I met him and was surprised that he was actually quite softly spoken. I enjoyed the accent and a sort of understated self-confidence. My gut instinct, confirmed by what I'd heard from others, told me he didn't scare easily. I wasn't worried that he might be up to something. When he deployed with us, my concern was him understanding us, getting the 'feel' of how close everyone was in my group and what we were fighting for."

A.T. Hattingh, team leader, Zulu Uniform: "When Toit told me that a foreign journalist would deploy to the bush with us, I was very opposed to the idea. I did not have time to wet nurse a prima donna. It was soon clear, however, that he expected no privileges and could fend for himself. I appreciated Jim's dedication to his profession but could not resist pulling his leg by offering him a R5 whilst he was on the ground with us, following spoor. He would very seriously reply that he was there to shoot pictures, not people. After the contact where Ben van Tonder lost his leg to a heatstrim, I had to withdraw with my team to Eenhana to repair two Casspirs which had been damaged in that contact. I realised that Jim was not just along for the ride when he asked me if I minded if he stayed with the teams in the bush. He not only earned our respect, we came to regard him as a friend.'"

The day had started like all the others, the team stopping at one kraal after another, questioning the Ovambo farmers about the presence of Swapo insurgents, back into the Casspirs and on to the next. Attie's team were doing the same a couple of klicks to the east. Everyone knew that with the beginning of the rains small units of heavily armed insurgents were crossing the border. Digging them out was the hard part.

We had stopped at one more kraal. The trackers walked to the log palisade and began questioning the head of the family. The conversation became animated, the farmer gesturing angrily from inside the enclosure. Watching the scene, I thought his anger was directed at us. I couldn't have been more mistaken. One of the trackers shouted to Toit. Two insurgents had come the night before and taken a goat without paying for it. The farmer wasn't sure which way they had gone, but he thought to the east, pointing and snapping his fingers.

Toit was reaching for the handset when Attie's voice crackled over the radio. His trackers had found seven spoor less than a mile east of us. The tracks were only two or three hours old. The change in everyone was immediate, an electric energy sparking through the group. Minutes later, we rendezvoused with Zulu Uniform. The trackers jumped off the cars with their stubby assault rifles, paused to chamber rounds, then ran to join those already on the trail. The hunt had started.

Two hours later, the spoor was down to five, but these five, the trackers said, their walking sticks touching faint disturbances of sand or dead leaves, didn't know their anti-tracking techniques. Even on difficult terrain, we followed at a fast walk, Casspirs flanking us. Zulu Uniform disappeared into the bush. Within minutes they had picked up the trail a few hundred metres ahead and Attie made a radio call. We scrambled into the cars and raced to the position he had marked with a yellow smoke grenade, jumping out to take the trail once more. Zulu Uniform fanned out and pushed forward again on voorsny. Within a ten kilometre radius of us, other teams were also searching. Gavin Manning, Jack Bouwer's second-in-command in Zulu Tango was one of them.

Gavin Manning, ZT-2: "The 'Summer Games' of the infiltration season were in full swing. Rather than trying to picture what other teams around you were doing or, for that matter, what the insurgents those other teams were chasing might do, it was best to concentrate on finding spoor and then working hard to gain ground on them. Of course, there was always hope that some of those being chased by other teams would run into your path when you were out ahead doing voorsny."

Reports began coming in over the radios. "Zulu November has at least ten spoor south of us," Toit said as we kept pace with the trackers. "They think they're about an hour behind them. Zulu Papa has four more east of Nkongo." The radio crackled again. "Jack's team is following two or three spoor just a couple of klicks southwest of us."

There was another radio call from Attie; again billowing smoke marked the location of fresher spoor. The trackers, excited and sweating, dived back into the Casspirs, and again we accelerated, crashing through the bush to where the smoke lingered. We were closing faster and faster.

By now the insurgents could surely hear the growls of diesel engines growing louder. Their tracks showed they had turned towards the border. But for the pursuers the 50-metre-wide strip between the two countries was irrelevant. The insurgents had crossed the cutline to kill; their flight back into Angola would ensure neither escape nor sanctuary. Ten minutes later, I caught a brief glimpse of a Zulu Tango car off to the left before it swung away and was lost among the trees.

Gavin Manning, ZT-2: "There were multiple spoor and follow-ups all around us and it was difficult to gauge if they all were from a single group that had bomb-shelled after contact with other teams, or individual units of Swapo's 'Far East Detachment' operating in that part of Ovamboland. My trackers were still familiarising themselves with the particular idiosyncrasies of this group's spoor, when Angus, who was on voorsny, called to say his guys had picked it up farther ahead."

Angus Pursell, ZT-4: "Most of Zulu Tango's follow-ups had me, Gavin and Ox doing voorsny, and in most instances we would hit contact first and the rest of the team or teams would join in. On this follow-up we were maybe 300 metres in front of the rest of the team when we picked up three spoor. I got on the radio and informed the others. As soon as Jack got there, the trackers jumped back into my Casspir and we raced forward. I was thinking,

'Today people are going to die, and, God, please let it not be me.' The trackers found it again, which meant we are gaining valuable ground and time. Then they said we must scramble the gunships because the gooks were close."

Angus and Gavin's calls alerted Toit and Attie to their presence beyond the trees, but there was no slackening in the pursuit. For now it was a running spoor, Zulu Quebec's trackers sprinting through the thick bush, slowing only when they lost the trail for a moment, milling, then taking off again at a dead run. Somewhere ahead of them, the insurgents were running flat out and desperately.

Toit ordered me into his car. Knowing we were behind them, chances were good they would start setting antipersonnel mines along the trail. The squat, pineapple-sectioned POM-Zs seldom killed, but the shrapnel could inflict terrible wounds. In a fast-moving chase like this, an exploding "pom-zed" could bring the follow-up to halt as the wounded were tended and helicopters scrambled to casevac them. At the very least, trackers from other teams nearby slowed as they began looking cautiously for trip wires. Neither Toit nor any of his men could trust my experience in spotting one.

François du Toit, ZQ-1: "Being on the ground with my men was part of being a leader, showing I was ready to take the same risks. It gave them confidence and a sense of competition. It was always risky to run on the spoor of the enemy, never knowing if we might trigger a POM-Z. They had a devastating effect, but never deterred us. Why? Because we were challenging death. There is absolutely nothing in this world that can beat the adrenaline high of knowing you are chasing an enemy who is either waiting for you in an ambush or has placed mines that could blow you to kingdom come. It's addictive."

Climbing into the car, I heard "casevac" on the radio. Running easily next to the Casspir, Toit shouted up to me, "Zulu November's just had a contact. They took out seven terrs, but one of their cars was hit with an RPG. They've got six wounded and at least one dead. Gunships can't take that many. They've had to scramble the Pumas from Ondangwa!"

I dropped into a seat and quickly checked the cameras. One had only a dozen shots left. I rewound it and loaded a fresh roll, swearing as the film tail kept slipping out with each jarring bump and sway of the car. I finally threaded it, shook out the debris and snapped the back closed just as we hit the yati, roaring across the cleared strip into Angola. Toit immediately advised Zulu 2 that we had gone "external" and to put the Alouette gunships on standby.

When the Casspirs and running policemen started going over their own tracks, it was clear we had to be right on top of the insurgents. But they had bomb-shelled, each taking off in a separate direction and circling, hoping their spoor would be lost in the torn up bush and sand behind the cars. Toit, sweating heavily through a layer of grime, swung into the Casspir and dropped into the hatch behind the gun turret.

"They're here!" he yelled, quickly checking the .50 calibre Browning and pulling the locking pin from the mount. "They're right here!"

Not more than 300 metres away, a completely separate act of the drama was nearing its climax.

Jack Bouwer, ZT-1: "We were chasing spoor, my vehicle and another flanking the trackers. We hit some very thick bush, which slowed us down and allowed them to get ahead of us. Suddenly, there was one hell of a bang right in front of my car. Smoke, sand and leaves filled the air and I knew immediately that one of the spoorsnyers had tripped a POM-Z."

Gavin Manning, ZT-2: "I yelled at my trackers, '*Ronda, ronda, na tiyeni!*'— 'Get in, get in, let's go!' As soon as they were aboard I shouted down through the command hatch at my driver, Sgt. Thomas Elumbe Phineas, '*Shinka, shinka! Komesho!*'—'Drive, drive! Straight ahead!' We hit a patch where the bush thinned and I saw yellow smoke above the trees half a klick away. As I stood again—*Doof!*—the unmistakeable dull bang of a POM-Z amid the crackle of R5s."

Angus Pursell, ZT-4: "That's when I heard the *bang* of a POM-Z and then gunfire behind us and 'Contact! Contact!' on the radio. There was that sudden, familiar rush of adrenaline. I immediately cocked my twin .30 Brownings and shouted to the driver to turn around and head back to the contact area. We started to circle it as I squeezed off bursts of flashing fire into any thick bush that might be hiding a gook."

Cutting along the edge of a kraal complex, we heard the muffled explosion. I looked in the direction it came from, but saw only thick bush.

Surrounded by the trackers of Zulu Hotel, Jasper Genis interrogates
captured Swapo insurgent Martin Haungula.

Prisoners Petrus Hatutale and Martin Haungula with Zulu
Hotel in Angola, New Years Eve 1986.

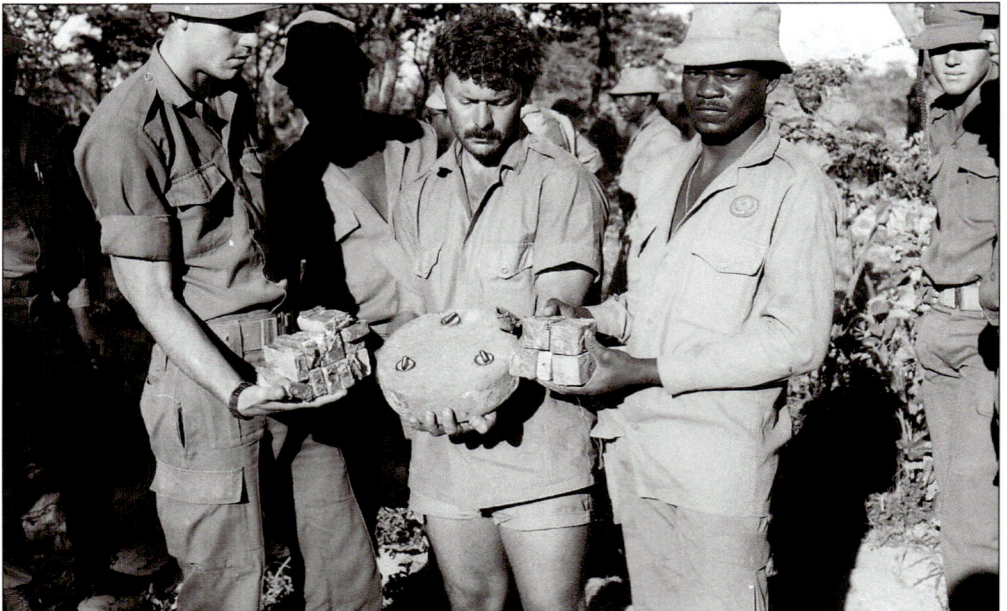

Flanked by army sappers, Tony da Costa and Zulu Hotel's senior Ovambo
warrant officer pose with a Yugoslavian TMA-3 anti-tank mine and
blocks of TNT from a Swapo cache 60km inside Angola.

Gunships lift off after refuelling deep inside Angola.

An injured SADF national serviceman is stretchered through
a mohango field to a waiting Alouette helicopter.

With the casevac on the floor behind him, Rick Dooley, 15
Squadron, heads for the SADF base at Nkongo.

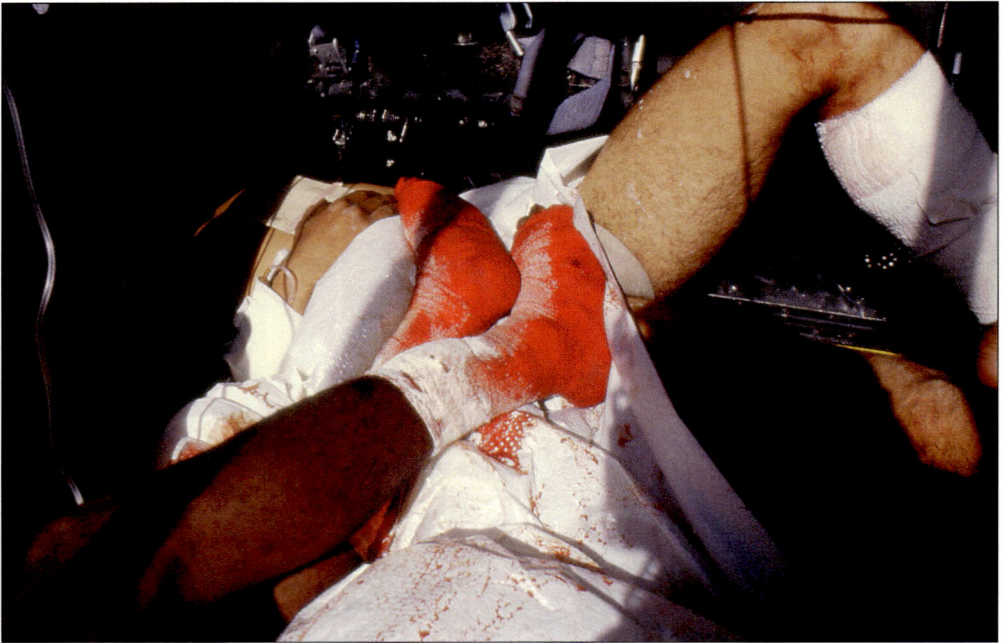

Wounded by a POM-Z anti-personnel mine, a Kavango volunteer from the SWATF
701 Battalion and a white South African conscript are flown to Eenhana.

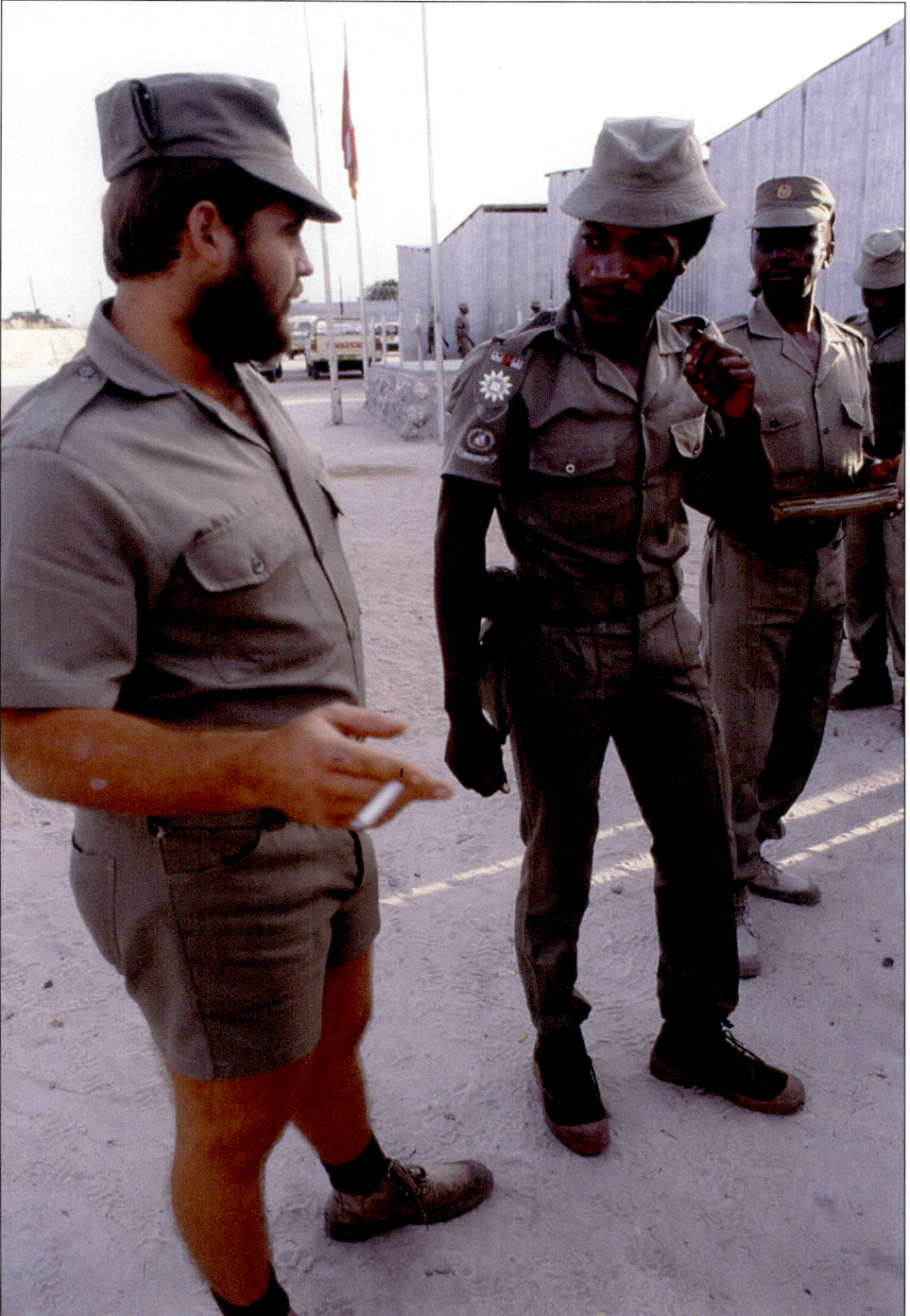

Angus Pursell and Johnny Mwashitinayo of Zulu Tango after a morning parade.

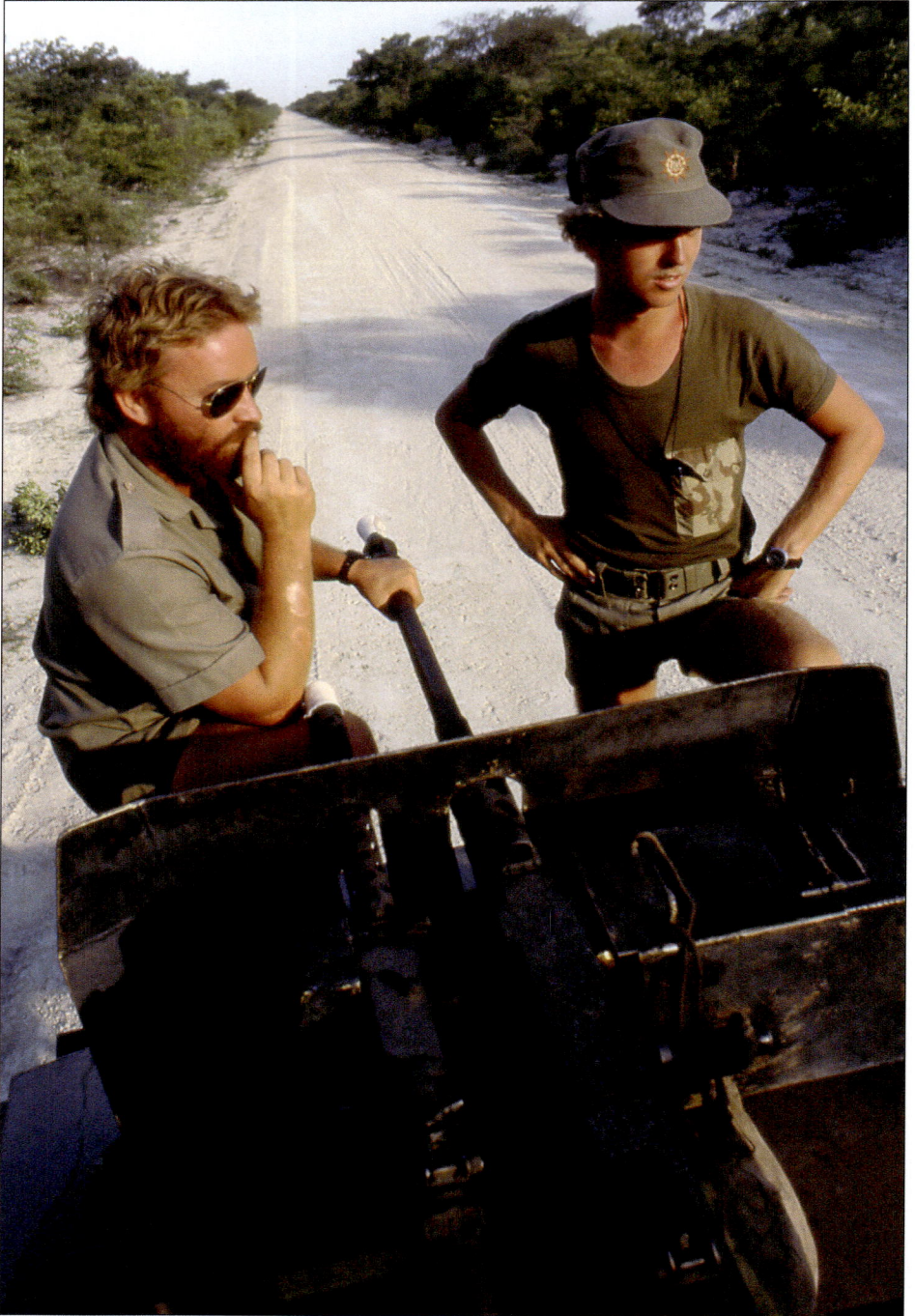

Team leader Jack Bouwer and 2iC Gavin Manning of Zulu Tango stop on the Oom Willie se Pad while one of their Casspirs changes a tyre.

Another team marks its position and Casspir and trackers continue the follow-up.

Tasked with keeping an eye on the author, Zulu Tango's Petrus
Hangula, WO Frans Ananaii and Kapinya enjoy the wind.

Gavin and Jack discuss the day's operations with Zulu Uniform's Attie and Adriaan Hattingh.

Johannes Quiero Kalimba, ZT

Angus Pursell, ZT

Thomas Elumbe Phineas, ZT

Ox du Preez, ZT

Morning prayers before departing Eenhana. From left, "Short Botes" Botha, Ryk "Ryno" Botha, Michael "Peanuts" Kennard, Attie Hattingh, David Absalom Aviva, Frikkie Steynberg, Ben Davis, François du Toit and William Handukeme.

Shikongo Oholiko, Zulu Uniform's best tracker, takes the lead on following spoor.

Michael "Peanuts" Kennard examines WO Carlos Sizando of Zulu Uniform after the contact where Attie Hattingh's car was hit with a heatstrim.

Exhausted after a long day that ended with a contact, Toit and
ops medic Ryk "Ryno" Botha take a moment to relax.

Zulu 1 Juliet's Theron de Wit points to the helicopter landing to casevac Riaan de la Rosa. Toit's driver, Frans "Bokkie" Filemon, shields Riaan's face from flying sand.

The effect of an RPG-75 on Betoger's Casspir.

Flight engineer "Grobbies" Grobbelaar stands to the left as Toit
and Ryno place Porky on the floor of the Alouette.

Toit and Zulu Quebec trackers follow spoor while Attie
Hattingh overtakes them to continue spoorsny.

Trackers from Zulu Quebec point to clear spoor with their "walking sticks."

Knowing the spoor they have been following is less than five minutes old, the men of Zulu Uniform prepare for a contact.

Contact! In the haze of gunsmoke and dust kicked up by bullets, Attie Hattingh's Casspir is seconds from being hit by a heatstrim.

"What was that?" I shouted at Toit.

"Pom-zed!"

A chill went through me. People had to be hurt; people I knew.

The radio crackled. "Jack says he's got lots of wounded from the pom-zed!" Toit shouted. "He's scrambling the choppers to casevac them out! We can't get gunships till they're finished!"

Jack Bouwer, ZT-1: "I jumped down to the ground and found nine of my guys had been hit. Fortunately, most were non-lethal leg wounds, but one was serious. I ran to my car and called for casevacs, then ran back to them and started giving first aid. From where I was kneeling I could hear the radio in the car and follow what was happening all around us. Ox was a few hundred metres ahead on voorsny and his voice came over the speaker. 'Contact!' and I heard the sound of his .30 Browning. Then he reported three terrs killed. *Yes!* I thought, and hoped the one who'd set the POM-Z was among them."

From somewhere ahead of us I heard a sudden burst of machine gun fire. Over the radio came the inevitable, "Contact! Contact!" and the driver automatically turned towards the firing. Toit drew his pistol from where it hung inside the command hatch, eased the slide back to check a round was chambered and reholstered it. With the opening shots, the trackers on the ground had pulled back or taken cover. Now it was up to the cars.

I wondered what the insurgents were carrying. Heatstrims? RPG-7s or the new RPG-75s? Who had been killed in the other contact? How badly wounded were the others? Is this the day it happens to you? Another explosion of gunfire broke out to our left front, and we swung towards it, Toit gripping the spade handles of the Browning, eyes darting back and forth. The two trackers still with us were down inside now, the muzzles of their assault rifles jammed through the pigeon holes.

Suddenly faced with an impenetrable wall of bush, the driver turned the wheel hard and took us between two trees. We came to crashing stop, all of us in the back thrown forward with tools, weapons, and ration pack tins. The car's nose had slipped between the trees, but the body had jammed. The men in the back leapt out with machetes and began chopping at one trunk while Toit pulled leaves and twigs from the ammunition belts. The tree toppled over and we were moving again.

The radio was screeching, crackling, *"Contact! Contact!"* I stood at the back of the Casspir, eyes trying to penetrate the bush, ears assailed by engine, guns and radios, nose absorbing dust and cordite. Attie and Adriaan's cars appeared, disappeared, in and out of bush and shadow 40 metres to our left, angling towards us. Heavy firing again, the shadows ahead filled with the blue-grey haze of gun smoke. Tracers blazed between the trees, cutting split-second, red-orange streaks through the haze to disappear abruptly or ricochet into the air. Toit was firing, aiming to the right of the two converging cars, the heavy Browning chopping down bush and raising exploding geysers of sand.

Where are they? I can't see them!

Still farther to the left, Zulu Tango was engaged with its own quarry.

Gavin Manning, ZT-2: "By now we were charging into the smoke near where the POM-Z had exploded. I had cocked my twin .30 Brownings and removed the turret's stopper pin, when, seconds later, we joined the contact proper. Through the trees I saw Ox and Angus's cars, and then trackers, some standing and shooting, one limping, another sliding for cover on his rump. My biggest fear was our guys mistaking a friendly spoorsnyer for the enemy. Flooring a tracker from another team would not be a crowd pleaser.

"I ordered Thomas to swing out to the left to try to pick up any escaping gooks. Behind me, Indakalute and Johannes Quiero Kalimba yelled and pointed at a clump of dense pepper bush under some msasa trees. Then I saw it—the barrel of a PKM machine gun. I gave it a good burst of about 15–20 rounds. Thomas saw where I was firing. Ignoring the possibility of a heatstrim coming through the windscreen, he drove the Casspir straight into position, smashing everything to pieces. God, that took guts. We rolled over the hiding place, but just to make sure there was no longer any threat, Indakaluthe and Kalimba leaned over the back and raked it with their R5s. We swung around and stopped alongside. I yelled a warning about it being booby-trapped as the trackers jumped out.

"Kalimba picked up the trashed PKM and other kit wrapped in a camo ground sheet and threw it all in the back of the car, then Thomas took us the 200 metres to the POM-Z scene and we busied ourselves with bandages and drips while the rest of the cars cleared an LZ for the choppers."

Angus Pursell, ZT-4: "A minute or two later our contact was over. We had quite a few wounded from the POM-Z and Jack told us to clear an area for a chopper to land. We then returned to where the guys were been treated. It was not a good feeling seeing our guys hurt, but this is what we had all volunteered to do. Somewhere off to our right we could hear the gunfire of another contact. It had to be Toit and Attie's teams."

Camera poised, others swinging around my neck in the shaking, swaying Casspir, I held tight while dodging branches that scraped over the top of the car. I jumped to the left just in time to avoid one, only to be hit by another that caught me solidly across the side of the head, knocking my glasses askew and numbing my ear. I quickly resettled them and saw the two cars had swung further towards us, firing, firing, dust from the impact of the bullets ahead adding to the thickening haze.

A.T. Hattingh, ZU-1: "I saw the terr with the SKS too late, and didn't have time to swing the turret with the 20mm and .30mm Browning in his direction before he fired. Everything turned into slow motion as I was looking at him, expecting the worst. I do not know if a branch deflected the heatstrim, but it went low and detonated against the front wheel hub. The explosion was very muffled through the radio's earphones, but I saw the flash when the heatstrim exploded, and felt the vehicle rock from side to side."

There was a sudden, bass-like explosion and Attie's car stumbled 20 metres away, hit with something, then swerved and shuddered to a stop. The firing reached another crescendo, overwhelming even the sounds of racing engines and screeching radios. Toit dropped inside and I followed suit, ducking below the armour as bullets ricocheted off the side of the Casspir. Then he was up again and firing into the gloom of shadows, gun smoke and dust.

A.T. Hattingh, ZU-1: I realised with relief that we were okay and shouted to 'Shorty,' my driver, to turn left so that I could get the terr in my gunsights. He shouted back that the vehicle was very sluggish and that he was battling to turn. I only realised after the contact that the left front wheel was flat. Fortunately one of the other vehicles took the terr out before he could get me into his sights."

François du Toit, ZQ-1: "The sound of a heatstrim exploding would send chills down my spine. All my senses would be at full alert, eyes scanning back and forth, and then one of the guys was shouting, 'There! There!' and shouting back, 'Where? Where?' praying I would see the enemy before he launched one of those deadly rifle grenades. And he would point and shout, '*There!*'"

There! I saw one running and diving to disappear into a thicket. We drove directly at the spot, Toit screaming at the driver, "Right! Right!" then "Stop! Stop! Don't run over him! Fuck, man, stop!"

We braked to a shuddering halt alongside the thicket, dust rolling over us from behind. Toit went over the side and I dove through the rear doors, hitting the ground hard, boots tangling in broken saplings to send me sprawling full length into the sand. Scrambling to my feet, I turned to follow, then saw the wounded insurgent roll over behind a pepper bush, trying to cock his SKS assault rifle. Bent low, Toit ran at him, pistol held forward, everything happening in slow motion: one running, the other jerking at the rifle in his hands; one sprinting slowly through the bush; the other looking up, then down, struggling to draw back the bolt on the rifle; the pistol in the hand coming up, only feet away …

Move! For fuck sake, move!

A shot, the muzzle jumping; another shot, and then a third. The weapon slipped from fingers that slowly opened. Then Toit, eyes bulging and lips drawn back from dirt-blackened teeth, was standing over him, the pistol at his side.

Attie and Adriaan came running from their cars, both wide-eyed and stoked to their fingertips on adrenaline. Aside from the rifle grenade that hit Attie's car, Adriaan's windscreen and gun shield were starred and dented from AK-47 fire.

"There are more over there that we took out!" Attie pointed, talking in quick bursts. "One of them hit us with a heatstrim! Shit! I didn't see him until just before he fired!"

From the bush around us the trackers began to emerge. A medic supported a black warrant officer, his back bleeding from a dozen or more places. Toit radioed for a chopper and sent the cars to clear a landing zone.

Michael "Peanuts" Kennard, ZU-4: "The pigeon hole that we used to shoot through was stuck because of sand and rain. In the contact one of the buddies was a bit too eager and tried to shoot the pigeon plate open but instead sent bullet fragments ricocheting inside the car. Carlos Sizando got some pieces in his back. Not too serious, but they needed to be removed and the wounds cleaned up, so we casevacked him."

Gavin Manning, ZT-2: "When we got to where our guys had tripped the POM-Z, I saw that Kapinya, one of my favourites, had taken a big piece of shrapnel through his calf. Aside from being one of ZT's best trackers, he was a natural comedian who could keep everyone laughing. There definitely wasn't going to be much fun around the campfire tonight. Not far from him Ryno Botha, ZQ's medic, was getting a drip going for one of the other wounded, the same one I'd seen sliding on his rump during the contact. Ryno's NCO medical bag was spread on top of flattened shrubbery. I grabbed a field dressing out of it, propped Kapinya's foot on my thigh and wrapped his calf as tightly as I could. By the time I'd tied the ends, blood was already seeping through the pad. It took another two dressings before the bleeding stopped. I reassured him by saying that the wound was "fokkol" and that he wasn't going to lose the leg. He relaxed a little, but by now the adrenaline had worn off and he was in a lot of pain. Even though he was sweating, his skin had taken on a dull look. This worried me at first, but he wasn't complaining about being cold, which made me confident he wasn't going into shock. He was thirsty, though, so I sent one of the trackers back to the car for my water bag and then held it to his mouth to make sure he didn't gulp down too much.

"Jack shouted to hurry up and load the wounded into the Casspirs and take them to a kraal clearing about 300 metres to the east. He was already talking on the VHF to two "Giants" that had picked up the wounded from ZN's contact. There was no way the gunships could take all our guys, so the Pumas were heading for us. After Kapinya and the others were loaded I stayed with Ryno in case he needed help. He was squeezing a Lactated Ringer's solution drip into his patient when the big choppers roared 50 feet directly above us. I saw them roll out hard left to set up their approach from the south.

"It wasn't long after hearing them land that I saw a SAMS doctor run into our clearing. I was impressed; he must have sprinted those 300 metres from the LZ. By now the guy on the drip had gone into shock and Ryno updated the doctor on what he had given him. After a quick examination he said we needed to move him as a lying casevac.

"My car was closest and we all lifted and passed him to others inside. The doctor insisted on laying him on the Casspir's black rubber seats. As badly wounded as he was, he frantically tried to arch his shirtless back off the seats, with the doctor trying to hold him still. In the summer sun at midday, those seats were hot enough to blister bare skin. I realised what the problem was and yelled at the doc to move him. We immediately shifted him onto the layer of twigs and leaves covering the ammo cases in the centre aisle and he calmed down, poor bugger.

"The Pumas were waiting, engines shrieking, when we got there. Our guy was carried from my Casspir to the open door and passed to the ZN sitting casevacs. The doc jumped in and was already working on him when the flight engineer slid the door shut and the pilot pulled pitch. I turned and ran towards my car, sand stinging the back of my legs. When it was gone, I saw Kapinya's blood on my hands and thigh, and thought what a shitty day it was when it took two Pumas to casevac our wounded."

The near and distant sounds of Alouettes and Pumas faded, the first west towards Eenhana, the others south to Ondangwa. Where our part of the wide-ranging contact had taken place, rifle grenades and RPG warheads were heaped together. Toit kneaded a handful of Soviet plastic explosive found on one of the bodies, laid it across the pile, then crimped a detonator onto a five-minute fuse with his teeth. Pushing it into the oily explosive, he lit the fuse and we trotted to the idling cars. We were a few hundred metres away when it went off, the explosion muffled by the dense bush.

I imagined the debris settling over the bodies lying where they had fallen, wondering what dreams and futures had been abruptly ended for the sake of this backward and little-known land. Another day finished as we rumbled back across the border.

14

Reality Check

Michael "Peanuts" Kennard, ZU-4: "To say we liked the idea of a journalist going with us would be a lie. We did not expect the government to allow it because sometimes we went over the yati. Up to then, these were covert operations, and no one was supposed to know about it. Once we were on a spoor it would be very difficult to stop at the cutline just because an outsider was on board. When I heard about this reporter deploying with us, I thought that he would be hiding under the floor carpet when the bullets started flying. Then I saw him hanging over the Casspir's top, taking photos during one of the contacts. Bliksem! That's when my opinion started to change."

By now, I'd been in a dozen contacts, snapping away with my cameras and ignoring the possibility of injury. More than once, the Ovambo policemen had tried to drag me down inside the steel hull to safety, but I'd shake off their concerned hands and stay where I was, looking for that Robert Capa shot. And each time I would be even more convinced that I was charmed, that I could stand up and wave if I wanted to and they still couldn't put one into me. The bullet with *my* name on it hadn't been made. "Cosmic protection," I smiled each time at their shaking heads. And I believed it.

"Listen," I'd tell them, "If we hit a contact, tell your people back here not to pull me down, okay? I can't get my pictures from inside." And they'd look at me for a moment, shrug as if to say, It's your arse, pal, and pass the word.

Chris Pieterse: "Jim and I were having a beer at the Okave Club and he was quite upset that the Ovambos kept pulling him down during a contact. I tried to explain to him how much lead was flying around at that moment. Because the terrs rarely showed themselves, the troops would lay down a wall of bullets to kill them before they could fire a heatstrim or RPG. I tried basic arithmetic—clearly not one of his majors at college. 'Look,' I said, 'you've seen what happens in a contact. Our guys shoot any place that might be hiding a terr. If everybody gets into the action, you're going to have at least 36 R5s, half-a-dozen .30 calibre Brownings and the odd .50 calibre

Browning or 20mm shooting at the same time, and that's on top of what the terrs are loosing off. This is not a good time to poke your head and shoulders above the armour plate.' But he was a slow child, and remained adamant. I gave up and I relayed his request to the guys to allow him to get shot if he wanted."

January 17, 1987

Rain during the night had softened and washed the ground clean, making the spoor so clear even I could see it. We stopped briefly at a kraal and a young woman with a baby on her hip pointed north and shook her hand rapidly. She had seen them pass not more than an hour earlier. From that point on, the outcome was inevitable—signed, sealed and delivered.

> **A.T. Hattingh, ZU-1:** "We picked up the spoor at a kraal complex after an Ovambo woman told us which way the terr had gone. I actually thought that he must have done something to piss them off tremendously. This was contrary to normal behaviour because the PBs knew what the repercussions would be from the Swapo cadres should it be known one of them had passed information to us."

The tracks led us past farmers preparing fields for planting. Yoked oxen snorted and shied, shaking their heads when the cars roared by. We crossed old fields, the cars shuddering over last year's furrows. Farmland and scattered mopani gave way to stunted tress that grew taller and thicker. The cars spread out in battle line abreast, each leaving flattened pepper bush and uprooted saplings in its wake. Between the Casspirs, trackers zigzagged through the bush as the men in the cars shouted encouragement. The spoor was growing fresher and fresher.

> **A.T. Hattingh:** "The terr's inexperience was evident as after approximately two kilometres he started running. I knew that he had signed his death warrant. A running spoor was the easiest to see and the trackers were able to run at quite a pace during the follow up."

I watched them dodging between the thin trees, ducking under branches as the Casspirs kept pace alongside. One of them, his face streaming with sweat, shouted to Toit: "Gunship! Kontact kom now-now!" It was time to scramble the choppers; we weren't more than 15 minutes behind and closing fast. He made the call that would send the flight crews at Eenhana running for their helicopters.

Toit had already pulled the locking pin from the gun mount and swung the guns left and right as we crashed through the bush. The men around me drew back the bolts on their weapons to double-check that rounds were chambered. Safeties snapped down and muzzles were pushed through the spring-loaded gun ports. The encouraging shouts of a moment ago were gone. Faces tightened as the tension became almost palpable, ratcheting pulses higher and higher.

The insurgents could hear the growls of pursuing Casspirs growing louder. How experienced were they? Would they stop to set an ambush? Would the next moment stop forever in the flesh-shredding explosion of a heatstrim burning through the side of the car? Hands tightened on weapons and eyes peered through the thick glass. At the chattering whine of a helicopter, I looked up to see an Alouette passing diagonally over us.

The trackers on the ground slowed and dropped back. I pushed the start button on the cassette recorder Velcro-ed to the front of my camera jacket. Any minute now…a-n-y minute. The hell with it. I hoisted myself onto the rear deck, camera in one hand, the other arm deflecting branches that threatened to sweep me off.

Chris Pieterse: "I had deployed to Eenhana as ops officer and was monitoring the radios as ZQ and ZU followed spoor a few kilometres west of the base. When they scrambled the gunships, I hopped on the command chopper and we were over the follow-up within ten minutes. Attie had timed the call for air support well, and after flying a tear-drop formation for a few minutes one of the cars hit contact."

Now!—with the sudden, staccato explosions of gunfire as Attie's cars hit the contact less than 30 metres ahead of us. As we rolled into it, I could see the familiar grey haze of dust and gun smoke. I'd raised a camera, looking for something to snap, when automatic-weapons fire started coming from our left.

Michael "Peanuts" Kennard, ZU-4: "I spotted the enemy and I started to turn not to be in the line of fire. Unfortunately my driver went the wrong way and I yelled to steer him in the direction where the enemy was. Everything was happening in slow motion, adrenalin pumping and thinking of the enemy lying on the ground, waiting to fire an RPG or a heatstrim. Adriaan and I were in the two front Casspirs when suddenly all hell broke loose. I opened up full blast, pouring fire into possible hiding places. That was when Toit's car crossed in front of us and my driver swerved to the right and went underneath a tree. I ducked, but a big branch struck my arm and turret at that moment and it set off a burst of rounds and the next moment I heard that Jim was hit."

One bullet clipped the edge of the camera vest over my chest, leaving a half-moon hole I wouldn't find until later; another struck the bevelled top of the Casspir and ricocheted upward. It was as though I'd been punched by a huge fist, the blow knocking the right arm sideways, camera falling to the end of its sling. The arm dropped, paralysed. In slow motion I pulled up the sleeve of the T-shirt and stared at a red hole in the side of my biceps—a biceps gone flaccid, hanging loose and formless as though it belonged to an old woman. My mouth opened and I let out a piercing scream—not from the pain, there wasn't any—but from the shocking realization that I'd been hit! *I'd been hit!*

My head dropped again—again in slow motion, it seemed—to look with embarrassment into the car, hoping no one had heard my wimpish cry. Then I realised that if I had caught one bullet, the possibility of another wasn't entirely out of the question. Swinging my legs over the edge, I dropped inside, landing in a sprawl between the seats. The sounds of screaming radios, blaring engine, shouting men, and assault rifles spitting bursts of automatic fire were deafening. Simon, the Ovambo ops medic, caught my eye and beckoned me forward. Sure that a bullet had broken the bone, I made my way up the aisle, slipping on empty casings, arm hanging uselessly. The car swerved and I toppled sideways across two men, one of whom straight-armed me to the floor without a backward glance.

Simon was already ripping open a field dressing when I reached him. He threw a rucksack out of the seat across from him and curtly motioned me to it, then sat alongside and eased the sleeve up and over my shoulder. Toit took a quick break from his Browning and ducked down to ask what the hell had happened.

François du Toit, ZQ-1: "The last time I looked back I saw Jim sitting outside, which I didn't think was very clever. A minute or two later, one of the Ovambos yelled at me that the shirumbu was hit. My first thought was that he was dying and I dropped inside to see. Fortunately, it was just his arm."

"ARM'S BROKEN!" I yelled over the firing. He gave me a withering look, grabbed the radio handset and spoke briefly. I caught the word "casevac." Another disgusted look in my direction, and he returned to the fire fight going on around us.

After a few more bursts he ducked down again and shouted, "ARE YOU SURE?"

I looked up at him and nodded violently. "ARM'S BROKEN!"

"WHAT HAPPENED? YOU FALL OFF THE CAR?"

Having last seen me on my precarious seat at the back of the Casspir, it was a reasonable assumption, but not part of the script I'd imagined for the scene.

"NO, GODAMMIT! I'M SHOT! I'M SHOT!"

"NO SHIT?" he yelled back, and returned to his guns.

A.T. Hattingh, ZU-1: "I heard Toit say over the radio that Jim was wounded. My first thought was that there was an accidental discharge of a firearm inside the Casspir. When I later heard that he was exposed at the back of the vehicle, a saying that Ian Richardson always had came to mind: 'In for a penny, in for a pound.'"

Chris Pieterse: "Everything looked as usual from the gunship. Lots of dust, Casspirs driving around randomly pouring fire into possible cover. Shortly after things calmed down, the voice of one of the Ovambos crackled over the VHF: 'Jim es geskiet!' (Jim has been shot!). Oh shit! I thought. How are we going to explain a dead Yank?"

Simon circled the biceps with gauze. I tried to move the arm. Nothing. I tried to open or close the hand. Nothing. I leaned back and closed my eyes for a moment. Then it struck me. What I had worked towards for the last year was finished. A broken arm would take months to heal, months before I could use it again. The project was over.

"FUCK!" I bellowed, smashing my good fist against the water tank in fury. Simon jerked his hands away and looked at me questioningly. "Sorry, tati," I said, shaking my head. "It's okay. Sorry." *Dammit!*

As quickly as it had started, the contact was over and three cars were flattening the bush nearby. Frikkie Steynberg, Zulu Uniform's ops medic, appeared with his first-aid kit. He unzipped the canvas case as Simon scrubbed my shoulder with an alcohol swab. Tapping the syringe he had drawn with Sosegon, he reversed it and with a downward flip of the wrist drove the needle into the shoulder muscle.

Frikkie pointed towards the back of the car. "Let's go!" he shouted. I followed him out of the Casspir and towards the helicopter that was sinking into the freshly cleared landing zone. Eyes narrowed to slits, we entered the downwash and stinging sand. Then I realised I could move the arm. I tried again. It was working; not very well, but I could definitely raise it a little. I tried to make a fist. No good, but the two little fingers moved slightly, curling inwards.

"IT'S NOT BROKEN! IT'S NOT BROKEN!" I yelled over the scream of the engine and flat thudding of rotor blades. I stopped and turned away from the sandstorm to show him the movement.

He grabbed my left arm and got me going again, yelling something in Afrikaans. I didn't understand it, but the look on his face said he wanted me on the chopper and out of his hair. As I settled next to the pilot, Frikkie latched the door from outside, gave me a grin and thumbs up, then turned and ran low under the blur of the blades. The pilot drew up on the collective control, and we lifted off.

The flight engineer placed a set of earphones over my head. "How's it?" pilot Dave Atkinson hissed over the intercom. He and I had been drinking in the air force compound the night before. "What happened?"

"Fucker shot me!"

"Genuine? Shit, we heard you'd broken your arm!" He released the intercom switch for a moment and spoke to Eenhana. "Okay, I've just told them you're hit and we're on the way. They'll have a medic waiting. Relax."

There was no pain anywhere around the wound, but the hand was burning and aching badly. And in spite of the cool wind whipping through the open door, beads of sweat trickled down my face. Ten minutes later, we settled on the tarmac. Pieterse and an army medic were there.

Chris Pieterse: "As soon as everything was under control on the ground, we flew back and I was waiting as Jim was helped out of the other chopper. He was as pale a ghost and obviously in a bit of shock. I asked him what it was like getting shot for being stupid. For once he was at a loss for words."

Pieterse was shaking his head. "Well, well, it's Mister 'If-I'm-Standing-Up-Taking-Pictures-Don't-Pull-Me-Down.' Tell me, Dumbshit, how's it feel?"

"Not too hot."

"Okay, give me your kit and go with this guy."

I handed over everything and followed the medic to the sick bay. The doctor unwrapped the bandage, noting cheerfully that there was no exit wound. "Looks like it's still in there," he said with an insouciance that was quite inappropriate from my point of view. The burning sensation in the hand, he explained, was "referred pain" due to damage to the median nerve. He applied a fresh dressing and I headed for the air force compound, passing small groups of pink-cheeked national servicemen in brown uniforms. The blood-stained gauze stood out against my dirt and tan.

"Koevoet," one whispered. I scowled, looking straight ahead until I'd left them behind. Rounding the corner, I cradled the forearm with my other hand. *Goddamn, this hurts.*

Dizzy, nauseous and soaked with sweat, I dropped into a chair under the camouflage net. Dave Atkinson came out of the SAAF tent, leaned over me and did something to the front of my T-shirt. I looked down. Pinned to it was a canvas swatch hastily scissored into the shape of a heart, coloured dark blue with a ballpoint pen and edged with red ink. He stood back, saluted and gave a spirited, if somewhat inaccurate, rendering of *The Star Spangled Banner*. I couldn't help grinning. My first purple heart.

The doctor arrived to say that a Puma should be scrambled from Ondangwa to pick me up. I shook my head, imagining messages zipping between various commands about committing a "Giant" to casevac one lightly wounded foreign journalist. The last thing I wanted was to call attention to myself by receiving special treatment. I could picture some staff officer going through the ceiling and urging higher ups to have my access curtailed or cancelled altogether. It would not only make things awkward and embarrassing for the people here, but also drag my name across the desks of senior army and air force officers. Knowing that it was always easier and safer for someone to say no than yes, I said I'd wait for the first Casspir driving back.

Major Brooks came up with the perfect compromise. A Bosbok spotter plane was scheduled to make a road reconnaissance down to Ondangwa. It was leaving in a few minutes and had an empty spare seat. I followed the pilot, who looked about 14 years old and bore a startling resemblance to my brother Bill, who had flown a very similar aircraft in Vietnam. It struck me that when Bill had been hit in 1969, his wound was in almost exactly the same place as mine. The difference was he had very nearly lost his arm. It was something I drew little consolation from as I pulled myself awkwardly into the back seat; my major concern at that point was not embarrassing myself by puking all over the inside of the airplane.

Less than an hour later, we touched down, taxied up to the deserted flight line and stopped not more than 50 metres from where I'd stepped off the Namibair flight seven weeks earlier. The pilot shut down the engine and climbed out. I climbed out behind him. He walked off in one direction. I walked off in another, looking for the bevy of nurses that would descend on me with soothing hands and words.

I spotted Bernie Ley scanning the flight line. His relief at seeing me intact and ambulatory was obvious. I smiled bravely. We'd have to wait for the doctor, Bernie said. He'd gone down to the flight line right after the Bosbok landed but missed me because I had gone off in the wrong direction. He was still down there, searching. A few minutes later, an ambulance pulled up. A trim, young fellow climbed out dressed in jogging shorts, flip-flops and a T-shirt advertising a bar in Durban. He strolled casually up the ramp.

"You the American journalist that's been shot?" I nodded, keeping a keen lookout for the bevy from the corner of my eye. This hand was hurting like a *bastard.*

"Well," he said, yawning, "let's see if we can find someone to X-ray that arm."

Right away I could see I'd walked into the wrong script again. Here I was, wounded in combat, begrimed and reeking of cordite, in pain—and this guy was yawning! I was tempted to affect a 1,000-yard stare, but gave it up as a bad idea—I might miss the bevy, hope for which was already fading with depressing rapidity.

The X-ray showed a jagged object lodged against the median nerve and artery. I was lucky. The bullet had broken up when it hit the edge of the Casspir, and only part of it had hit me. After snipping away tissue around the entry wound, he probed the hole with his little finger. It disappeared down to the second knuckle before he stopped. I saw Bernie turn slightly pale.

"You'll probably need neurosurgery to get that out," the doc said, "and we don't have the facilities here. In the meantime, I'll tell the infirmary at Okave to give you a shot of morphine every six hours."

Five days later I hied myself to a clinic in Cape Town where the offending object was removed. Didn't have a bevy of stunning nurses down there, either.

15

The Flower of Their Youth

February 12, 1987
Onaimwandi

Sugar,
Returned yesterday from a week in Cape Town and a spot of micro-neurosurgery.
When I came out of the anaesthetic, a plastic specimen jar was on the bedside table.
In it was a piece of bullet jacket the size of a fingernail wrapped with fibres of green
cloth. It had not crossed my mind to wonder where the hole in my T-shirt had gone.
Both were pressing against the artery and median nerve. A contusion to the latter
has left me with a hand that is numb on the surface, but "Sort of like razor blades
inside?" the surgeon suggested. Yep.

There have been two deaths since I've been away; both South Africans, both
long-serving good operators. They died in a head-on collision while driving a bakkie
between Ondangwa and Oshakati. The vagaries of fate.

The worst thing (I think) about my absence is that I've missed a lot of stories
and photos. Things have very busy. Yet, there's something niggling at the back of my
mind that tells me I would have been hurt far more seriously had I been in the veld
these last couple of weeks. Superstitious? Not me. But at Eenhana the night before
I was hit, a gushing thunderstorm passed over and not long thereafter, a full moon
threw a rainbow into the retreating edge of the rain. (I swear to God. We all stood
there and marvelled, none of us ever having seen a rainbow in the middle of the
night, making silly, drunken comments about "what it meant.") And prior to this
latest new experience, part of my singing-in-the shower repertoire was "Swing Low
Sweet Chariot" and "Bury Me Not on the Lone Prairie." You can bet I haven't sung
either since. But don't ever accuse me of being superstitious.

The infiltration is in full gallop, and multiple contacts are everyday events
in Ovamboland, especially in the central and eastern regions, where intelligence
reports say that Swapo's "Typhoon Detachment" is preparing to come across. They
haven't been seen since 1985, when they tried and then withdrew in tatters after
being badly mauled by Ops K and 101 Battalion. Still, by Swapo standards, they
are the elite, trained especially for base attacks and ambushes.

A captured insurgent revealed there were more than 100 of them at Namakunde, waiting for orders to come down. "Yes! These will stand and fight," the guys here tell me, rubbing their hands together. "What a pleasure."

Letter addressed and stamped, I popped a Voltaren and wished I was still on the shots of morphine. The razor blades were a constant. I lay on the bed and picked up *Mafeking Road*, a book of short stories borrowed from Bernie Ley. Set in the dorps—small towns—and farms of South Africa in the early 1900s, the tales revealed much about the Afrikaner mindset. I almost leapt out of my skin at an almighty crash on the door.

"Come out here, you bloody Englishman!"

I opened the door to find Zulu Delta's team leader, Hennie Nel, and his 2iC, Dean Viljoen. "I'm American."

"Same thing," Nella said.

"Kom, man, time for a drink."

"I really don't feel like…"

"You're coming to the Okave Club. Let's go."

"And bring your tape recorder. We have some stories for your book."

I'd been there only once before, in the company of Chris Pieterse, but the frowns and backs that turned towards me made it obvious that I was not welcome. This was where they could drink and let their hair down without worrying about an outsider overhearing. When we walked in this time, there were still a few looks of disapproval, but the atmosphere was less arctic than three weeks earlier.

"We were making bets about you coming back," Dean said.

"Who won?"

"Not saying."

Marius Brand joined us and pointed at the other end of the bar. Louw van Niekerk, the giant with the scarred cheek, was in animated conversation with some others.

"Louw wants to buy you a beer," Marius said. "But you'll have to ask in Afrikaans, 'cause he doesn't speak much English."

"What do I say?" I asked stupidly. Brand told me and I practiced it a couple of times. Standing in front of Van Niekerk, I looked up and repeated, "Ek moer jou nou." This doesn't make much sense when translated literally, but in the Afrikaans vernacular means quite specifically that, "I'm going to knock you on your arse right now."

Whether he spotted the grins on the faces behind me or decided I was hallucinating from too much sun, he patted my shoulder and handed me a Castle. Two hours and more beers later, I was feeling remarkably little pain. And the story telling was in full flow.

"Remember Simon?" Dean said. "He was the Ovambo radioman you met with Zulu Mike last year. Incredible tracker and really good guy. We were on a follow-up and he saw the trip wire for a pom-zed. He stopped, but one of the other trackers walked straight into it. The top of the pom-zed hit him under the arm and went all the way through his chest. He walked about five steps and died."

"It was our first night back after a really good week," Nella was saying some time later. "Three contacts, four terrs killed. We threw a fancy dress party here in the club. I was wearing top hat and tails. After trying to drink the place dry, I went back to our barracks and woke up Dean here, but the Baileys had dried my throat. He couldn't understand what I was saying and told to me go and sleep it off. This made me angry and I stormed out. On the way to my place I stopped to have a pee, looked up and thought, 'Hell, that's a big shooting star trail.' It passed west to east and there was a big explosion, and that's when I realised it was a 122mm rocket! The next one took out the main sewerage pump station next to the barracks. I got a good bearing and ran in to wake up Dean. Then I jumped in the Landcruiser and found Sheshe, our Blesbok driver, and told him to get all the team to the stores, no matter their condition. He said, 'Santie, make sure the commanders have the Casspirs ready and our rat packs loaded,' and he took off. When everyone gathered, there was a lot of laughing at my top hat and tails. After a quick briefing we headed out of town at dawn and soon found a B-10 launch pad. The army arrived and we started the follow-up. It had started to drizzle when we found the 122mm launch pad and seven spoor leading away from it.

"It went into a grassy, wet shona. We came out of it into a mohango field. Nothing. Everyone spread out and a couple hours later, Willie 'Kaffertjie' Venter in my number 2 car picked up two spoor. Des Allen and Tony da Costa from Zulu India arrived and I gave them a sitrep. I got out of my car and went into the mohango with just a walking stick."

"And still wearing his tails," Dean laughed.

"Bandito, one of my best spoorsnyers, was in front of me with his walking stick and a P-38 pistol, and Johnny Magodi and another behind me. Then I saw something strange—deep spike-like tracks going in the direction of a large kraal in the distance. I signalled Gerson, who was driving my Casspir, to move forward into the mohango with us. Emmanuel was behind the .50 Browning. We got to the kraal, entered and turned right. There were some men in the centre compound, but I decided to search the grain storage bins first. While I was looking inside them, I saw a small hut. I went through a curtain and there were two terrs lying on their backs and pointing AKs at me. The sight of me in tails must have confused the hell out of them. I reacted on instinct, running at them and hitting them with the stick. Bandito and Johnnie entered at that moment and we had them. We also found the women's high-heel shoes they'd been wearing to disguise their spoor.

"We took them back to Dean's car and everyone wanted info from them. They were terrified and admitted they were part of a group of 10 that was supposed to RV northwest of Oshikuku, about 12 kilometres away. We got going and about an hour later the drizzle turned into heavy rain. Suddenly, all hell broke lose just south of the tar road opposite Oshikuku, when Dean, Des, and Tony hit a contact and floored two terrs. In the middle of it all, our number 2 car had taken the embankment too fast and rolled onto its side, fortunately with no casualties. Dean used his Wolf to pull it back on its wheels and we started following three other spoor towards the yati. After Zulu Victor and Zulu Oscar made contact and killed two of them, I decided to call it a day.

"We'd come back from a week's deployment only the day before and I could see everyone was exhausted. When my team and Zulu India got back to Okave about 17h00, we had another celebration. I finally changed from tails to T-shirt and shorts and told everyone to take the next day off. Then Dean, Tony, Des, Kaffertjie and I drank until the wee hours of the following morning.

"Speaking of which," Nella frowned, lifting my beer and shaking it, "you're empty. Don't you bloody Englishmen drink?"

"American."

"Same thing." He stepped to the bar and returned with another round.

"One night only a couple days after you left last year," Dean was saying, "the terrs revved Ohangwena. Did you hear about it?"

"We were TB-ed about 20 kilometres west of Two-One-Delta," Nella said, "and the sound of mortars actually woke us up. I switched on the radio and heard Z2 giving a sitrep to Bakstein's Zulu Victor and Zulu Oscar, who were about five kilometres south of the base, and then a sitrep from Ohangwena that they had repulsed the attack. When we RV-ed with them east of Oshikango, they had about 20 spoor going towards Namakunde, but we picked up 12 more on their left flank. There were lots of shonas—"

"Same area where you got stuck with Zulu Alpha last year," Dean interrupted. "I pulled you guys out."

"Quiet, man," Nella insisted. "Anyway, I sent Dean and Kaffertjie ahead on voorsny. Kashima, Dean's senior Ovambo, saw someone in the water and the next thing I heard on the radio was 'Contact!' We went forward and then— shit!—we were stuck in the shona! I saw movement on our left and started giving covering fire. When I saw that Dean was on the ground, I jumped out and went into the water with Bandito, Santos, and our medic Thomas Shilongo. Gerson was next to me, carrying the radio. We made contact and killed one carrying an RPG. Then I nearly drowned when I went into a shona that was deeper than I thought."

"We were wading across this shona, the water was right up to our chests in some places," Dean said, "and suddenly one of the Ovambos was pointing and saying, 'There, there!' Man, we had terrs in the weeds right in front of us, and they were firing, and we were firing, and the cars were firing behind us, water was kicking up all around us. There were more terrs in the bush on the other side of the shona, and they were shooting. Shit, we were getting machine guns, mortars, RPGs, everything thrown at us. There were about…"

I held up a hand to stop him. "Wait, wait, I have to turn the tape over."

Nella paused until the cassette recorder was rolling again and I pushed it in front of him. "There were about 30 terrs," he continued. "The gunships arrived just then and opened up with their 20mm guns right above us. Looked like fairy lights when those shells hit the ground and exploded. It was complete chaos, with guys from different teams scattered around. I got comms with the pilots and ordered them to stop. We had 15 confirmed Victor Yankees. I was sure there were at least six more that we'd killed in the water, but no one did a sweep as everyone wanted to get on the ground for the follow up. Gerson, Johnny Magodi, Bandito, myself and two Ovambos from ZV and ZO picked up six spoor. One of them was bleeding and about a kilometre-and-a-half later we found him. The other five were now running towards Namakunde. Right after the gunships left to refuel, my car, with Emmanuel, Shilongo and Thomas caught up with us, and then cars 2 and 3, plus the Blesbok. By now we were low on ammo, so we grabbed fresh magazines. The terrs split up, three going north and two NNE. We marked the two spoor and followed the three. We had them cut off from Namakunde, so I radioed Bakstein and Dean to patrol the tar road north of Namakunde to prevent them getting to the FAPLA base at Ongiva.

"We had to stop again because of more deep shonas, and got out to follow on foot. About 15 minutes later, the spoor showed they were walking. Johnny Shidute, Ishmael, and Johnny Cleopas, who were on the ground, called the cars to join us. With Emmanuel leading the way in my car, they worked their way around the shonas. Right after they caught up with us, we had the next contact and recovered one RPG and two AK-47s.

"We drove back to the marked spoor, which Kaffertjie and the Blesbok were following. The terrs were anti-tracking in thick bush, which made it difficult for voorsny. At a kraal we got info the terrs were just ahead. I called in the gunships and one of them got a visual about 600 metres in front of us. He asked if he could shoot and I said yes, because we needed to protect the trackers. The flight engineer opened fire and suddenly he had a runaway 20mm. Just then, one of the terrs fired a SAM-7, but the recoil from the 20mm was pushing the gunship to the right and the SAM went under it. A few minutes later, we caught up with the terrs and took out both of them.

"When all my guys were accounted for, we joined up with the other teams and went back across the yati. The army commander at Etale radioed and invited us for a well deserved beer and braai. It was a nice evening, everyone talking about what they'd seen and done. We later learned that the terrs called themselves the 'Stalin Detachment' and were trained specially for this attack. Their plan was to overrun Ohangwena and capture a white policeman."

"Man, you should have been there," Dean said. "Afterwards, we were saying you really should have been with us. You could've really got some good coverage there."

Brand, who had been giving covering fire to Dean and Nella as they waded across the shona, shook his head sympathetically at my missing it.

Long after midnight, I deserted the party and managed to get lost on the 100-metre walk back to Z3.

February 14, 1987

The next morning, not sure which hurt more, the head or hand, I begged a ride in a replacement Casspir heading for Eenhana. Not up to spending the rest of the week riding through the bush, I decided that if something were to happen,

I'd catch a lift with one of the helicopters and join the follow-up from there. In the meantime, I had more than enough backlogged tapes and scribbled notes to type out one-handed. And at night I'd be able to throw my sleeping bag on the floor of the air-conditioned ops room, kept cool for the sake of the radios. A rare treat.

Lt Chris Ronne, team leader, Z1J: "With Betoger as my second-in-command, we had worked north of the yati the first few days and picked up lots of spoor. Zulu Uniform, Zulu Lima and Zulu Quebec came up to assist and we had six or seven contacts and got at least a dozen kills. It was the most successful week our group had had since its formation in August 1985. There were still a few days of the deployment left, so we headed to Zulu 2 to rebunker and make running repairs to our vehicles. Quite a few other teams also TB-ed outside the base, and that night there was a reasonable party. I planned an early start so didn't spend much time and went back to sleep next to my vehicles."

Theron de Wit, car commander, Z1J-2: "We were a good team. I had already done my two years of national service as an ops medic in the SADF. When I joined Koevoet in 1984, I was one of the founders of the *voetspanne*—teams working on foot at night with the latest night vision equipment from Krygkor. General Dreyer eventually cancelled those and I was selected to be part of a new team with Lt Ronne, Betoger, and Claassie Claassen. We recruited our buddies—the spoorsnyers—and started training them. There were no new Casspirs available, and the old ones kept breaking down so there was a lot of work to get them in good operating condition. When we armed them, Betoger, was who second-in-command, liked the Russian RPDs, and he fitted two of those on his car. Claassie had two LMGs, and Ronne and I had twin .30 Brownings. That first year we struggled a bit, but Ronne pushed us hard and as we got to know each other better, our successes grew, which saw us recognised by the older teams. Ronne was a good leader and kept us motivated. Even though he was an officer and I was a constable, he treated me like a friend. Betoger and I met in Windhoek when I joined the task force. We were both born in South West Africa and got along very well. I met Claassie the day he arrived from South Africa and we immediately connected. He passed on his investigation experience, which we continued to use to our advantage even after he left to become Zulu Juliet's team leader."

On the afternoon I arrived at Eenhana, half a dozen groups rolled in to rebunker with diesel and water and set up camp outside the base. Aside from fuel and water, Eenhana offered fresh meat and beer. A braai was always the order of the evening, followed by a few beers with the air force. That night, about 20 men sat either side of a row of expanded metal tables, everyone wanting to hear the tape I'd made of being hit. My scream raised roars of laughter and demands to hear it again.

"How's the arm, Englishman?" Betoger asked, wiping his eyes.

"Arm's fine, but the hand still hurts," I admitted.

"So where did it hit you?"

I lifted my arm and pulled up the short sleeve.

Betoger, whose real name was Christie Fourie, leaned forward and peered closely at the red scar. "Hell, how did you get hit there?"

"Well, I had the camera up like this," I started to explain, holding an imaginary camera at eye level, "looking for a shot and…"

"You must have been surrendering!" the 24 year-old Southwester butted in. "You weren't looking for a picture, you had your arms raised. Hey," he said, looking around, "we've got a hands-upper here. What kind of journalist did we get? A surrendering journalist! I'll bet he's the only white man in Ovamboland with tanned armpits!"

The heavy humour was, I realised, a sign of at least partial adoption. Even the "Englishman" label was a nuanced insult. Raised on stories of the Anglo-Boer War and the infamy of the British-built concentration camps, Afrikaners used the term as a post-Civil War southerner would "Yankee"—damning or cautiously welcoming. In this case, it emphasized that, though I was and would always be an outsider, my return to operations represented a rite of passage, an honorary initiation into the bottom rung of an exclusive society.

"You really disappointed us for a few minutes, though," Betoger said.

"Why's that?"

"No, the first thing over the radio was you'd broken your arm."

"Yeah, well, that's what I tho…"

"And all of us were saying what a clumsy fuck you were. *No* one breaks his arm in the middle of a contact, man."

"Yeah, but … "

"And then we heard Toit say that you had been hit, and all of us said, 'All *right*! He's not such a clumsy fuck after all!'" He crossed his arms and looked around at his audience. "Toit said this Englishman kept shouting"—Betoger pitched his voice high—'I'm shot, I'm shot!'" He doubled over as everyone dissolved into laughter, a couple of them choking on their beers.

I waited for it to subside. "Thanks a lot. That's great. I really appreciate the concern."

"But you want to take it easy, man," counselled another, trying to keep a straight face. "You're not as young as you used to be, you know."

I glowered for effect and took another pull at the beer. Some took great delight in reminding me that, at 42, I was 20 years older than their average age. I stared at the braai and pretended I hadn't heard.

"By the way, you got any daughters old enough for me?"

"Bastards," I hissed, while they fell about laughing again.

"So what did you think when you got hit?" a grinning Attie asked.

"Surprised the hell out of me. I just never thought it was going to happen," I said, a little mollified that someone was taking it seriously. At least Attie was all right. Someone you could always count on.

"Listen," he said, "it's not the one with your name on it that you have to worry about, it's the one that says 'To whom it may concern.'" There was a brief rise at the old joke. "But, man, you can ride on the back of my car anytime."

"Thanks, but I think I'll take my pictures from inside next time."

"No, no," he said. "Genuine. You can ride on the back of my car anytime you want. In fact, I'd really like it."

"Why's that?" I asked, eyeing him suspiciously.

"No, if they see an old and easy target like you, maybe they won't shoot at me!" he roared, ducking as I threw my beer at him.

In the morning, the group leaders and car commanders came in to plan the day's movements and get the latest intelligence. Sitting around the outdoor tables, they sipped coffee and gnawed on dry rusks while discussing where they would be operating for the next two or three days. Toit and Attie would work to the west, towards Ohangwena. Three other groups, none of whom I knew well, would be heading east. Info from the local population placed at least one group of up to ten insurgents between Eenhana and Nkongo.

I started on the thrice-daily cleaning—blowing dust out of crevices with a can of compressed air, polishing lenses, checking batteries. Porky, the tall, cropped-headed teenager I'd met during my two-week introduction to Koevoet nine months earlier, sat next to me with his cup of coffee. Now wearing the Zulu Juliet insignia and more comfortable using English with me, he was still as gawky and quiet and painfully shy as when I'd first met him. Why, he asked, did I carry three cameras, each with a different lens? I passed them over. He carefully held up each in turn and looked through the viewfinder. Big, jovial Betoger ambled over to watch, a rusk in one hand, chipped enamel mug in the other.

"Goeie môre, Hands-upper," he grinned at me.

Porky gently placed the last camera back on the table, looking at it enviously. He asked shyly if I would consider selling one to him before I left. Betoger put down his mug, shoved the rusk in his mouth and picked it up. Clowning, he sighted through the viewfinder and pretended to take a picture an inch from Porky's nose.

Betoger's merciless teasing was part of what made him one of Koevoet's much-loved characters. A widely told tale concerned the time he and a friend emptied a bottle of brandy between them and decided to set off two 200-gram blocks of Soviet TNT they'd "forgotten" to turn in from a contact. They slightly miscalculated the charge and placement. When the smoke and dust settled, a portion of their barracks was gone. The next morning, they were standing rigidly at attention in front of Brigadier Dreyer.

"What the hell did you think you were doing?" he shouted at them. The boss was no man to be trifled with at the best of times. The boss in a temper sent people running for cover. It was commonly held that suffering the wrath of the Almighty might be infinitely preferable to facing the "Brig" when he was seriously outraged.

"Sir, we didn't mean to … "

"You're fired! Pack your bags," Dreyer snarled. "I'm sending you back to South Africa."

"But, sir, you can't do that!" said Betoger, drawing on heretofore untapped courage. *"Please* don't send us back," he blinked, trying to hold back the tears. "I promise I'll never do anything like it again. Never. I swear. But please don't send us back." The pleading and grovelling went on until Dreyer relented and banned them to the Koevoet satellite base at Ongwediva. Before they could draw a sigh of relief, he pointed a finger at them and sighted down it. "If I see either of you, or even *hear* anything about you, you're fired, and that's a promise. Now get the hell out of my sight!" Their exile lasted three months before Dreyer allowed them back to Okave.

Someone who blew up his own barracks, however innocently, was not the sort I was keen to see playing with one of my cameras. I held my breath until it was safely back on the table, then snatched it up and draped the sling over my neck. These guys were nice enough, but their exuberance tended to get out of hand at times.

> **Chris Ronne, Z1J-1:** "I woke up early and wanted to get going, so walked into the base to tell the ops room where we'd be working. When I got there, Betoger was talking to the journalist. I had a quick cup of coffee and as we walked back to the cars Betoger asked if we could invite him on our next deployment. 'Hy is allraait vir n Engelsman,' he said. ('He's alright for an Englishman.') I told him I'd think about it, though truthfully I wasn't keen on having an outsider with us, as one never knew if there was a hidden agenda.
>
> "We were the first group to pull out at about 0630, heading east along the Chandelier Road towards the Oshakati Cuca shop about four kilometres from Eenhana. My plan was to cut for spoor along a known infiltration route south of the road. We were still short of the cuca shop when my black group leader, who had amazing eyes, yelled to stop. He jumped out of the vehicle and ran back in the direction we had come from. After a close look at the ground, he identified seven to nine spoor, not more than five hours old, going south. I got on the FM to Zulu Lima and the main comms network to report what we had found, and then started the follow up."

Toit, still waiting for his cars to finish with their rebunkering, walked over to the ops room with Riaan de la Rosa, who had just returned from leave. I poured another cup of coffee and followed. Toit almost knocked me over as he and de la Rosa ran out.

"Lieutenant Ronne's found a fresh ambush site the terrs left this morning. They've got spoor just 15 minutes from here. You coming with us?"

Something I'd not felt before held me motionless for a second. *What was that?* I wondered, as whatever it was slipped away. I looked at Toit, who was waiting impatiently for an answer, shook my head and told him that I'd be riding out with the choppers when they were scrambled.

"Okay, see you later," and they went pounding down the muddy road to get their group saddled up and moving.

So what the hell's the matter with you? I thought. *You afraid of something? Oh right, sure,* I smirked in denial. *I just don't feel like it is all.*

J.C. Lesch, team leader, Zulu Juliet: "We were working on one of our cars at Eenhana, when Chris Ronne called and said they had hot spoor. We got going immediately and rushed down the Chandelier Road and into the bush.

Chris Ronne, Z1J-1: About three kilometres south of the road we came to a kraal complex. The spoorsnyers got very excited, saying the terrs had left in a hurry only 20 or 30 minutes earlier and that I should put the gunships on standby. Zulu Lima contacted me to say they were just five or six minutes behind us and that Toit and Lesch were also on the way.

Jack Bouwer, ZT-1: "We heard Z1J report spoor east of Eenhana, but we had picked up our own spoor that led north and were already following it. Three or four other teams were heading for them so we stayed with what we had."

I ducked into the radio room to check the grid reference of the teams that had called in, then stepped over to the air force tent, where the pilots were pulling on flight suits and shoulder holsters. The flight engineers were already out on the hardpan pre-flighting the helicopters. There was nothing to do now but wait for the word to go. "If they're that close, we should be in the air *now*," Dooley grumbled.

Sitting with the crews under the ever-present camouflage net, I swapped flying stories and other lies, checking my watch every two minutes and affecting an air of boredom. But feet tapped, crossed legs bounced up and down and hands made constant tiny adjustments to webbing and zippers, all in nervous anticipation of coming action. Or maybe it was only me. No matter how many times I did it, the heart started beating just a little faster, the palms became just a little damper, as the wait began. Only this time it was worse. I couldn't put my finger on it, but—*then what's the matter? I don't know, it's just that, I don't know—but I feel something. Something's wrong.*

Of three hand-cranked field telephones inside the air force ops room, only the one connected to the Koevoet ops room had any significance. The word to scramble would come over the Ops K radio net and then be passed to the pilots via that one special phone. To my ear, they sounded exactly the same, but for the air crews, each had its own distinctive and immediately recognizable tone. If the wrong one clattered during a conversation, the speaker would smoothly carry on. I never did get the hang of it. Every ring would have my head swivelling round to stare at the open door to the ops room.

"Army ops," someone would say good-naturedly at my sudden start.

"Right," I'd say, and slide back from the edge of my chair.

Chris Ronne, Z1J-1: "The spoor went due east and then swung to the northeast. Two of us established the main direction, while Betoger in Z1J-4 and Theron in Z1J-2 headed east-southeast. By this time we were in very thick bush and I called them back to cover my left flank. They were on their way when Zulu Lima's lead car arrived and I told him to move his entire team to my left as well. He had just taken his position when Betoger came out of the bush about five metres from him. We later established that the terr was lining up on ZL-1 when Betoger pulled in between them. There was no missing at that range."

Theron De Wit, Z1J-2: "Ronne ordered me and Betoger to move forward with our cars. Betoger was about 100 metres ahead of me when his car was hit through the front left window just ahead of the mirror."

J.C. Lesch, ZJ-1: "It wasn't long before we found Z1J's spoorsnyers. Betoger's car was on my left and Porky on the other side of him. Just as we stopped, there was a loud *BANG!* as Betoger's car was hit with an RPG. Gunfire was heavy and I sent Porky forward. Less than a minute later, I got a call on the radio from him. 'Lesch, Lesch, Porky.' 'Go,' I answered. 'I think I've been shot!' he said. I asked where he'd been hit and where he was. There was a long pause. The next voice on the radio was his driver. 'Sante Porky hy's geskiet ek dink hy's dood!' Porky's been shot and I think he's dead!'"

Chris Ronne, Z1J-1: "My driver raced forward and hit the biggest tree in the area, leaving us with the front wheels off the ground and stuck in the middle of the contact area. Cars from Zulu Juliet and Zulu Quebec arrived, everyone shooting towards where the RPG had been fired, adding to the fire from my team and ZL-1. His car was only about five metres from mine. I jumped out and ran for it. With all the gunfire, those five metres felt like 100. I got to his car and between me and Toit, we managed to restore some order and call for a casevac."

One of the pilots was in the middle of a story when the telephone rang. He stopped and heads lifted, waiting. We heard the radio operator answer. He came running out.

"SCRAMBLE! THEY'VE HIT AN AMBUSH! THEY NEED GUNSHIPS AND CASEVACS NOW!"

Chairs screeched backward on the concrete as everything else was forgotten and three crews sprinted the 100 metres for the choppers, holding on to flapping equipment and struggling with zippers on the run. *It's happened. Whatever it is, it's happened,* as I ran behind Dooley.

Rick Dooley: "I clearly recall that day. Despite our incessant requests to get in the air, they were ambushed prior to calling us out. When it came through, we scrambled to the already prepared helicopters. I buckled up, hit the starter and rejoiced in the whine of the turbine engine as she came to life, the blades gathering momentum in concert with the adrenaline pumping through our veins."

Then we were there and settling in, the helicopters coming alive, trembling and shaking as checklists were completed. A final thumbs-up from the flight engineers sent the ungainly machines taxiing one by one out of the revetments and onto the runway. A rolling take-off, then the tails came up and we were airborne, noses tucked down and racing southeast just above the trees.

Something *was* wrong. This time it was all different. Terribly different. I knew it, felt it in my bones. What had happened out there? Okay, people were hurt, but how many? How badly? And the worst question of all: did I know them? Some indefinable dark monster had slipped into my chest, claws grabbing and slowly tightening.

Relax. Everything's okay. It's only because it's the first time since you were hit. Take it easy. Do something.

I bent over my cameras and gave the lenses a final wipe, opening Velcro pouches on the camera vest to double check which held the colour film and which the black and white. I clenched the aching hand, willing it to feel and work, my breath starting to come in short jerks. Finally, I took the headset, settled it over my ears and reached up to plug in the jack.

Dooley thumbed the mike button, his voice distant and metallic. "Sounds bad," turning his dark visored helmet towards me. "They're saying they hit an ambush and took some casualties."

Whatever had been building in me started to accelerate. "How bad?" wondering at the sound of my voice. *Why was it suddenly effort to talk?*

"Really bad."

The monster I now knew for what it was grabbed hold inside my chest and squeezed. My words, even allowing for the distortion of the intercom system, came through strained and tight. "How far out are we?"

"Five minutes."

Sitting on the aft-facing seat, I watched Grobbelaar, the flight engineer, as he leaned across the machine gun, scanning the bush and trees flashing under us, his face a blank. How could he look like that? Didn't he feel what I was feeling? Was my own face as blank? Whatever had crawled into my chest was really there now, squeezing harder. I twisted around to stare out the Plexiglas nose.

This is part of what you came for, boy, I started telling myself. *This is what you came for.*

We banked sharply, and I saw smoke from a white phosphorus grenade billowing out of the bush about two kilometres in front of us. Coming up was an open, grassy pan surrounded by thick bush. There they were, half a dozen Casspirs and Wolf Turbos scattered across it. As we decelerated and began a straight-in approach, the other two choppers broke off to set up top cover orbits. Then dust and grass were blowing away under the down-wash of the blades, and we bumped and settled heavily. I scrambled out, squinting against the stinging sand, latched the door and ran towards the nearest cars. Dooley immediately lifted off behind me.

Toit was standing on top of his car, handset against his ear, his face set in an expression I'd not seen before. He pointed with a jerk of his free hand towards the rear of a Casspir at right angles to his own. Gathered around the back, a dozen trackers stared inside. They made way for me as I came up.

A body lay on the narrow floor, head towards me. Theron De Wit kneeled straight-armed above it, pressing powerfully and rhythmically on the chest. Ryno Botha, ZQ's medic, had the head tilted back and at every fourth push covered the open mouth with his own, filling the lungs, then pressing his fingers in search of a carotid pulse.

God, don't let me know him, I thought stupidly, as though it would make it less real, *just don't let me know him.*

Theron motioned for help, and two trackers climbed quickly inside. Each took an arm to help lift the unconscious body from the cramped car. Above, two helicopters orbited, their turbines and slapping blades adding to the screech of radios and idling diesel engines on the ground. Only the sound of voices was absent as we all watched silently.

Theron de Wit, Z1J-2: "During the contact the number 4 car had radioed that a shirumbu was injured, but there was no way I could get to him. When the firing stopped, somebody ordered me to fall back to an open area where I could help. He was unconscious when I got there, but I couldn't see any wounds. It wasn't until we moved him out of the car that I saw a bullet hole in the upper side of his back. There was no exit wound so I was sure the bullet had hit his heart or punctured a main artery. He had died within a minute or two from massive internal bleeding."

Take a photo. No. Come on, isn't this part of it? Take your pictures. I can't. It's too private. I can't do it. I twisted away, not wanting to see, feeling for the first time like an intruder, a filthy, horrible voyeur. When I turned back, he was face down and Simon, ZQ's black medic, was cutting the shirt up the back. The shirt came off, and I saw the two closely-spaced bullet holes in his side. As they pulled him back over, his head rolled to the side, blood smearing at the corner of his mouth.

Oh, God, no, not Porky! Not quiet, skinny 19-year-old Porky. I was just talking with him! And as they kept working on him, I had to walk away, joining the knot of men who stood stiffly and quietly to one side.

Ryno knelt at Porky's head, one hand behind the neck, leaning down to fill lungs that still refused to work on their own. Theron straddled Porky's chest, crossed hands driving downward over the heart. Simon lifted an arm to wrap it with a blood-pressure cuff and listened with his stethoscope, all of them working with silent desperation. Above, helicopters still orbited protectively in the clear morning sky.

Simon placed his fingertips on Porky's forehead and raised an eyelid with his thumb. He covered the eye with the other hand, then quickly removed it. The pupils were fixed and dilated. He spoke quietly to the other two. Theron lifted his hands from the thin chest and stood, swinging one leg over the body. Ryno looked up, his eyes stricken and unbelieving. He looked back at the body and slowly rose to his feet, wiping Porky's blood from his own lips.

Then Dooley's chopper was landing again. Seven Ovambos and South Africans reached down to gather the body into a bier of black and white arms.

With Toit cradling Porky's head, they stumbled towards the Alouette. I ran after them, camera snapping in the blur of sound and movement, the body anonymous. Only a pair of green-stockinged feet protruded from the cluster of men. As I neared the helicopter, I saw another body already on the floor, soaked in blood from the waist down, the head turned away. They laid Porky gently on his back next to Dooley, his head against the seat I had held on the way in. In the downwash of sand, dust and grass, I stared at him inside the Plexiglas shroud as the chopper lifted and turned towards Eenhana.

> **Rick Dooley:** "We landed and the first body was loaded in the back, blood gushing over the floor. He'd been hit in the lower abdomen with an RPG and I could see his internal organs. He was still alive but unconscious. Then Porky was loaded in front. I remember Jim standing behind the men, the expression on his face mirroring the human tragedy being played out. We raced back to Eenhana, our friends now the flotsam of war, understanding how fleeting life can be. On arrival, the medical teams were waiting and jumped into the helicopter. Porky gazed at them through dead eyes, his head lolling in time to the helicopter's movements as medics frantically pumped drips into the other body."

When Dooley lifted off, I looked around and saw de la Rosa, shot through both arms, face slack with pain and shock, supported from behind by one of the Ovambos. Theron was tying a tourniquet around his upper right arm. Three other men with minor shrapnel wounds were being treated by Simon and Ryno. They would go out on the next choppers. *What the fuck did they hit?*

Toit was still on the radio, talking rapidly with the ops officer at Eenhana. He took a deep breath as he slipped the headset around his neck. "Porky's dead," he said with cold fury. "Betoger was hit with an RPG that came through the front of his car. Three of the Ovambos are wounded. De la Rosa's hit. They rolled right into the fucking ambush. Another car was shot out with heatstrims. The trackers have found where the terrs were waiting. We've got at least seven spoor. You staying or you want out on the next chopper?"

"No," I shook my head, "I'm coming with you."

"Porky called his own casevac," Toit said as we started rolling. "Right after they hit the ambush, I heard him say over the radio that he'd been shot. I told him I'd already called for a casevac and asked him who'd been hurt, and he said it was himself. Then one of the Ovambos got on the radio and said, "Hurry! The shirumbu is dying. He needs help."'

Lesch's voice came over the speakers, saying they were returning to the ambush site. The next report was that they'd found two bodies, along with a PKM, AK-47 and the empty launcher for the RPG-75 that hit Betoger's car. Zulu Juliet's trackers had picked up another spoor leading away from the contact area.

An hour later, Toit heard the update from Eenhana and looked down at me from his position behind the guns. "Betoger's dead. Nothing could have saved him." Then, a few minutes later, "You're really quiet today. You okay?" I nodded.

Because this isn't the way it happens. Because someone's going to tell me that they'll be okay, that this isn't real. Betoger's the one who pleaded with the boss to stay, he can't be dead. And Porky's not really dead, either. I was talking to them this morning.

"Are you sure?" Another nod. "Want to go back?"

"No, I'm okay. No sweat," I said, hardly recognizing my own voice.

Jack Bouwer, ZT-1: "We listened to the other groups report about Betoger and Porky, but we were already near the yati and decided to stay on the spoor we had. At about 1300 my group and Attie's ZU were in voorsny when I heard 'Contact! Contact!' on the radio. It was Angus and they had just killed two insurgents. Soon after this I hit another one hiding under a bush and carrying an AK-47 with a heatstrim on the end. When we pulled him out, he was badly wounded. He told my senior Ovambo warrant officer, Johnny Mwashitinayo, they were sappers and their mission was to plant landmines and blow up power lines. He admitted that there was a cache not far away, and that they had planted a mine on the yati. Following his directions, our two teams uncovered a lot of TNT and detonators and lifted the mine."

Soon after the ambush, Zulu 2 radioed Toit to say Brigadier Dreyer didn't want any of the seven making it back to Angola. "What the fuck do you think we're doing," Toit snapped. There was no question in anyone's mind about these people escaping.

Thirty minutes later, we hit the first one. Perhaps he knew there would be no surrendering because he came out of the bush squeezing the trigger of his AK-47, shots going wild and blowing out one of our tyres before a dozen bullets took him down. His head snapped back as he half twisted and dropped. An RPG-75 rolled away from him, its shoulder strap shot in two. The head pressed forward into the blood-spattered sand as one leg drew up.

I followed the trackers out the door and turned towards the scene, flinching at the unexpected burst of automatic fire. It was from Betoger's driver, who had been wounded by the RPG but refused to be casevacked. Face contorted and eyes narrowed to slits, he emptied his magazine into the dying man, the high-velocity bullets plucking and lifting the camouflage uniform away from the shivering body like a narrow, concentrated wind rippling across it.

Betoger had been his friend.

By mid-afternoon, I had forced myself out of the car alongside the trackers. It was the only way.

> **Theron de Wit, Z1J-2:** "That evening I spoke to the doctor in Eenhana and he told me that Betoger was so strong his heart just keep on beating, but the injuries were so great there was nothing they could do to save him."

> **Rick Dooley:** "The only way of coping was to keep busy. After each mission we immediately refuelled, rearmed and briefed at base as we knew that the Koevoet teams would not let one insurgent survive. We hunted them systematically over the next few days, killing them one by one, until all were accounted for."

The third day after the ambush, the last of the ambushers fell under Koevoet's guns. It was rumoured that at least one had tried to surrender, but in a contact, someone explained patiently, in the *confusion* and everything, well …

Beneath the camouflage net of the air force canteen at Eenhana, an exhausted and filthy group of policemen bowed their heads in memory of Porky and Betoger. They would not be spoken of tonight, but as heads and cans of beer lifted to offer a final toast, eyes blinking back what was there, something escaped to trace a furrow down a dust-caked cheek.

16

Questions and Clichés

So why was I there? I asked myself often enough and was asked over and over when I returned. It seemed such a simple question that there should have been an easy answer. But there wasn't, there really wasn't. Posturing? That's what a lot of it was, I suppose: I'm here, I'm cool. Though, God knew (I hoped), there was more to it than that. It was convenient to pass off my presence there as a search for the truth of a little-understood African war; that was actual, that I was doing. It wasn't until later that I realised I had gone there to learn the truth of myself as well. All the questions and clichés of "grace under fire" were part of the search, and when I finally thought I had it, had passed my own examination, there was a sense of belonging, with all that went with it That featureless spot on a world map my eyes would once have passed over without hesitation became the centre of my universe.

Acceptance and belonging didn't come easily, but they came. Of course, it helped being a little unique. I was a foreigner and a journalist (or a writer when I was feeling particularly pretentious) who went into the bush with them week after week, unarmed and dripping with cameras; which made me a novelty, and a little special, but special only in a different way from anyone else who was there or passed through. I had come of my own volition to live amongst them, to tell a story from an insider's view, a story that couldn't be told honestly any other way. Or at least that's what I said I believed. I came looking for what I was born to, and that I believed totally.

In my time there I saw only one other journalist arrive to take the measure of the war. He came escorted from Windhoek, inarticulate and posturing with the best of us. It was understandable posturing, but I didn't like it or him.

I'd just been wounded for the second time by then, and he avoided me like I carried the plague, eyeing the bloody bandage distastefully and saying nothing, at least to me. I wanted to know why they let him in: this was my story, my people, he was a trespasser, but I kept my mouth shut, hoping childishly that when they took him out it would be a dry run. Contacts were my province, goddammit, he didn't have the right to one; I'd earned them with my sweat and fear and blood. But the second day in the bush, the group he was with found a single spoor and there was the inevitable conclusion.

When his escort officer, waiting in Oshakati, heard about it over the radio, he decided his boy had seen as much as he needed and sent a chopper to collect him. Big Bez from Zulu Whiskey said when he was told there was a helicopter in-bound, he had his gear stacked in about 30 seconds flat; he was ready to get out of there, no shit. Smart man. When Bez told me that, he laughed conspiratorially in a way that made me feel better. Not a lot, but some; I was too greedy, too selfish, too puffed up with my own self-imagined uniqueness to be entirely appeased.

A few days later, we saw the piece he had written. I couldn't read the Afrikaans, but the photos told me more about him than the copy. After the contact, he'd posed on one knee next to the body, holding the dead insurgent's rifle. The photo was there, implicit in its suggestion. It was good for another laugh, and I was perhaps less than charitable, mentioning it more often than was necessary, with all my own implicit suggestions about myself. Just who did he think he was fooling? I wanted to know. Of course, I was too cool: *I* wouldn't have had a photo like that taken of *me*.

Until I thought about it, and saw that he was behaving only slightly more obtrusively than I, perhaps. Just who did I think *I* was fooling, I should have asked. It was still *I'm here, I'm cool,* and I guess he had as much right to it as anyone else. But I saw in the photo (would the article have exonerated him?) the pose of white superiority (who did he think were the heart of Koevoet, did most of the killing *and* dying?) that many within the unit—yes, even here— believed as well, but were too involved, too sensitive, perhaps even too aware of the contradictions to flaunt. Still, he was neither the polarized kaffir-baiting thug nor the hands-thrown-in-the-air moral hypocrite. In fact, he was probably more like all of us, black and white, than I, at least, was prepared to admit at the time.

Out of the bush, you never really thought about dying. Of course, it was possible, but you never thought it could happen to you. Getting hurt?—well, who didn't get hurt occasionally? No big thing, you said pompously after it happened the first time. But even then, you never thought about getting hurt seriously. That and dying just didn't exist. They did, of course, but were so deeply repressed they couldn't touch you. Most of the time, anyway. Sure, there were times you were frightened (frightened? try terrified), and it was okay to mention it—as long as you didn't mention it too often. "Yeah, I'm afraid sometimes," Bez said. "Heatstrims, those scare me." And that was the only time I heard it, at the end of a drinking session that suddenly turned serious. But in the morning it didn't exist again, and good manners prevented pursuing it further.

"Aren't you scared?" Jackie asked me not long after we'd met, and I laughed and said, "All the time." But that was before I understood what he was really talking about, before the naiveté of a schoolboy adventure wore off and it became something else entirely. Man, was I dumb. Later, I felt it so badly on two occasions—after Porky and Betoger were killed, then again at Ohangwena—that I was crippled; not by the fear of dying, but by the need to *live*. Yet afterward, I understood that I had never been so aware of being alive. Never. Another cliché, but there it was.

"Violence freak, adrenaline junkie," said an accusing journalist disapprovingly after I'd come out, which wasn't entirely correct, nor completely wrong either, as far as it went, but he would never really know. It was certainly the fashionable thing to say, and I understood why he had to say it. As a political child of the Sixties, though, at least he could have smiled just a little when I agreed by quoting Mick Jagger at him: "Violence gives you a buzz." I was ready to drill him with sharper homilies from his folk heroes of the peace-and-flowers era until I saw it would be wasted effort; he simply wasn't prepared to acknowledge the paradox, and instead glared at me with furious self-righteousness. Had he been more honest, he would have understood that we were co-sinners. It wasn't my covering the war that got to him; it was whom I chose to go with. Real journalists pick their sides more carefully, is what he meant to say. And sides, of course, was what it was all about.

Had he been willing to listen, I would have tried to explain that in some ways, it was all pure fantasy; since when did middle-aged American writers find themselves with unheard-of dispensations that allowed them to go charging through the bush of Namibia and Angola with an elite counterinsurgency unit? But the fantasy was real; sometimes altogether too real. And that was the opiate: the proof of the risk.

And risk, of course, was what it was all about, too.

There is no one who goes into it—chasing war or adventure (war correspondent, if you please)—who doesn't get at least a tingle from being seen as different, as somehow a little special. "Boy, it must take real balls to do that. You wouldn't get *me* out there." And you smile or frown and say, no, it's just a job, you know, denying the image as custom requires. Which of course only plants it all the more securely, convincing them that not only are you insanely brave, but modest too, and wrong on both counts, if they only knew. Sometimes, for those who matter, you try to explain that what they do is what requires the courage: a family, a secure nine to five and all the rest you've run away from all your life. You tell them that what you do requires no courage because it is an obsession over which you have no control. It's not courage, but an overwhelming *need*. And because they haven't the need themselves, cannot conceive of a reason for having it, you're stuck with the image they've conferred. Which is exactly what you wanted all along anyway, however fraudulent.

Every man in the world hugs to himself a secret image of who he is or what he wants to be. It's not given to many to take it out, give it a dusting and look at it critically. In the end, it was everything I'd hoped for, and more, and still not nearly enough.

Piet Cronje and I walked away from where we had pitched camp at the foot of the tall, granite outcropping. We followed the cold, clear stream that gurgled through the rocky, alkaline desert of the Kaokoveld. To the west and north, mountains rose sharp-spined and purple in the fading light. Somewhere among them was the source of the brook that tumbled along the deeply eroded defile. The brutal starkness of the terrain, so unlike the flat, monotonous bush of central and eastern Ovambo 160 kilometres to the east, was enough to take the breath away: a land designed for awful contemplation.

We stopped alongside a deep pool and stared for a long moment at the darkening moonscape. Piet hunkered down, the rifle that seemed a part of him resting across heavy thighs.

"I worked out here for almost four years," he said, breaking the silence. "Most of it on foot." His mutilated right hand released the rifle for a moment and traced an arc along the horizon. "Good places to get ambushed."

I waited. Piet didn't volunteer a lot. "Were you?" I finally prompted.

He nodded. "Walked into one not so far from here. Nineteen gooks." His eyes moved slowly across the land before he stood and balanced the rifle over his shoulder. "Started shooting right in front of us," he said matter-of-factly, pointing to a stunted bush not more than 15 metres away.

I turned with him and we started back. "So what happened?" I asked, unable to hold back the question.

"No cover, no place to go except forward. We floored seven. I killed four myself. Lost one of my boys, five wounded."

Silence returned. There was only the grate of our boots on loose shale and sand. The stocky figure next to me paused and we looked back at the jagged, silhouetted mountains. "The worst one was right after I started working out here. It was about this time of day, and we were driving along a trail out there." His chin lifted towards the mountains. "There was a dry river bed on our right, a tall *kopje*—a rocky hill—on the other side. I was at the back of the Casspir when we were hit. Two RPGs went through the front of the car, and two cars behind us were shot out. My car was already burning as we went off the trail and into the riverbed. I thought the driver was doing it, trying to find cover. The rest of us got out and started firing towards the *kopje*. The driver and gunner didn't come out, so I went back in to get them. I was going to pull the driver out first, but when my hand went halfway through his neck, I knew he was dead. When I pulled the gunner out, his left leg was gone and the right one was hanging on with just a little muscle.

"I put a tourniquet around the stump, then cut off what was left of the right one and tied that off, too, and got a drip into him. The fire in the car made a good target, and the gooks started shooting mortar bombs at us. I had to crawl back to the other cars to treat the wounded and start drips for the ones who needed them. The terrs finally stopped shooting, but we didn't know if they had run away or were moving around to hit us from another direction. We had to wait there all night before the casevac Pumas got to us." He shook his head and looked at me. "The gunner died. I thought I could save him, but he died before the choppers arrived."

We started back down, loose rocks skittering away under our feet. Scattered across the sand of our oasis camp below, cooking fires glowed red and orange, sparks twisting frantically to disappear into the cold night air. Halfway down the slope, he coughed into his claw of a hand and cleared his throat.

"But that was when I was still a youngster," he said shyly, embarrassed at having talked so much.

"How old are you now, Piet?" I asked, the story still echoing in my head.

"Twenty-three," he said, shifting the rifle in his arms.

17

Blood Moon

Had I deployed with Zulu Whiskey as planned, I would have missed the first part of it altogether. But they were pulling out a day early and, in a classic example of how the banal can embrace fate, my laundry wasn't ready. Getting dirty, fine, that I was used to; but starting off with stinking clothes was just too much. Bez, ZW's team leader, pondered my fastidiousness for a moment and offered an easy solution. "Catch a ride with Lesch and Zulu Juliet tomorrow," he said. "They'll be RV-ing with us in the veld, and you can join us there."

When I asked Lesch if he'd mind my hitching a lift, he said, "Sure, Jim, no problem," and Wednesday morning my laundry was ready and so was I. But then one of his cars had a turbocharger problem, and off it went to Zulu 12 for repair. Lunchtime at the garage came and went but a compressor gremlin still had the mechanics scratching their heads. Lesch finally said the hell with it, we'll take our time working up to Ohangwena, wait there for the car and RV with Bez on Thursday. Which was what we did, pulling off the tar road at the small Security Branch base late in the afternoon. And that's when the next seemingly inconsequential step towards what was coming clicked firmly into place.

> **J.C. Lesch, ZJ-1:** "When we arrived at Ohangwena, Zulu Lima had taken our usual spot right outside the wall, so we set up our TB about 50 meters south of them near the Kwanyama Tribal District offices."

An hour before sunset, Lesch's fourth car, turbocharger restored to good health, arrived and cooking fires were soon going. Waiting for them to burn down to coals, we slipped into the base for a beer and a shower. What a pleasure, I thought, even if it did seem an unnecessary luxury. Standing under the trickle of cold water, I noted shrapnel holes through the thin walls of the toilet and shower block, evidence of the attack right after I'd left eleven months earlier. No one had been injured, but the damage was enough to stir the imagination.

Afterwards, we sat on the concrete patio and accepted beers from the young base commander. The pigs I'd seen the year before were gone—most likely on a braai—and the dogs older and more restrained. I cast a wary eye for Bobba the grumpy baboon and spotted him and his companion near a tree on the east side of the base. The semi-circle of scars he'd left on my arm was a reminder of that first week with Koevoet. "Africa's a tough place," Marius Brand said instructively afterwards. I never anticipated just how tough subsequent lessons would be. That I'd managed to stumble more or less successfully from one test to the next was undoubtedly a source of wonder for all concerned.

But even now, after all that I had seen and shared, there remained a subtle barrier that kept me truly apart. I could joke with them, and my presence was no longer considered remarkable, but I was still an *uitlander*. Aside from being a non-combatant—a waste of space in the crowded cars—there was also the language. Amongst the Ovambos I met, only Jerry Mbwale knew more than a pinch of English, and of the whites just a handful were completely at ease in the language. Often what I perceived as cool reserve was shyness about stepping outside the comfort of Afrikaans.

Although I had a nodding acquaintance with most of the teams, it wasn't until I deployed with one that they became more than faces and passing hellos. Each had its own personality. One might enjoy a reputation for aggressiveness and cold-blooded efficiency, another for the skills of its spoorsnyers, yet another for being laid back and easy going. There were high scorers, usually commanded by grizzled veterans in their mid-twenties who had learned their trade under founder members; there were others that slogged along, seldom shining but doing the grinding, dirty and dangerous work that contributed to Koevoet's reputation. Each was a unique micro-culture within the Koevoet subculture; each a fascinating study of men at war. Tonight, I contemplated Zulu Juliet's car commanders as I cleaned my cameras and nursed a beer.

Marius Clark—another "Apie"—stood inside the wire cage, feeding potato crisps to two vervet monkeys perched on his shoulders. Their shrill scolding when the pack ran empty set him to clucking soothingly as he opened another. Short and round and sporting a goatee that looked as out of place on an otherwise beardless face as the pistol on his hip, the 28 year-old's placid nature made him the unlikeliest candidate for Koevoet membership of anyone I had met in the unit.

Charles Labello, on secondment from the SADF, was the team's SAMS ops medic. Of medium height, with curly, black hair, he was the son of an

Italian immigrant to South Africa. Half of his voluntary one year assignment to Koevoet was already completed. When the next six months were over, he told me, he was going back to South Africa to continue his university studies. After that, he'd be pleased never to see the operational area again.

The new cop on the beat was Boeta, who had joined the team after Porky's death. The tallest and youngest of the car commanders, he came across as the prototypical farm boy. Still learning the job and eager to prove himself in the way of new guys everywhere, he approached everything with single-minded determination.

Acting Inspector-Lieutenant Victor Nghihepa, the team's senior Ovambo, sat alongside Lesch and they discussed the next day's plan. A teetotaller, he declined a beer, and then returned to the TB. "Very serious guy," Lesch said. "Keeps everyone on their toes."

Blond and carrying too much weight from the beer, Lesch was one of those with a quick, easy laugh and a joke for almost any occasion. No one could ever really accuse him of being too serious. A four-year Koevoet veteran, he had taken over as Zulu Juliet's group leader only three months earlier when Herman Claassen, the previous commander, had been badly wounded by a POM-Z.

Still convalescing, "Claassie" was always there to meet them when they returned from the bush, leaning on his crutches and favouring the broken leg with the fresh, shiny scar tissue. In spite of a fractured wrist and serious nerve damage that kept both his forearm and lower leg in steel and plastic braces, he was constantly pestering Dreyer for permission to return to ops. It was a long time afterward when he told me what had happened.

Claassie Claassen, team leader, ZJ: "We were near Eheke that morning, about 12 kilometres north of the yati, when we picked up two spoor going south. As we closed the distance my old team, Chris Ronne's Z1J, joined us on the follow-up. At around noon I scrambled the gunships—I remember Captain Koch was in one of them—but the Swaps kept changing direction and anti-tracking. I was on the ground with the radio to keep the rest of the group updated. Then it was a running spoor and I ran back to the car to get my 9mm. I rejoined them and just as I jumped over an old fallen tree, one of the trackers to my right tripped the POM-Z. I remember a loud *bang* similar to a hand grenade, a lot of dust and then I was on the ground and people were moaning all around me. I had shrapnel in my right arm, more in my abdomen, and my leg was broken."

Theron de Wit, Z1J-2: "There was an explosion, smoke and sand in the air, and then a deathly stillness. When the dust settled I saw 11 wounded comrades scattered around the path. I got to Claassie, saw it was very serious and immediately began applying first aid. He had been with our team before he took over ZJ, so I knew him well and was very worried. He asked me how it looked and I lied, assuring him that it was okay, that he was in good hands."

Claassie Claassen, ZJ-1: "I told Theron that my leg was stuffed, but he kept trying to draw my attention to the right hand that was bleeding where shrapnel had gone through it. It wasn't until I was on the gunship when I started feeling pain. Every time the helicopter turned at a certain angle, it felt like a hammer hitting my leg. At Eenhana, we were all stabilised and then flown by Dakota to Ondangwa. That's where the pain in my stomach became severe and I could not breathe properly. The doctor looked at the X-rays and said they'd have to shorten my colon because of shrapnel damage. The next day, I was flown to 1 Military Hospital. One of the trackers lost a leg from the POM-Z and another died a year later from his wounds."

I never got to know Claassie well, but he always struck me as genuine, committed and deeply caring about his men and the civilian population. I still remember him standing in front of the storerooms that day, crutch under one arm and waving with the other as we pulled away from the empty parade ground.

Walking back to the TB after our beers, our attention was captured by a deep-orange full moon pushing its way out of the horizon. "That's a hunter's moon where I come from," I said. "Blood moon," someone corrected me.

J.C. Lesch, ZJ-1: "Because our weekly rations included fresh meat that wouldn't keep, we usually had a braai the first night of a deployment. Braais are part of our culture and we Afrikaners like our meat well done. Jim was treading on holy ground when he said we didn't know how to properly barbeque good steak. 'The only way to eat beef,' this uitlander told us, 'is knock its horns off, wipe its arse and put it on the table.' Naturally, we ignored him and kept the meat sizzling over the fire."

Lounging around the glowing embers, replete and mellow after our meal, we talked of this and that, the conversation always coming back to the intensity of the present infiltration. Lesch admitted there hadn't been anything like it for a long time. Even allowing for more than 200 Swapo already killed or captured since the beginning of January, Koevoet's losses of 15 dead and over 40 wounded were high.

"We're definitely bleeding this year," he said, "The ratio isn't good."

The moon was higher now, metamorphosed from orange to yellow to a silvery-white disk bright enough to throw shadows. Perfect in lighting the way for large groups crossing the cutline.

"You know, the gooks revved this place last year just a couple of days after you left," Lesch continued. "Two or three mortar bombs landed inside the base, and the water tank was hit with an RPG, but no one was hurt. Fourteen of the Swaps were killed on the follow-up the next day." It was a story I'd heard from Zulu Alpha's Thys Loedolff, who had set off from Eenhana with one Casspir packed with trackers to follow the spoor. Later, over beers at the Okave Club, Nella and Dean Viljoen had added their recollections of wading through shonas under fire, with Marius Brand giving covering fire.

"One mortar landed right behind the toilets and showers," said Lesch, "You see the holes in the walls?"

"Wouldn't have wanted to be sitting there when that happened," I laughed. Charles wondered aloud what would be the best thing to do in a mortar attack. "Lie down and don't move," I said, as if I knew what I was talking about. Looking at the large maroela tree spreading over us, I imagined mortar rounds exploding in the branches and shotgunning anything below. "But first get away from trees like these," I added off-handedly.

Lesch leaned forward to stir the coals. "They hit the place right after midnight. When the last mortar bomb landed, they tried a ground assault. Two of 'em were killed outside the walls, and the rest gapped it back into the bush. We found out later that their plans were to capture at least one white, load him in a Casspir, and force him to drive them back to Namakunde."

I stared into the embers and tried to imagine it. Explosions, streams of tracers crisscrossing in the night, murky figures slipping through mopani bush and high grass towards the base. *That would really be something,* I thought, regretting that I'd missed it.

Apie climbed under his mosquito net alongside the Blesbok, Charles and Lesch settled around the back. A Casspir was parked parallel 10 metres away, and I lay on my cot between the two, wrapping my shirt around the diesel-stained feather pillow. Boeta stretched out on his ground sheet between me and the others. The fire slowly died, talk of contacts and women and contacts and women dwindled with it.

"You know, it's probably about time for another rev here," said Lesch. "Full moon, middle of the infiltration. Never know." He laughed.

I zipped up my sleeping bag and looked at the sky. "Anyone know which of those two constellations is the Southern Cross?" I asked, pointing an arm overhead.

"It's that one, the lower one," said Boeta.

"No, it's the higher one," said Charles. We slept.

March 12, 1987

0330

The Typhoon unit of more than 40 men probably crossed the yati not long after the moon was high enough to light the way. Even with the weight of mortars, base plates, ammunition, machine guns and RPGs, they would have been in position not long after we dropped off to sleep. One cluster of three mortars and crews took its place in scattered mopani bush a few hundred metres to our west, the range to the Kwanyama Tribal offices probably paced off long before. The second crew, tasked with bombarding the base, set up somewhere to the northwest with two tubes. They would not be as accurate, over-estimating the range by just enough to send their rounds at least 50 metres farther than planned. By design and accident, there were now two 82mm and three 60mm tubes aligned on Zulu Juliet's TB. The rest of the enemy force comprised an assault group that slipped into position east of the base, ready to go in as soon as the mortars stopped firing. As in the attack a year earlier, one of the priorities was the capture of at least one white car commander and a Casspir.

Perhaps it was their enthusiasm or over-confidence that brought them too near the berm too soon, or possibly a simple error in navigation. Someone may have coughed, stumbled in the dark, dropped a piece of equipment. Whatever it was, the baboons saw or heard them. Alerted by Bobba and his mate's furious screams, a sentry spotted movement and opened fire, killing two insurgents carrying RPGs, and then another. Half a kilometre away, there must have been confusion at the unexpected sound of a machine gun. Surprise had been lost. From somewhere in the shadows, two PKMs opened fire on the base as the Cuban-trained mortar crews went into action, dropping rounds down the tubes as fast as they could.

I came awake as the first two shrieked out of the night, exploding on hard, packed clay somewhere behind me. My eyes snapped open to see streams of tracers flashing overhead from the north and east. Rolling off the cot in my sleeping bag, I thought, This really isn't happening. The guys in the base, they're just playing a practical joke, the bastards, and they better stop it right now. But it was no joke and it didn't stop.

> **J.C. Lesch, ZJ-1:** "I was awakened by a very loud explosion. I leaped from my bedroll and tried to work out what the hell it was. Then I heard the distinct sound of distant mortars being fired. *CHOONK! CHOONK!* and all hell broke loose! Suddenly there were white flashes everywhere. The explosions were all around us, some very close, and they kept coming down; you could hear the whine—*zzzzzzz*—as they fell and then see the white flashes of the explosions and feel an immediate slap of air from the concussions."

> **Marius "Apie" Clark, ZJ-2:** "I was woken by explosions very close and saw our buddies scrambling for cover. They were shouting, 'MORTARS!' and 'REV! REV!' I rolled out of my sleeping bag and under the Blesbok, ending up at about the middle of the vehicle right under the centre of the V-hull. A lot of our buddies were also there. Everyone was trying to get under cover, and I soon found myself being steadily pushed back until I was lying between the rear wheels."

Rounds were dropping right on top of us—*whu-WHUMP! whu-WHUMP!*— so near and closely spaced there was nothing to do but flatten against the ground. *whu-WHUMP!UMP! whu-WHUMP!* Close enough to feel the solid punch of shock waves through the ground and air, knowing to stand was to die and in the moments between explosions hearing the *crack!* of bullets and warbling whirr of shrapnel.

> **J.C. Lesch, ZJ-1:** "My first thought was to order everyone to get under the Blesbok and the Casspirs, but they were already taking cover wherever

possible. The explosions were so close together that the flashes were almost like a constant, bright light."

In their TB seven kilometres to the east, Zulu Bravo and its new 23-year-old team leader were shaken from their sleep.

Gavin Manning, Zulu Bravo commander: "I came awake, instantly alert. For a second I lay there, peering out from under my bivi and wondering what was wrong. Then to our west I recognized the unmistakable sounds of mortar rounds landing in quick succession, some louder and heavier than others, with the distinctive, sharper 'boommmm' of rocket propelled grenades punctuating the rest. I crawled out and saw white flashes lighting up the horizon. It had to be the Security Branch base at Ohangwena. Fuck, I thought, they're getting 60mm and 82mm mortars and RPGs. From around our TB there was muffled laughter and the odd *'Aauw haitee!'*—'Oh, man!'—exclamation each time another explosion flashed in the distance. They were excited, knowing there would be plenty of spoor and that it was going to be a busy day. I looked at my watch. Almost three hours before there would be enough light to find that spoor. I immediately started planning which way we'd go and ordered my senior Ovambo, Inspector Simon Hidimbwasha, to be ready to move at 0500. It would still be dark, but by dawn I wanted to be in position to intercept the terrs on their way back to Namakunde."

Michael "Peanuts" Kennard, ZU-4: "The day before we had gotten one kill about 20 klicks south of Ongiva, and then TB-ed near St Mary's Mission, just four of five kilometres northeast of 21D. We could clearly hear the mortars."

And the explosions kept coming, each one sending a hard ripple through the ground under my chest. I heard Lesch yell "JIM ARE YOU OKAY?" and yelling back "I'M OKAY!" only shit scared *whuWHUMP! WHUMP!* then Lesch again "GET UNDER THE CAR!" and screaming back "I'M OKAY HERE" knowing if I moved they would kill me, eyes squeezed shut, then one so close that everything went orange through my eyelids, the blast inflating the sleeping bag like a balloon and my left forearm suddenly gone numb and thinking it was from the concussion, no pain, just the concussion, it'll be all right in a moment. There was the hiss of tyres hit by shrapnel and over that the sound of a steam kettle high pitched and constant and at first I think a radiator's been holed but the cars are cold it can't be a radiator, it's someone screaming, someone's been hit…

> **J.C. Lesch, ZJ-1:** "About five of my spoorsnyers were with me under the Blesbok, and the explosions were coming even closer together, some so near that the concussion made you gasp for air. Then one exploded just behind us. Through the ringing in my ears there was a very load hissing noise from the rear tyre of the Blesbok. I was trying to figure out what it was when another one exploded right next to us and I was hurled against the rear diff and covered in dirt, feeling like hot lead had been poured over my back. I roared from the pain, just as another hit behind us and the men on that side were slammed against me and I went into the rear diff again."

> **Marius "Apie" Clark, ZJ-2:** "Mortars were exploding all around us and then one detonated so close I felt pain all over my body, with my upper body numb. I heard guys moaning around me, but there was nothing I could do because the mortars were still coming down."

A flare burst over the base, separating into three slowly descending lights, turning everything blood red around us. Oh shit, that's one of theirs, it's a Russian one not one of ours and then I recognized the sound of return fire from inside the base.

> **J.C. Lesch, ZJ-1:** "I could hear someone gurgling next to me and someone else screaming. I rolled over and in the flashes saw that it was Stephanus, one of my trusted old hands, next to me, blood gushing from a severed artery in his neck. I tried to stop the bleeding, but then his body went limp and he stopped breathing. Behind me someone else had blood frothing in his lungs. It was Johannes. I tried to help him but couldn't find a pulse. I was alive because they had taken the blast and shrapnel. The mortars were still coming down and if I was going to live … I pulled the body of my friend Stephanus close to me, and then I lost consciousness."

Still in my sleeping bag, I lizard-crawled under the car and bumped into someone not moving and a couple of feet away the sound of ragged, wet, shuddering breaths, blood bubbling in chest and throat. "IS ANYONE HURT

THERE ARE TWO BAD ONES HERE!" I screamed, and Apie shouted back "LESCH IS HIT! I'M HIT! LESCH IS HURT BAD!" and Boeta yells "I'M HIT BUT I'M OKAY" and I yelled back "WHERE'S CHARLES IS HE OKAY WE NEED HIM!" and Apie, "I DON'T KNOW I CAN'T FIND HIM I DON'T KNOW WHERE HE IS!" and I started wondering if the terrs were coming in on the ground, how many of them, and I thought of all the weapons still in the cars. "DOES ANYONE HAVE WEAPONS?" Then some of the trackers were firing, aiming into the bush and grass to the south and east, yellow-orange muzzle flashes punctuating the dark and finally there was a lull in the explosions. I rose to one knee—*whu-whump!*—and I'm down again, seeing streams of tracers coming in, searching, lower and lower.

Marius "Apie" Clark, ZJ-2: "Some of the buddies had run through the mortars to the Casspirs and I heard guns on the cars firing."

Fire from the trackers and from inside the base was going back along the same paths and then there's no more incoming and someone was shouting in Afrikaans, "Nee skiet! Nee skiet!" Stop firing! and bit by bit it tapered off and suddenly everything was still. We wait, the only sound the moans of the wounded. I looked at my watch, angling it to catch the light from the moon. The face was grey with cordite. Wetting a thumb, I wiped some of it off and saw the time was just after 0400. The attack had lasted more than 20 minutes. Stephanus, the Ovambo I had bumped into under the Blesbok, is dead, the other, Johannes, is badly wounded and unconscious.

Marius "Apie" Clark, ZJ-2: "When the mortars stopped, I got out from under the Blesbok with some guys from our team and started looking for everybody. One of the trackers was lying where I'd first crawled to when the attack started. Shrapnel had been diverted down on him and he was dead."

J.C. Lesch, ZJ-1: "The next thing I can recall was hearing voices. We were well outside the base and at first I was afraid that the terrs had been bold enough to attack us on the ground. Then I realised they were speaking Afrikaans. I got up and starting checking who was wounded and who was okay when I saw the tail of an 82mm mortar sticking out of the ground less than two metres from where I'd been lying. If the terrs hadn't forgotten to remove the safety pin from the detonator cap it would certainly have killed me."

"Where's Charles?" I asked, wondering at the calmness in my voice. "We need him."

"Maybe he's already gone over to the sick-bay," Apie says just as quietly.

We climbed cautiously to our feet and looked towards the base. Something was burning, flames reaching high above the berm. The smell and smoke of cordite hung everywhere in the moonlight. All around us are shallow, frosty-white depressions left by exploding mortar rounds. Someone would later count almost 200 impact points. The tyres on the Casspir and Blesbok either side of my cot are flat, and the windows starred from shrapnel. Bright gouges show on the armoured sides.

"Careful where you walk," Boeta says, flashing a dim torch around us. The plastic tail fins of three unexploded pencilstrims, anti-personnel rifle grenades, protrude from the hard ground; the insurgents had forgotten to unscrew the safety caps. Within 20 metres of where we'd lain, at least five mortar rounds, half buried, had also failed to detonate.

Christ.

It's only when I try to help move Johannes from under the car that I realise there's something wrong with my hand. I can make a fist, but the hand drops at the end of the wrist and the fingers won't open. In the light of Boeta's torch I'm surprised to see a puckered and bloody hole high on the forearm. *Shit. I've been hit.* I pull a camera from my duffel bag and awkwardly fit the flash to it. The duffel bag has at least half-a-dozen holes through it. My cot and the shirt I'd used as a pillow case are snowy with feathers blown out of the pillow by shrapnel. It took a long time to appreciate that what made those holes had passed barely a foot to either side of me. How many were even closer? Pointless to speculate.

Inside the base, one of the Casspirs is blazing; a mortar round had landed inside it, setting off white phosphorus smoke grenades and rupturing fuel lines. The flames cast a reddish glow across the compound. The elevated water tank, hit twice with RPGs, is emptying itself noisily in two arcing streams. Groups of uninjured men stand with their weapons, laughing with the brittleness of relief, coming down from fear-induced highs.

The two vervet monkeys, eyes wide and screaming in fear and bewilderment, lie on the floor of their cage. Both their spines have been severed by shrapnel.

In the shock of the aftermath, they're ignored. Later, they'll be mercifully shot amid the empty potato-chip packs.

When we reach the small sick bay, soldiers and a SAMS team carry medical kits from a brown Casspir bearing the 101 Battalion insignia. They've come the four kilometres from Etale, where the sounds of the exploding mortars would have been very loud. That they've arrived so soon means they were on their way within minutes of the last explosion. Not knowing if the insurgents had prepared an ambush in the dark, that took some balls.

Walking wounded are clustered in the square of light thrown from the open door. I edge my way through them. Inside, the seriously wounded lie on a concrete floor streaked with blood, broken arms and legs already bandaged and held rigid in inflatable splints. A doctor in army browns, R4 slung over his back, concentrates on Johannes, tilting the head back to insert a breathing tube. A thick field dressing around his head is already oozing blood. Two Zulu Lima ops medics, one Ovambo and one South African, his neck streaked with caked blood, work side by side on others, putting in drips, splinting more shattered limbs, applying pressure bandages.

> **Marius "Apie" Clark, ZJ-2:** "We found Lesch at the sickbay. He was lying on the floor and I could see that he had a lot of shrapnel wounds. Someone told me I was also bleeding, but I felt no pain at the time. No one knew where Charles was, so two of us went back to the TB to look for him. About 20 or 30 metres from where we'd been sleeping, we found him lying in a pool of blood and moaning. I ran back to my sleeping roll and grabbed the ground cover canvas. With the help of two more buddies we lifted Charles onto it and carried him to the sick bay."

I had just stepped outside when Apie and three trackers arrived, each at the corner of a ground sheet. At the weighted centre an inch or more of blood has pooled around the body. Pink and grey intestine bulges from his side, and there is a deep shrapnel wound across his forehead, the frontal lobe exposed. His body carries another dozen terrible wounds. In spite of it all, he is still quietly conscious.

"He must have run when the rev started," Apie says. "A mortar bomb landed right next to him. He was still trying to crawl away when we found him."

But first get away from trees like those, I'd said. Oh, God, did he remember that?

Boeta limps from two pieces of shrapnel that had passed through the fleshy part of his thigh. Lesch's back and right side are flayed from literally hundreds of tiny fragments of shrapnel and grains of sand driven into him by the exploding mortar round. Had Stephanus and Johannes not been between him and the blast, he would be dead. Had I taken cover under the car I would be dead—shrapnel had hit the V-hull and ricocheted down on them. Of at least a dozen razor-sharp fragments that hit the duffel bag and cot on either side of me I have a single piece in my arm. Was it the absolute belief I would die if I moved that kept me from scuttling under the car? Whatever, I am very lucky.

In the radio room, messages have gone out to Okave, Eenhana and Ondangwa Air Force Base, reporting the attack and listing the casualties: one dead and 16 wounded. Three of the wounded are Priority 1, which means they require immediate casevacking. The base commander, a young Security Branch lieutenant, sets the microphone back in its clip and stands, his ankle zigzagged with lines of coagulating blood. Limping towards the door, he hesitates, then almost as an afterthought, turns to show me his assault rifle. The lower yoke of the folding steel stock is broken cleanly in two.

"How did that happen?" I ask.

"Shrapnel," he says, shaking his head and staring at the break.

In the middle of the attack he had seen the mortar round land inside the Casspir, setting it afire. In an almost fatal gesture, he and another had left their cover and sprinted to the other cars parked alongside it. As he was crossing the parade ground, a mortar exploded next to him. A small fragment hit his ankle, a much larger one was stopped by the assault rifle. He looks at the weapon and then at me.

"Knocked it right out of my hands," he says, trying to grin. The corners of his mouth twitch and settle, the effort wasted. He shrugs and limps out the door. More luck.

Gavin Manning, ZB-1: "There was no point trying to sleep so Simon Hidimbwasha and I brewed up some coffee. We climbed into my Wolf and switched on the radios. The Ohangwena base commander was reporting the number of casualties, their status, and that the 'Giants'—Pumas—had been scrambled. He also described the damage, which seemed minimal considering the hammering we'd heard, and the direction the mortars had come from. As soon as he finished his sitrep at least half a dozen teams popped up on the net, discussing where they'd RV. Simon checked his watch and went off to make sure everyone was ready to move."

The NCO and officers' mess is turned into a ward for the injured who have already been treated. Mattresses are dragged in. Lesch settles on one, lying on his unwounded side, his face tight with pain. Acting Inspector-Lieutenant Victor Nghihepa squats in front and quietly briefs him on the extent of the casualties. His hand moves slowly over Lesch's wounds to keep the flies from settling. The youngest member of the group enters through the screen door, his wrist and hand heavily bandaged. He starts to sit on the concrete floor.

"Nee," said Lesch, shifting over and patting the mattress. "Hier, tati. Kom." The boy lies next to him, staring blankly at the wall. Apie is handing out cups of steaming coffee. He offers one to me, then stops. "Look at your camera, Jim." I turn it around. The lens filter is cracked from a piece of shrapnel that clipped the metal ring on its way through my duffel bag.

Claassie Claassen: "Whoever was on duty that night called me at home and I got to the ops room as quickly as possible. All I could do was listen silently to the reports coming in from 21D and think, 'God, let them live.'"

An hour and a half later, two Puma helicopters thunder low overhead. But for the risk of men dying, they would not have come until the sun was up and the area around the base secured. The heat signatures from the engines make them especially easy targets at night for a SAM-7 heat-seeking missile. They come out of the darkness, bellies and rotor blades briefly illuminated above the base, then vanish. Our ears follow their low, tight orbits as they come around to land in the glare of Casspir headlights, a vertical windstorm of dust and sand enveloping them as they settle one after the other outside the berm.

Figures rise from the surrounding shadows, men in brown and green uniforms bending to lift stretchers. They move into the stinging sand, their shouts blown away under the scream of turbines and the staccato bass of whirling rotor blades. The stretchers are slid awkwardly through the doors. Walking wounded are helped on board. I follow the doctor into the second Puma and we lift off for the 30-minute flight to Ondangwa.

The high-pitched whine of engines running flat out makes conversation impossible. We sit on the cold floor, those of us at windows watching the barely visible terrain flashing by just below. Halfway there in the first thin light of dawn, Johannes goes into cardiac arrest. A medic gives him mouth-to-mouth, the doctor applies external heart massage as the rest of us watch numbly. Both men sit back on their heels and nod: his heart is pumping and he's breathing again. The pitch of the blades finally deepens as the nose of the helicopter lifts, and we float across the long runway at Ondangwa.

We land in the predawn grey and medical teams are waiting on the flight line. Johannes and Charles are immediately transferred to a waiting ambulance and rushed to the intensive care unit. The other seriously wounded are carried or helped into the remaining ambulances for the 50-metre trip to the trauma centre. As the rest of us climb tiredly from the decks of the Pumas to the tarmac, the cheerful, willing faces of the medics are ignored; the world outside the last three hours has become irrelevant. What we've seen and felt and heard has become the focus of our existence, and for the moment, there is nothing capable of intruding into the experience. Tomorrow something might replace it, but for now it's all there was or ever would be in our lives, and we walk quietly and singly across the tarmac, each lost in his own thoughts.

"All the casevacs are flown into the hospital there," Henk had said as we passed the base the year before.

Under a double-layered steel mesh canopy outside the operating rooms, ten triage stretchers are quickly filled. The sickly sweet and coppery smell of blood mingles with the hospital odour of disinfectants while doctors and nurses work over shattered black and white bodies. A team of three concentrates on Charles, whose critical condition has been worsened by a collapsed lung. Because of the head and chest wounds, they cannot give him an anaesthetic. Still semi-conscious, he grimaces as an incision is made between his ribs and a chest tube inserted. In the middle of it all, I take photos automatically, trance-like.

In the intensive care unit, a stretcher rests on a bed, two doctors and a medic alongside. The medic stands clear of the metal frame and presses defibrillator pads against Johannes's chest, stepping back as the unconscious body bucks under the electrical surge. The heart monitor is silent. He steps in again; there's another spasm. Nothing.

Come on, man. Live!

A third time. His body seems to bounce off the mattress under the jolt of electricity. The heart monitor beeps. Everyone holds his breath. Another beep, then another and another. The doctor nods and the medical team lean over the bed, hiding him from view.

Claassie Claassen: "When I got to Ondangwa, it was chaos. The wounded trackers from Zulu Juliet and Zulu Lima were all mixed up. Jim was shaken by what happened. I remember him standing next to me alongside Johannes, whose head was in a pool of blood."

I return to the triage area. Gurneys with broken bodies are being rolled from the X-ray room into the operating theatres, the surgical teams working non-stop. My own X-ray shows a bullet-size piece of shrapnel lodged two inches above the elbow, four inches from where it hit my forearm. I'm told that I'll be the last to go under the knife.

A medic is carefully cleaning Lesch's raw back. His bush shorts are eased off, and we're all suddenly aware of the blood on the front of his underwear. Lesch follows our eyes and blanches. He reaches down quickly to pull the elastic waistband forward and check. The elastic snaps back, and he sighs. The blood is from another of his wounds. As witnesses, we sigh with him, a nervous chuckle going around the stretcher.

Half an hour later, I walk back into the ICU to check on Johannes. The stretcher and white mattress underneath his torso are soaked in blood. Depressions in the mattress where the feet of the stretcher press into it are red pools. The screen of the heart monitor peaks and beeps rhythmically. Tubes carrying whole blood and saline snake from his arms to overhead sachets. His chest rises and falls in concert with the rhythmic hiss of a respirator. A medic, sandwich in hand, sits at his side, keeping check on the life-support systems.

I'm standing next to the bed when his heart stops for the last time, the monitor emitting a steady tone, the screen showing a flat unbroken line. The medic puts down the sandwich and wearily begins to turn off the machines. *No! They can't stop now. They can't just let him go!*

"We couldn't do anything more," he says. "It took us ten minutes to get his heart going when we got him in here. He was already brain dead. We just couldn't do anything more," his voice pleading.

My eyes lingered on Johannes, then turned to the next bed where a wounded insurgent lay, captured the week before. Here was one who would applaud, who would laugh, at the death of him and Stephanus, both of whom had been wounded next to me and died next to me. And Porky and Betoger.

Remember them, you bastard? The last of the wall I've tried to keep around my emotions crumbles. Staring at him, I raised a hand and drew the forefinger slowly across my throat, lips drawn back in irrational, animal hatred. Frightened and helpless, he looked away and pulled the starched sheet over his face.

"*...maybe I'm being idealistic too, but I can't imagine seeing or experiencing anything that would make me lose a basic sense of humanity ...* "

"*And I hope you never do,*" Bernie had said. "*Because it's something you'll never forget.*"

Ashamed, I walk quickly outside and lean against the wall, sliding down to sit in the sand. As I cradle my arm, the tears come and I weep silently. For Stephanus and Johannes, whom I didn't know, for the wounded and maimed, and perhaps most of all for me; a loss of innocence.

I didn't come for this. Yes, you did; this is exactly what you came for: the adrenaline, the fear, living on the edge, the image. Just what did you expect? You love it. Don't deny it. Yes, but I didn't come for this. Tell that to someone else. All right! But let me love it tomorrow.

I look up and Simon, one of the wounded Ovambos, is squatting patiently in front of me. " 'Sawright, tati," he murmurs, handing me his Coke, " 'Sawright, tati."

I take a swallow and cough half of it through my nose, spraying both of us. Embarrassed, I wipe my face against my shoulder.

"Kom, tati," he says, rising and helping me to my feet. "Kom."

We walk back inside, and I see Johannes being rolled out of the ICU. Outside, two medics and a chaplain struggle to slide the tall, lifeless figure into a body bag. I notice the teeth on the zipper are broken. For some reason, it suddenly becomes terribly important to me.

"It won't work," I say, pointing. "There's some teeth gone. It won't zip up; it won't *work.*"

The medic, the same who had switched off the machines attached to Stephanus, looks up, his eyes wet. "Then I'll just have to sew it up, won't I," he snaps, standing abruptly and walking away.

Their way still lit by a hunter's moon, at least half the attackers escaped into Angola and the safety of the Namakunde Fapla base. By dawn, Casspirs and Wolf Turbos were criss-crossing the bush on both sides of the yati. Unknown to any of us in the hospital, a Romeo Mike team from 101 Battalion has already hit the first contact. One insurgent is dead and a SAM-7 ground-to-air missile recovered. The army establishes blocker groups along the cutline while nine Koevoet teams begin hunting for sign. Zulu Bravo was one of them.

Gavin Manning, ZB-1: "We went north and had more spoor than we knew what to do with. Thinus and Zulu November joined us and when the terrs bomb-shelled, I was left with three cars—mine, Werner Mouton in ZB-2 and one from another team. We took two running spoor. They were taking care to tread in each other's footprints, but the trackers saw through that pretty quickly. We were about 15 kilometres north of the yati when they gave up all pretence and started running flat out.

"We suddenly burst out of thick bush into a clearing about half the size of a football pitch and the spoor disappeared in the grass at the edge of it. At its centre was a hand-dug water hole, sort of an inverted cone about four metres deep from the top of the low sand wall that circled it. The wall was surrounded and topped with a thick layer of dried branches to keep animals out, and on the far side an entrance of two forked trunks holding a long pole. Just outside that lay a hollowed-out log the PBs kept filled with water for their cattle.

"They couldn't have been more than five minutes in front of us, and the anti-tracking when they reached this point would have taken precious time, which meant they were very close. Whilst our gunners watched the trees four of us climbed down from the cars with our R5s and chambered rounds. Shikufunde and Daniel David went to the right, circling between the water hole and the edge of the clearing, Gherson Nderura and I went left. We were on opposite sides of the wall and piled-up brush when I saw Daniel signalling me urgently. Gherson and I ran around and met them at the drinking trough. All four of us crouched against it and Daniel pointed his walking stick at a tiny scuff mark in the sand. He then raised it towards the water hole and whispered very softly, 'Ek dink hulle is binne.' I think they're inside.

"We backed away to my car. One of the guys in the Wolf tossed a white phos grenade down to me. I pulled the pin, leaned back and took a long throw into the dried brush, hoping to set it alight. There was the usual orange spray of burning phosphorus followed by dense white smoke. We waited as it slowly dispersed in the still air. The branches had stubbornly refused to catch fire. 'Kom ons kyk,' I said. Let's look.

"The four of us spread out in line abreast to do a clockwise sweep, with me nearest the water hole. We hadn't gone very far when, less than three metres in front of us, there was sudden movement. I nearly fucking swallowed my balls as two figures in faded Libyan camo came to their feet from where they'd been hiding under the brush. Everything went into slow motion, the rising figures registering on the brain like a film advancing frame by frame. I saw their AKMs lifting and had a vague impression of Gherson, Daniel and Shikufunde scattering. The muzzle of the nearest one swung towards me; in half a second I was going to die. I don't think I've ever moved quicker in my life. Without even thinking about it, my R5 was already on him. The selector was on single shot and my finger a blur of contractions on the trigger. I put three or four rounds into his chest and a red mist blew from his mouth. He was already going backwards over the sand wall as I brought it across, still firing. The second was turning towards the water hole, looking for cover, and my bullets entered his side, twisting him away from me and the next ones taking him in the back. He disappeared over the edge and died facedown where he fell.

"Before I could even draw a breath ZB-2 came charging in from behind, Werner screaming at me to get out of the way so he could fire. I merely stepped about three paces to my right as I knew I had killed them both. It was then that the fear of a few seconds earlier exploded into fury and I began shitting out my guys for leaving me exposed. Hidimbwasha came running over from the car and calmed me down, saying they thought my bullets would cause the heatstrims and pencilstrims in the terrs' chest webbing to explode, which could have killed all of us. That's how close we were. We collected the weapons and ammunition, searched them for documents, and pushed on in search of the others who'd hit 21D."

François du Toit, ZQ-1: "Attie and I had gotten to Ohangwena at first light. Bez and Zulu Whiskey arrived right after us and we discussed which direction the terrs might have gone. We knew most of them would have headed for Namakunde, but at least five Koevoet teams and the army were already working spoor north of the cutline. Should we join them, or was it possible that some of the enemy might have taken advantage of the confusion and gone the other way? On a hunch, we decided to head south."

Michael "Peanuts" Kennard, ZU-4: "That morning there were so many teams chasing spoor north of the cutline that we decided to go southwest. About ten klicks later, I stopped at a kraal to question the PBs. No one knew anything, but the way one of them kept glancing at me gave me the feeling there was something wrong. As I drove away, I mentioned my suspicions to Attie over the radio and he told me to go back and question him again. We turned around and I saw the guy coming after us on a bicycle. He told me that he'd seen a group of terrs going south the night before."

As teams hunted north and south of the yati, the Ondangwa hospital was transitioning from intense focus on saving life to treatment. Initial assessments had been done, a priority list completed, blood types matched, X-rays examined. Men were shifted one by one from stretcher to gurney and wheeled into the operating theatre. I sat against the far wall with a coffee and watched. Though the arm throbbed, it was a dull ache, not the sharp intense pain of the first time. But there was no upward or lateral movement in the wrist and I couldn't grasp anything unless it was first pressed into the palm with the other hand. After seeing what others had suffered, it was an inconvenience I could live with.

It was late afternoon by the time a nurse took me though the swinging doors. An exhausted surgeon was examining my X-rays. "We're out of general anaesthetic," he said apologetically, "so my colleague will do an axillary block." Flat on my back, arm extended to the side, I watched the anaesthetist slip a long needle into my armpit. A little extra push to puncture the nerve sheath and an electric shock went down to the fingertips as he injected a local.

A few minutes later, he was tapping the back of my hand with the point of something. "Feel that?" Nope. He moved higher. "That?" Nope. "There?" Nothing. "Good." The surgeon leaned over the elbow with a scalpel. "I'm following the path the shrapnel took," he murmured from behind the surgical mask. The nurse pressed a gauze sponge into the wound. He went back to work. "Can't be sure, but it may have nicked the radial nerve." Then, "A little more … and … got it." There was the clink of metal hitting the bottom of a kidney pan. With a tiny spoon he began removing what looked like bright strawberry jam. "Bullets, shrapnel, they leave a trail of mush," he said, flicking each runny gobbet into the pan. "If we don't get rid of it everything goes septic." He straightened to ease an aching back. "Next step," picking up a length of flattened, opaque tube and showing it to me. "Penrose drain." He leaned down again. "This goes into the incision … there. You'll have a lot of bleeding the next few days and it needs a way out." The nurse handed him a surgical suture and with practiced twists of the forceps clamped on the needle he sewed the wound closed. The nurse snipped the thread, placed a thick wound dressing over the arm and wrapped it with an elastic bandage. "Right," the doc said. "Done. Off you go."

I stepped through the swinging doors into the triage area. Bernie Ley was waiting. He took in the sling and dressing that was already turning dark at the elbow. He pulled a face. "Coming down here every couple of days to fetch you is getting boring. If I'd known what a fucking metal magnet you were …" He shook his head. "You okay?" I nodded. "Okay, let's get back to the house. You could use a drink."

I didn't even think to ask how the teams were doing.

François du Toit, ZQ-1: "We picked up around ten spoor and followed it the rest of the day. By noon the next day my team, Attie's Zulu Uniform and Bez's Zulu Whiskey were about 20 kilometres north of Oshakati. It's open bush around there. Scattered trees, anthills, patches of mopani. The trackers were spread out. I was behind my guns, with just one of my buddies in the back. DB Koch in ZQ-3 was following a little ways behind my car.

"Then I saw the trackers' body language change, very alert and moving forward in a crouch. I had seen it many times before, the way they could sense that the enemy was very near. You could *feel* the tension in them. I double-checked my .50 Browning and told my driver to move quickly to the right, into a low thicket so I would be in a better position to cover them. What I didn't know was that a few weeks earlier the PBs had cut a lot of the mopani here for firewood.

"We accelerated and suddenly came to a stop, the diff guard sitting on a stump and the Casspir's front wheels high off the ground. I was swearing at my driver when I saw movement and looked down. Right next to the car were insurgents leopard-crawling like crazy to get away. Not only were we immobilized, but my .50 and .30 Brownings were pointing at the sky! It was the worst nightmare for a contact. No time to throw a smoke grenade to mark our position. I grabbed my R5 with one hand and the radio handset with the other to warn everyone, but when I squeezed the key all I got was a high-pitched screech.

"At that moment, I saw another insurgent stand up not more than ten metres to my left, staring directly at me. Everything went into super slow motion as I watched him raise an RPG to his shoulder, take aim and fire. I saw it coming and waited for the explosion, knowing it was going to take my legs off. I braced myself, but, incredibly, there was no explosion. A second later, 'DeeBee' Koch came racing forward, the guns on his Casspir blazing and knocking the terr off his feet. He switched targets, laying down short bursts of saturation fire into the mopani alongside my car. There was the sound of gunfire all around, then a tremendous explosion—not single *BANG!* but a loud, ripping, roaring kind that went on long enough to scare the shit out of everyone. I'd never heard anything like it. Mixed in with that was AK-47 fire and the distinctive sound of a Russian PKM."

Michael "Peanuts" Kennard, ZU-4: "We were about 50 metres ahead of Toit on voorsny and had passed well to one side of the terrs without seeing them. I suddenly heard firing behind us and then a big bang when something exploded. I shouted at my driver to turn back. More cars were turning and heading for the contact when I saw Johannes Kanjamotu, one of Toit's trackers, lying on the ground east of the contact. He'd obviously been hit. I jumped out and yelled at my driver to stop between him and the other cars—I was afraid in the confusion they might think he was a terr and finish him off. When I got to him, he was bleeding badly from his leg. I pushed my finger against the artery above the wound, then saw Frikkie running towards us. When he arrived, I ran back to my car to give him covering fire as there were still some terrs running around like mad. Bullets were flying everywhere. Frikkie stayed there in the middle of it and he saved Johannes's life."

When ops medic Frikkie Steynberg saw Kanjamotu go down, he grabbed his NCO medical bag and R5, jumped from his car and sprinted through the crossfire. Johannes had been hit through the thigh, his femur broken and an arterial spray spurting from the wound. He was within minutes of dying from loss of blood. Ignoring the bullets cracking past him, Frikkie concentrated on stopping the bleeding and was soon joined by ZU's ex-Swapo medic. Tourniquet cinched tight above the wound, they started a plasma drip and applied a temporary splint, before loading him into Peanuts' Casspir and moving beyond the contact area.

When the firing stopped, the bodies of seven Swapo insurgents lay scattered across the contact area. The only other Koevoet injury was Kobie "Klein Sty" Strydom of ZW, who had been hit in the back by splinters from armour-piercing PKM fire. Johannes was a Priority 1 and the call went out for a casevac. At Ondangwa to the southeast, a Puma crew raced for the flight line.

Michael "Peanuts" Kennard, ZU-4: "When the shooting stopped, Attie came on the radio to ask if everyone was okay. At first all the cars except mine reported flat tyres. One of my buddies then told me that he had seen some terrs running out of the southern edge of contact area. I asked Attie if there was another car that could assist me. Then I heard Paul 'Short Botes' Botha of ZQ report that his car was okay, but Attie said that as large as the spoor had been, he wanted us to proceed with caution. He would change tyres as quickly as possible and join us. We went forward and quickly picked up two running spoor. It was so clear that my driver could follow it from the driver's seat. We went about 1,000 metres and just as I was preparing to stop and wait for the other cars I spotted the two terrs trying to hide in tall grass under a tree. I alerted Short Botes, and as we went forward they decided to put up a fight. We killed them and took the bodies back to the first contact point. Right after that the Pumas arrived and lifted our casevacs."

François du Toit, ZQ-1: "Afterwards, we walked around my Casspir and found the RPG rocket dangling from two thin branches. The tail fins had hit some mopani as it was leaving the launcher and deflected the warhead. It must have spun end over end as the propellant charge burned itself out, and finally came to a rest in those branches. Even if it hadn't been deflected, there hadn't been enough distance for it to arm itself. We were searching through the bush when we discovered what had made the strange explosion. DeeBee's bullets had ignited the solid fuel booster of a SAM-7 ground-to-air missile one of the terrs had been carrying! The back end of it was scorched and melted. Then we remembered the intelligence briefings that they were planning to shoot down a 'Flossie'—a C-130 Hercules—at Ondangwa. That's where they must have been heading when we found them. How thankful we were to get hold of that piece of ugly kit."

Twenty kilometres away at Okave, SAMS Doctor Poenie van Zyl had just finished changing the dressing on my arm when Chris Pieterse stuck his head around the door of the infirmary. "Some of the teams are coming in," he said. "They had a moer of a contact. Get your cameras and let's go." It was a ten-minute drive to the satellite base at Ongwediva. By the time we arrived, a dozen Casspirs were rolling through the gate, bodies lashed to spare tyres and wheel arches. As the men climbed down, some wore tan Russian bush hats taken as spoils of war. All were unusually subdued, no hint of the post-contact euphoria I was used to seeing. Toit, in particular, seemed strangely detached. When I greeted him, he looked through me and turned away. The bodies were transferred to a bakkie, which sped off to Z3, where their uniforms and equipment identified them as being part of Swapo's Air and Ground Force detachment. Photos would be taken and circulated in an attempt to put names to the faces.

I snapped my own photos, the last one of Toit, Peanuts and Attie standing to one side, their faces expressionless. They returned to their cars and the teams pulled out. It was Friday, only three days into the week's deployment. They were returning to the war.

Like the rev on Ohangwena a year earlier, this one had been planned by commissars with no understanding of what their ill-prepared men would face, nor any regard for their fate. At least a quarter of the attackers died in exchange for two of Zulu Juliet's constables, a burned-out Casspir and punctured water tank. True to form, Swapo's propaganda radio claimed that the People's Liberation Army of Namibia had destroyed the Ohangwena police base and killed dozens of South African racist soldiers. They forgot to mention dropping mortar shells on an Ovambo school dormitory east of the base, killing two young women and wounding another eight.

Johannes Kanjamotu reached the primary trauma centre at Ondangwa in time to save his life, but damage to the femoral artery and subsequent loss of blood supply to his leg resulted in it being amputated. After weeks convalescing at 1 Military Hospital in Pretoria and being fitted with a prosthetic, he refused to accept medical retirement and demanded to return to Koevoet. His persistence convinced Attie Hattingh to bring him back as co-driver and gunner for Zulu Uniform's Blesbok supply vehicle.

And he would see more action. The war had another two years to run and hundreds of young, poorly-trained insurgents would die for Swapo's vision of a Marxist state—as would a score of friends dedicated to stopping them.

Gavin Manning, ZB-1: "Of all the contacts I had with both the SADF during my national service and later with Ops K, the one at the waterhole has stuck with me the most. Not because of how close I came to dying, but because of the tragedy that followed. We returned two weeks later to find the area around the site resembling photos I had seen of the DMZ in Vietnam. Scorched earth. In all my time in the operational area, I'd never come across anything like it. There must have been 20 or 30 PBs, mostly children, looking lost and confused. The adult men were chopping down small trees to build shelters, the children trying to find fallen fruit from the eheke and maroela trees. We found an old woman sitting dazed and starving under one tree and I asked her what happened. She explained that the waterhole lay where a number of kraal farmlands met and was shared by those families. When they found the bodies of the two terrs, each headman felt it was the duty of the others to bury them. As a result, they were left in the waterhole, which was now cursed because of their deaths there.

"Some days after they'd been killed, she said, a Swapo commander from the base at Mongua, north of Ongiva, arrived and discovered the decomposing corpses. He was infuriated by what he saw as a lack of respect for his 'freedom fighters.' 'Why should we respect Swapo?' the old lady asked me with what seemed faultless logic. 'They are fighting for Namibia, we live in Angola.' The Swapo commander, a champion of the people, did not see it that way. In retribution, he ordered his cadres to torch every kraal within about a two-kilometre radius of the waterhole. At least ten families had lost their homes. Even the stores of mohango that would keep them fed until the next harvest had been burned.

"It was strictly against regulations, but I had Simon Hidimbwasha distribute two cases – 24 units – of individual ration packs. It was pitifully inadequate, so I gave her 400 rand, my week's allowance for paying informants, and told her to go across the border to Ohangwena and buy supplies for their children. I knew that before we got back to Okave at the end of the deployment, I'd have to do a little creative paperwork to account for it, but I couldn't just ignore what had happened. We TB-ed nearby that night and Simon went over to visit them. When he returned, he had a message. They had asked him to tell me that, 'You are a good man and a good shirumbu.' Afterwards, my guys would come up to me and murmur in a mix of Afrikaans and Oshivambo, 'Dit was mooi, sante. *Oshidi shiidi*.' That was nice, sergeant, and that's the truth."

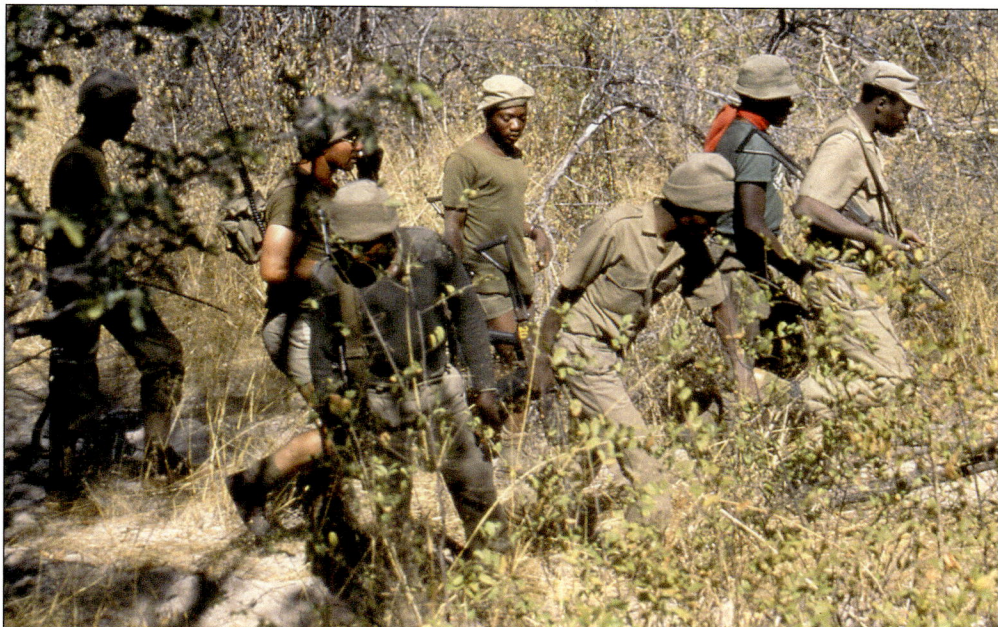

Carrying only a radio to coordinate Zulu Uniform's Casspirs,
Attie Hattingh joins his men on the spoor.

Casspir windscreen hit by heatstrim rifle grenade.

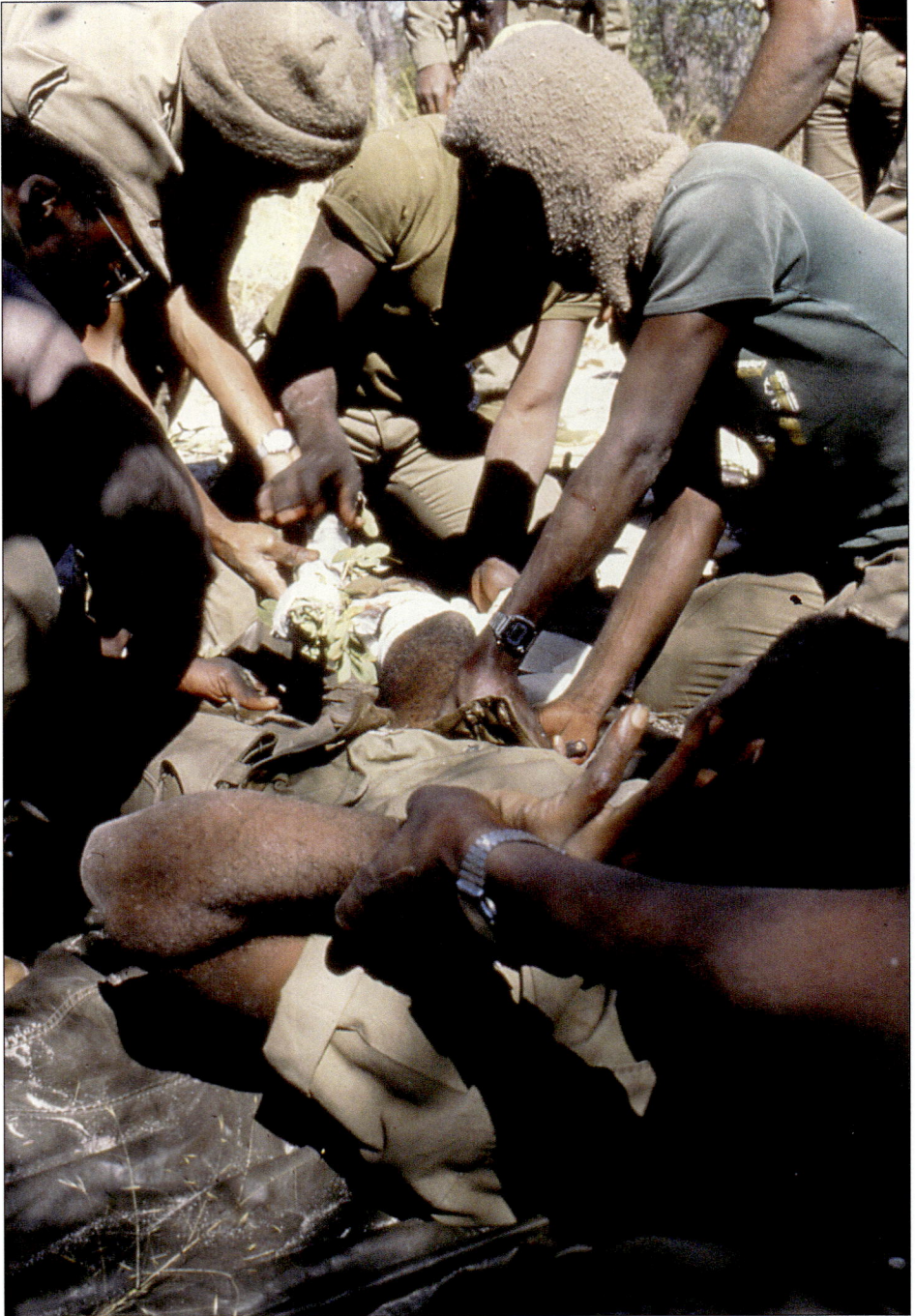

The heatstrim's slug deflected down to hit the driver below the knee.
His comrades apply a splint as they wait for a casevac chopper.

Alouette gunship orbits over Casspirs and Blesboks.

Attie marks a freshly cleared landing zone and talks to the pilot of
an Alouette coming in to casevac the wounded driver.

Bez Bezuidenhout of Zulu Whiskey holds a drip as the man is carried to the helicopter.

Casevac on board, the flight engineer monitors tail rotor clearance on lift off.

Chris Ronne of Zulu 1 Juliet, Toit and trackers examine the body of one
of the insurgents that ambushed their teams two hours earlier.

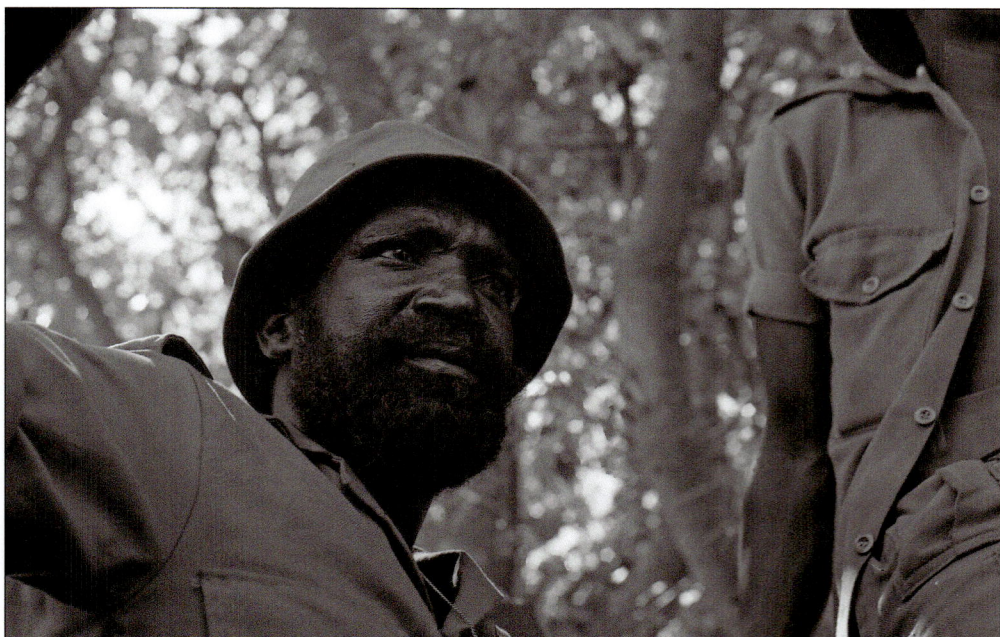

Zulu Quebec's senior Ovambo warrant officer, William Handukeme.

Zulu Quebec trackers reload the ammunition belt of their PKM machine gun.

After a day of multiple contacts during which two colleagues each lost a leg to heatstrims, exhausted WO David Absalom Aviva and Andre Snyman of Zulu Uniform take a welcome break in the Eenhana ops centre.

Trackers sprint through the soft sand as they follow a running spoor.

With temperatures of over 100F, a team stops to allow engines and trackers to cool.

Considered the best trackers in the world, these Ovambo
spoorsnyers follow the faint signs left by insurgents.

The aftermath of another contact. Zulu Uniform and Zulu Tango
cluster around the body of a Swapo insurgent.

Piet "Hand" Cronje and comrades pause in the far western province of Kaokoveld.
His Wolf Turbo is armed with a GA-1 20mm cannon and 60mm mortar.

Benny, ZG

Jackie Grobler, ZG

Flanked by Nick Coetzee and Piet "Hand" Cronje in the Kaokoveld,
MajGen Sterk Hans Dreyer takes a welcome break from his office.

Jan Smit, Z-1 radio operator

Marius "Apie" Clark, ZJ

Senior tracker Stephanus Abel leans on the backplate behind Zulu Juliet's
team leader J.C. Lesch on the fateful drive to Ohangwena.

A Casspir blazes at Ohangwena after a mortar round landed
inside and set off white phosphorus grenades.

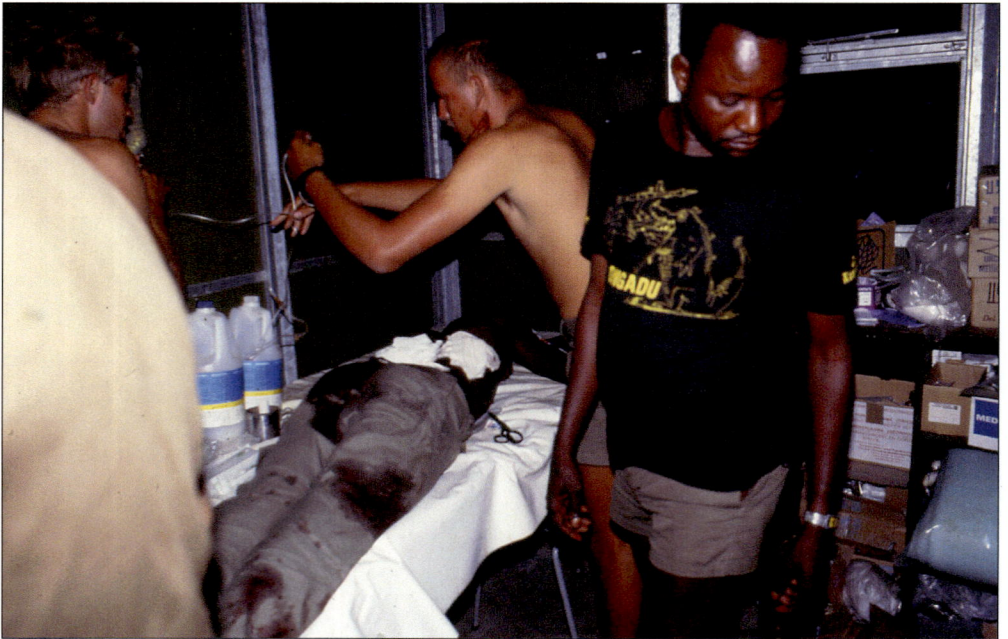

Zulu Lima's SAMS ops medic Jean, helped by Riaan Williams and the team's senior
Ovambo, WO Tau, treat one of Zulu Juliet's men in the Ohangwena sick bay.

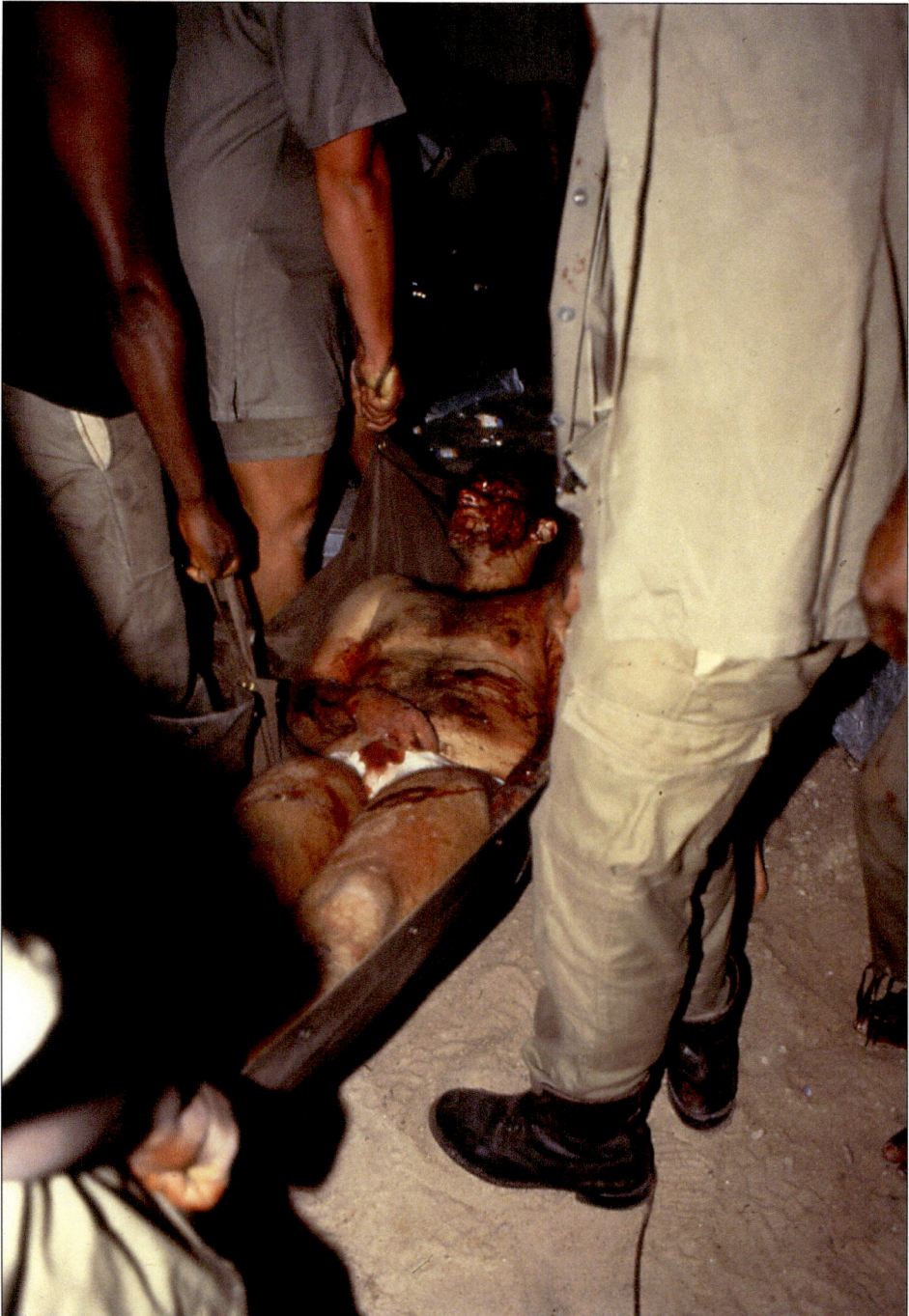

Following the attack on Ohangwena, Zulu Juliet's ops medic
Charles Labello is carried into the infirmary.

A SAMS doctor works to stabilise two of Zulu Juliet's men
critically wounded by mortar shrapnel.

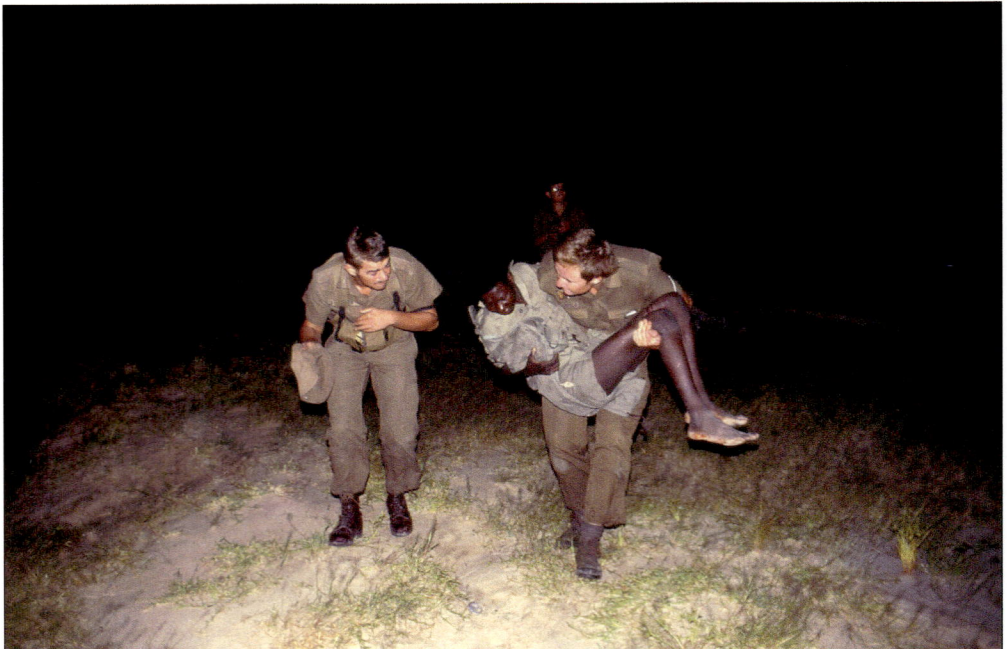

A SAMS ops medic carries one of Zulu Juliet's wounded to the casevac Puma.

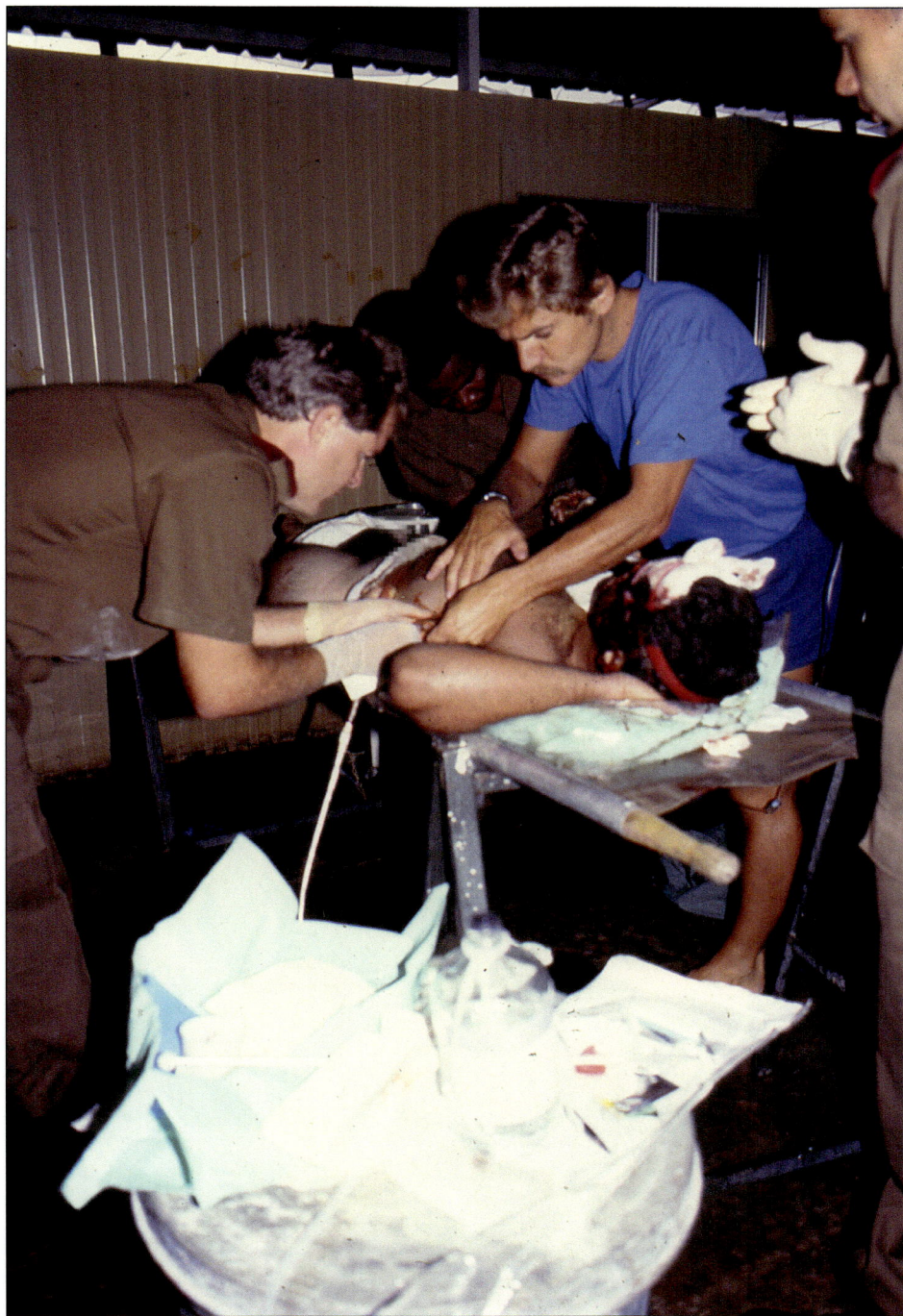

Flown to Ondangwa Air force Base, critically injured Charles
Labello grimaces as a chest tube is inserted.

Back in the Okave base, the faces of these men show the strain of
a week tracking insurgents and close-quarter contacts.

18

A Time to Go

Chris Pieterse: "The first couple of nights after he was hit, Jim stayed with Bernie and Marga Ley. But it was a strictly no-sympathy household. The first time Marga saw him on her new white sofa, she yelled, 'Don't get blood on that!' and ran to get a towel to put under his arm.

"One Sunday afternoon I was invited over and after lunch the Ley's retired for a siesta. I was shooting the breeze with Jim when he asked if I would do him a huge favour. Neither hand was working very well, the zip was stuck and he needed to pee. Would I get it loose for him? He stood in front of my chair and I made him a solemn promise: 'If anybody walks in now, you are a dead man!'"

Each morning I'd visit the sick bay where one of the medics would massage a cupful of black, jellied blood from the end of the Penrose drain. One morning, I looked up to see Kokkie watching. He caught my eye and shook his head. "Vasbyt, Jim," he murmured. Hang in there.

A few days later, the surgeon examined me again. By now I could lift the back of the hand, but the fingers wouldn't follow, folding uselessly into the palm. "Maybe it's only neurapraxia," he said encouragingly. "Could be the radial nerve's temporarily damaged by the shock wave when the shrapnel went through your arm. If the nerve itself wasn't hit, you should start getting recovery pretty soon."

So I stayed on, hoping the hand would improve enough to use the cameras quickly or hold on inside the cars. Of course, to have said that the only thing I wanted was to get back on operations, to record the action, to continue the story, might have sent a polygraph wild. I knew that to climb back into a Casspir and head into the bush would have taken more than I had shown so far. All I knew was that I didn't want to leave.

"Shrapnel Jim," Attie called me, but it wasn't just Attie who kept reminding me: "Left, right"—pointing to each arm—"centre," tapping the middle of their chests on the last: that's where the next one was going to connect if I went on.

You've used up plenty of your luck, they were saying; don't squander what you have on balance.

Even newly-promoted Major General Dreyer shook his head. "I don't think you should go back into the bush," he said. But it was only an excuse left hanging there, one I could pull down and wrap around me if the hand began working and I didn't want to continue. *Yeah, I'd really like to, but the general, he said I couldn't,* if that's what I needed.

By the end of two weeks, the drain was gone, the wound had closed, but there was no change in the hand and I knew I was just spinning my wheels by staying on. (It would take nine months and another operation in England before I could open it.) The infiltration had reached its peak, and I'd taken to hanging around the ops room, listening to teams calling in on the radio and following their progress on the map that covered one wall. Every "Contact!" I heard took me back into the bush, images strobe-flashing through my mind, while calls for casevacs twisted and knotted my insides with the newly learned questions and selfish hope: *Who? How bad? And if it's bad, if it's a really bad one, just don't let me know them.*

Then one day: "Ambush!" That was all, nothing more. My eyes darted from the group's last reported position on the map, to the radio and back again, the call taking me breathlessly out-of-body and riveting my feet in place until it was over and they were talking again. But it was all too agonizing. And vicarious. I had become a safe voyeur; non-essential. It was time to leave.

A few days before my departure, I walked into the ops room. It was crowded with grim-faced policemen. Dreyer was talking on the radio. I asked Smitty, the radioman, what was happening.

"Captain Koch's been hit—hit bad. He was in a gunship when they spotted two terrs. They came in low and didn't see three others. He took five AK rounds, and the flight engineer was killed. Three rounds went through the captain's body, and both legs were hit. He's already on the way to Ondangwa in a chopper. They don't think he's going to live."

The same Klaus Koch whose arm had been torn apart three years earlier when an RPG had exploded against his rifle. He'd been through three years of hospitals and operations to partially repair the damage, returning to Koevoet between each procedure. The surgeons still hadn't finished with him when this happened.

Two days later, we heard from the hospital in Pretoria. He was still in critical condition. By the end of the week, word came that he was going to make it, but they'd had to amputate one leg.

When the day finally came to leave, Jackie volunteered to drive me to Ondangwa. We stopped first at Okave so I could say good-bye to General Dreyer. As we were pulling away, I saw Johnny Mwashitinayo, the Ovambo warrant officer from Zulu Tango. I had just heard he was getting his own fighting group and was up for promotion to lieutenant. Jackie stopped the car, and I ran over to him. We met in the middle of the empty parade ground.

"Johnny, ek moet nou gaan," holding my hand out. I have to go now. It exhausted most of my Afrikaans.

He flashed a smile and took my hand, one of us not knowing enough Afrikaans, the other without English. Still gripping my hand, he fished in his breast pocket and withdrew a small ivory amulet, yellowed with age. He turned the hand over and pressed it into my palm.

"Gaan goed," he said—go well—closing my fingers on the good-luck charm. Not trusting my voice, I nodded, and turned abruptly for the car.

There wasn't much to say as we sped along the tarmac road. Scrawny cattle grazed on either side. Those tall anthills jutted from the landscape like silent sentinels among the scattered makalani palms. We passed the bars and cuca shops with the names already imprinted on my mind. OJ's Mississippi Satisfaction. The Happy Bar. The Sorry Bar.

Ahead of us was a column of green Casspirs. We overtook the first one and I saw Adriaan sitting behind his gun mount. I cranked down the window and leaned out to wave. He punched the air and gave me a thumbs-up. As we came abreast of each car, I was greeted with waving black arms and shouted good-byes. Jackie slowed alongside the lead Casspir. Attie, headset firmly over his bush hat, leaned over with that familiar grin and shouted something that was whipped away in the wind. Jackie accelerated, and I turned to watch them grow steadily smaller behind us. Before another hour passed, they would be in the thick bush somewhere between Ohangwena and Eenhana, hunting. I wondered where they'd TB tonight. Eenhana, I decided automatically, unless they found spoor that took them across the cutline into Angola.

It was four and a half months since I arrived, a year almost to the day since my first trip into the bush with Marius Brand and the men of Zulu Alpha. I had seen and experienced more than I'd ever bargained for.

"You know what Johnny said to the general about you?" Jackie said, breaking the silence. I shook my head. "He told him, 'We want to keep that shirumbu here.' You're going to be missed."

The road ahead almost blurred. *All right, goddammit, just take it easy.*

Jackie stopped at the gates of the air force base while new South African conscripts passed mirrors under the car to check for bombs. They stared at Jackie with barely concealed awe. They recognized the olive-green uniform. Their eyes widened as they took in my arm in its sling. They had heard plenty about Koevoet.

It was suddenly all too absurd. "It isn't part of your programme," Henk had told me. And then: *How was I going to do a first-hand account of counterinsurgency operations by hanging out with a bunch of cops?* Four months in the bush, the scars, the people, the association and now these kids at the gate thinking I was one of the dreaded Koevoet. The only cliché I had missed was the slap across the face and saying, Thanks, Sarge, I needed that. *Look, I don't want to go out on some Boy Scout camping trip,* I'd told Bernie Ley on that first day. Had I ever been that green?

"What's so funny?" Jackie asked.

"Nothing," I shook my head. "Really, it's nothing."

But I don't want to go, Jackie.

We pulled up in front of the dusty air-movements shack. Jackie unloaded my kit bag and typewriter case and checked them onto the flight for Pretoria. High above us, a four-engined C-130 was in a steep, spiralling descent. Two Alouettes chattered over the thin bush around the base, 20mm gun barrels projecting from the open doors.

"I've got to be getting back," he said.

"Sure."

"I wasn't just joking when I said you'd be missed, you know."

"Thanks. Listen. Say good-bye for me to everyone I didn't see this morning, okay?"

"Yeah."

"And keep your head down."

"You too," and he was gone.

The announcement came to board. Walking across the hot tarmac with the other passengers, I saw the Pumas sitting quietly on the hardpan. At the hospital just beyond the flight line, all was quiet: no medics rushing wounded into operating rooms. Then it was time, and I ducked through the door and boarded the flight that waited to take me away.

I stared out the window of the Hercules, face pressed against the Plexiglas until long after it all disappeared; another lifetime fallen behind. When I settled back in the seat, my civilian neighbour—a bureaucrat by the look of him—noted the sling and smiled patronizingly below a narrow moustache.

"Going home?"

"Yeah," not much wanting to talk.

"Defence Force?"

"Uh-uh, just passing through; journalist."

"Is it? So who do you write for?"

I told him, closed my eyes and leaned back, hoping he would shut up or disappear.

"So, what happened to your arm there?" he insisted, which was what he was really interested in.

"Shrapnel," I said, the tone suggesting he mind his own business. *Leave me alone.*

"Genuine?" he said, raising his eyebrows. He'd met someone who'd been wounded in the operational area. "What happened? Kaffirs get you?"

Suddenly, there was nothing about him I liked; not his thin moustache, nor his safari suit, not his double chin or soft hands or pale skin. Damned if I'd explain anything.

"Just kidding," I said. "Tennis elbow."

Eyes and nostrils narrowed. Lips pressed together, he returned to his girlie magazine. So much for South African-American relations on this flight.

Pretoria was like another world; crowded sidewalks full of staid and uninvolved South Africans, all going about their business, their knowledge of the bush war limited to what they read in the newspapers. Like Londoners reading about Northern Ireland. Where I had come from might have been a million miles away. On the moon, at least.

Bernie Ley arrived in Pretoria for a conference and on my last day there drove me to the airport. On the way we stopped at 1 Military Hospital and took the elevator up to the orthopaedic ward. In the visitors' room was Johannes Kanjamotu, the tracker from Zulu Quebec who'd been saved by Frikkie. His leg gone above the knee, he was sitting in a wheelchair playing cards with a soldier from 101 Battalion. He flashed a smile of recognition when we entered. We shook hands, and Bernie brought him up to date on what had happened in the unit since he'd been away. He listened eagerly, asking about different people. Yes, he knew Captain Koch was here; he had seen him that morning.

A nurse interrupted and motioned us to follow her. Koch brightened when he saw us come in. "Hoe gaan dit?" he whispered hoarsely. The respirator had only been removed from his throat that morning. Below his knee the sheet fell sharply to the mattress. *So what the hell do you say?*

"How's the arms?" he rasped.

"Hell, it's nothing. I mean, really, no problem. Nothing like—how about you?"

"No, I'll be okay," he whispered. "I guess I'm pretty lucky. Looks like I'll be here a while."

"Shit, you'll be back up there before you know it."

He shook his head slowly. "I'm not going back. My little girl, she told me, 'Daddy, please don't go back again.'" He turned his head away. "I'm finished with it. I've done my share." He looked back at us. "I've done my share," he whispered fiercely.

We stood awkwardly next to the bed, trying to ignore the missing leg and making uncomfortable conversation until some of his family arrived and we made our good-byes. Months later, I would hear that he had returned to Okave.

We rode the elevator down to the intensive care unit. Bernie explained to the nurse what we had come for, and she led us into the stainless steel and glass ward. Another nurse stood at a raised station, where she could monitor the life support systems and see into the five cubicles around her. The first nurse indicated the one directly in front of the station and we walked to the door. A black body lay on the bed, starkly outlined by the crisp, white sheets. A respirator mask was held in place by an elastic strap; dangling tubes and wires led away from him. One leg was gone below the knee.

"He's been in a coma since he arrived," said the nurse. "It's impossible to say if or when he'll come out of it."

"You recognize him?" Bernie asked.

"Yeah." But I didn't, really. I'd only been with the group one day when it happened. And the respirator, how could I tell with that over his face? All I knew was that he had been sleeping less than 50 feet from me when the first mortar round landed that night at Ohangwena.

I took one last look, then turned and walked away. I was going home.

Coming back was like I'd never been away. Everything was the same: the people, the places, the mind-sets. Only I had changed, and there wasn't any help for that.

There was an obsession to explain what I'd seen and done and learned; I had to tell them. Everyone. It was part of me now, and I wanted to grab the world by its shoulders and say: *Listen!* But not many really wanted to know, and when a reasonably intelligent and articulate friend interrupted with a whiskey and soda and asked, "But what does it all *mean,* old chap?" I finally slowed down, kept to myself and started writing.

Some asked, "So, how are things down there?"—already knowing the answers they wanted to hear, smug or annoyed when what I gave them fit or didn't fit the neat compartments they'd built to receive them. Both sides as convinced as if they'd been there, both sides equally unknowing. But experts; they *knew,* they had read it all, according to whichever gospel they chose to believe. They didn't have a clue.

The first couple of months were the worst, trying to come down, trying to put it on paper; re-adjusting, back in the flow, and listening to stories of what real life was all about: holidays, job frustrations, schools, and spring sales. "And I found the most darling outfit for next to nothing," Sugar Jones said, changing the subject to something more important.

I called Bez, Zulu Whisky's group leader, one night to ask how everyone was doing.

"No, everything's fine here," he said. "Really slow. Oh, yeah, Flip—you remember Flip?—from Zulu Foxtrot?—yeah, he was hit this morning. He was on the ground during a follow-up and got hit in the leg by a heatstrim."

I remembered Flip being caught on foot during the contact near Ondobe, and then climbing on top of the Strandwolf to warn Botes.

"What happened, how'd it happen?" I shouted down the line.

"Nothing special," Bez shouted back, "just a normal contact."

A few weeks after returning to the quiet English countryside, a letter arrived from Claassie. He was still waiting for his wounds to heal enough to return to the bush.

Hi Jim

I'm writing a short letter just to let you know that everything is still okay. On 1987/05/07 at 03h00 Swapo attacked the town with B-10s. Only two bombs fell inside the town. No casualties inside the town. By 07h00 the first terr was killed and 10h30 four more. (Zulu Foxtrot + India and Zulu November + Alpha were the groups that got them.) Two were captured.

Excuse my writing. The writing is bad, fractured bone in wrist still hurts a little. Also it's a long time since I'm writing English. One of Z5's cars from the Opuwa base was shot out on the tar road near Concor. The white group leader as well as the black driver were killed. I do not think you knew them.

Attie of Zulu Uniform was hurt by a POM-Z mine as well. Please tell the people overseas what's happening here.

Yours sincerely,

Claassie

Postscript

S et inside a shadow box on the wall of my study is a South African Police Medal for Combating Terrorism. It is flanked by a heart-shaped piece of canvas and a broken lens filter, dates and places noted. The medal, the only one ever given a foreigner, is undeserved, the others no more than an accident of time and place. Hanging nearby is a slab of African teak, elephants and makalani palms cut into its centre. Chiselled in the dark wood below is "To Jim Hooper From Koevoet 1987". It was presented in a packed Okave Club my last night in Oshakati, accompanied by shouts about being old and clumsy and an Englishman—"American, dammit!" "Same thing!"—that made it a treasured moment.

But memories are all that's left now. Save for the Southwesters who were there that drunken, rowdy night, everyone is gone. Even many of Koevoet's Ovambos, their lives at risk under a Swapo government, fled to South Africa. Their fate, known to few outside the brotherhood that rode into battle with them, is worth recording.

Only days after Koevoet repulsed the April 1st invasion, Attorney General Louis Pienaar visited Okave. Speaking to the assembled black and white operators, he saluted them on behalf of the South African Government for ensuring that free and fair elections could be held in Namibia. He also delivered a solemn promise from President PW Botha: should the political process go against them, the black members of Koevoet would not be abandoned, but relocated to South Africa as members of the SAP.

Swapo won the elections. In January 1990, General Dreyer and Lt Col Willem Fouche met the first group at the Pretoria train station and saw them bussed to a campsite near Rustenberg. There, they lived in tents and survived on ration packs until the government decreed that they would be employed by the SAP as "general workers." By now totalling some 700 warriors and their families, they were moved to an abandoned mining complex outside Rooiberg the following year. The Stock Theft Unit eagerly employed them and was so impressed with their successes in recovering stolen farm animals that it was decided to send them to the SAP Training College. But budgets were being cut and only 36 men completed it and were sworn in as constables. In 1992 alone, their tracking skills led to 14 farm murders being solved.

In the lead up to the country's own elections, the Convention for a Democratic South Africa (CODESA), attended by the major parties, began negotiations on the future of the country. Unsurprisingly, the military and police units that had been most successful in countering the communist onslaught against Namibia—especially Koevoet and the SADF's Portuguese-speaking 32 Battalion—were loathed by the African National Congress. The predominantly white National Party, which had promised protection to those who had given so much, acceded to most of the ANC's demands.

On 28 March 1993, SAP General Johan Koen arrived in Rooiberg to tell the black members of the old Ops K that CODESA refused to honour the guarantees made to them. The tracking unit was dismantled, the police college graduates transferred around the country, the rest given small retirement packages and abandoned to eke out a living as best they could. Disillusioned by the betrayal, LtCol Fouche went on sick leave and soon thereafter retired from the SAP as medically unfit.

Among those who haven't forgotten them is General Dreyer. I received an email from him not long ago, in which he wrote of hearing from some of the old trackers now and then. Contentedly settled on his farm and a regular gym user, he admits that old age is setting in, but his health remains excellent.

And what of others whose stories have been told here? Tragically, Adriaan Hattingh, Attie's brother, was killed the year after I left, only days after taking over as Zulu Quebec's group leader. Squint-eyed Bennie, Jackie's right-hand man and friend, and Daniel Taiko both died during the April '89 fighting when Swapo's president broke the United Nations peace agreement he had signed just four months earlier.

In 2008, my old friend Bernie Ley died of a heart attack. I miss him. Brigadier Rob Crowther, Defence Attaché at the South African embassy who opened that door to the border war for me, suffered the same the following year, while Jacobus "Apie" Andries' own heart betrayed him at far too young an age. Otto Shivute, the man sitting the other side of a Casspir the first time I crossed the cutline into Angola, died of kidney disease at a private clinic in Walvis Bay. Richard Charter drowned in a canoeing accident in 2004.

But I'm pleased to report that Otto's old commander, Marius Brand, is well and a regular correspondent. He is deeply involved in community development, training small farmers in every aspect of commercial agriculture, and promoting sources of inexpensive, alternative energy in remote areas. "We had coffee with General Sterk Hans recently," Marius wrote in an email. "He is still strong and upright. Most of the guys are doing well and believe in the future of the country. The most surprising thing that came out of this meeting was that we all agreed that our best friends in Koevoet were our trackers. Many of the guys are still in contact with their 'buddies,' as we called them. They were wonderful and brave and there was just so much respect between us." Of the others I rode with that first week, Thys Loedolff is still in the SAP, a lieutenant colonel in command of Middleberg's Cyber Crime Unit, while Christo "Skim" Schutte works for a private security company in Iraq.

Pierre Botha, who along with Boesman and Thinus, tried to convince the "Brig" that no one in Zulu November had enough English to accommodate an American journalist, is a security consultant in the Middle East. Lukas Kilino, the man who kept pulling me down during my first contact, returned to Angola in 1997, and is thought to have been murdered there. His son Tony recently contacted me, asking for photos and my memories of the man; it was a privilege to send what I had.

Not long before this manuscript went to the publisher another request arrived via my website. Like Tony Kilino's, it still prompts a moment of reflection whenever I read it.

Dear Mr Hooper.
I write to you from Namibia, and hope you are fine. My mother's brother fought as a member of Koevoet. I was wondering if you may have met him? His nickname was 'Betoger,' real name Christie Fourie. I can only remember him from when I was a small boy, and have been looking for more information about him my whole life. If you ever met my uncle, please send me some personal story about him. I so want to learn about him from the people he knew and had with him till his death. Thank you for your time, and any response would mean the world to me.
Yours Sincerely
Conrad Coertzen

After sharing my memories of the man who teased me about being a "hands-upper," I forwarded his email to all the Koevoet men in my address book. Their response has been magnificent.

Hennie "Nella" Nel left the SAP in 1990 and joined a company selling preventative maintenance products for the car industry. Five years later, he started his own company, and in 1997 began manufacturing his own range of environmentally friendly chemical products for the mining industry. He and his family live in Pretoria and are hopeful for the future of South Africa. Nella's Zulu Delta brother-in-arms, Dean Viljoen, has a company in Ellisras, casting reinforced concrete floors for clients involved in the new Medupi Power Station project.

Flip Fouche contacted me last year and proved enormously helpful in tracking down others I rode with. Following the war, he served in the Eastern Transvaal's bomb disposal unit, retired as a warrant officer in 1995 and for the last few years has been involved in de-mining in South Sudan for Norwegian Peoples Aid. Herman Grobler, who experienced his first contact the day Daniel Taiko spotted the ambush, lost a leg to a heatstrim the day Daniel died, and won a place in Koevoet legend: after the contact, he amputated what was left of his own leg with a penknife. He is today a colonel in the South African Police.

Jasper Genis, with whom I spent New Year's Eve 60 kilometres inside Angola, is, like Flip, involved in mine clearance in Sudan. I suspect there are few others in his line of work that can boast of surviving the blast of four cheese mines. Tony da Costa, my Afrikaans-English translator with the Swapo prisoners that last day of 1986, resigned from the police as a captain in 2004. He subsequently went into the private security industry in Iraq. In 2008, he joined the United Nations, and still works in the Middle East. Craig Rucastle, one of the teenaged army sappers that accompanied us on that trip to lift Swapo arms caches, completed his studies and set off to see some of the world. He and his wife live in London where he is a sales director for a cosmetics firm.

On his return to South Africa, Chris Ronne rose to the rank of lieutenant colonel. In 1997, he was forced to take a severance package after refusing to apologise for his years in Koevoet and the Security Branch. Along with former colleagues, he started Micro Finance Company in Durban. Its success led to Roof Caddy, a roof-rack manufacturing company that continues to expand.

Theron de Wit left the police in 1989, to start his own business as an insurance loss adjustor. A born-and-bred Southwester, he still lives in Tsumeb in Namibia.

Attie Hattingh resigned from the police shortly after leaving Namibia in 1990, refusing to associate himself with an organization that, contrary to its promises, left Koevoet's black colleagues to fend for themselves. It was, he still believes, a combination of betrayal and treason of the highest order. Soon after returning to Pretoria, he founded his own security company that has gone from strength to strength. As a mark of his own loyalty, most of Attie's employees are the men he shared so much with during those years in the bush. "Their expertise and commitment are always in demand," he says with evident pride.

Michael "Peanuts" Kennard moved from Zulu Uniform to take over as Zulu November's team leader, returning to Bloemfontein after the war. He remained in the police and is today a senior detective warrant officer. In a recent email, he revealed: "Well, I can only honestly tell you that I personally don't think that one of the enemy's bullets hit you that day. I cannot say for sure that it was from my .30 Browning, but it was your car in front of mine and I think you can do the maths. I really did not feel okay with this for a long time." I assured Peanuts I had only myself to blame, but the next time we met he was buying the beer.

A year after his charge through enemy fire to treat Zulu Quebec's Johannes Kanjamotu, ops medic Fred "Frikkie" Steynberg, was awarded the Honoris Crux, South Africa's highest decoration for bravery in combat. Today, he lives in Rhodes Village, a Victorian settlement in the stunning Drakensberg Mountains between South Africa and Lesotho. An internationally recognised sportsman, he owns Linecasters, which caters for fly fishing enthusiasts and hunters from around the world.

Bearing no physical scars from his years of combat, François du Toit returned to South Africa and a year later left the police to sell insurance. He married, had two children and rejoined the SAP, only to be diagnosed with PTSD and medically boarded in 1994. When a second marriage failed, he became a dedicated evangelist. "I do a lot of speaking engagements and counselling all over South Africa," Toit says. "Out of this was born a Christian fellowship called 'Walk the Way.' I really came to love God, my fellow man, and myself, but I'm still a work in progress." He attributes his surviving that RPG—and many other close calls during his Koevoet days—to the power of family and friends' prayers that he came home safely.

After several operations on his leg, Claassie Claassen eventually returned to the veld as group leader of Zulu November (after Peanuts was demoted for being exceptionally naughty). On April 1 1989, his team made first contact with the Swapo invaders, killing 33 and capturing one. After the war, he returned to Cape Town and joined the Housebreaking (Burglary) Unit, retiring in 1995 to provide armed protection for isolated farms. Of his wounds: "I am lucky as far as healing goes, but the rebuilt ankle is stiff and the right hand still aches where the shrapnel went through it." J.C. Lesch, who took command of Zulu Juliet after Claassie was wounded, lives in Knysna, which lies between the world-famous Garden Route and the Indian Ocean, one of the most beautiful areas in South Africa. His retail business took a blow from the current economic recession, but he has parlayed his love of cooking into a seafood restaurant that has proved a hit with both locals and tourists. My comments about his braai that night at Ohangwena were clearly misplaced.

After Koevoet, Marius "Apie" Clark took up his old job in the Peninsula Murder and Robbery Squad in Cape Town and in 1995 was medically boarded. He moved to Zambia, where he started a plumbing company that has enjoyed considerable success. In 2011, Apie, Theron de Wit and Claassie held a reunion in the Caprivi Strip, the first time they'd met up since the end of the war. The days spent on the Kwando River, reminiscing and bringing each other up to date was, according to all, such a success that they are already planning another.

Jack Bouwer of Zulu Tango retired from the SAP as a captain in 1996 and is still happily married to Soekie; it was her father, then-Major Willem Fouche, that gave him the unwelcome news about having to baby-sit a foreign journalist in the veld. After several business ventures, the last as a forensic psychophysiologist, Jack has recently settled in Natal. Angus Pursell left the SAP in 1997 as an internal prosecutor, and started his own company, ASP Polygraph, in Durban. He is a member of the South African Polygraph Association, as well as the British and European Polygraph Association. Gavin Manning served as second-in-command of the elite Durban Reaction Unit No 9, retiring as a captain in 1998. Auckland is now his home, where he works as the senior database consultant for New Zealand's largest hotel and casino group. His fluency in English, Afrikaans and Oshivambo (the latter so good that the PBs sometimes asked if he was an albino Ovambo), and didactic approach to tactics and terrain, were invaluable in painting a more complete picture of Koevoet's war.

Chris Pieterse, whose counsel about not standing up to take photos I foolishly ignored, took time from his wholesale dried fruit and nut business in Cape Town to read this manuscript, answer myriad arcane questions and offer advice. He hasn't let me forget I got shot for being stupid.

Rick Dooley resigned from the South African Air Force in 1988 to spread his wings in commercial aviation. Today he is director of operations for an air charter service in the Seychelles, flying state-of-the-art Eurocopter Colibri EC120Bs and a Patenavia P.68C Vulcanair over far more scenic vistas than Ovamboland.

Roelf Maritz left the SAP in 1994, traveled to America on vacation and settled in Texas, where he attended the police academy in Tarrant County. After successfully completing the course, he was hired by the Keller Police Department, later returning to Tarrant Country, where he was appointed a deputy sheriff. He also worked for Vance International Security Company as a tactical security officer. When his mother fell ill in 2008, he returned to South Africa. While there, he met his soul mate, married and today lives in Parys in the Free State. Like J.C. Lesch, he has gone into the restaurant business.

And did any of them leave embittered? you might well ask. And I would try to look wise and say: Yes, some, and predictably so; the rest simply philosophical about the years they lived through.

As for me, I still think about it from time to time—hard not to, really—a fractured mirror of moments and people: snatches of conversations, and the early morning smell of wet mopani mingling with blue diesel exhausts; hours of mind-numbing boredom inside a Casspir as it nosed its way through thick pepper bush and msasa trees; the tense anticipation on a running spoor; the sudden adrenaline rush at the first shots of a contact. Everything seems so clear still. Especially the people. The people. As though I could step through the mirror's frame and they would all be there, just the way they were.

If broken glass and shattered bodies could be put back together again.

When you leave somewhere it is gone forever; the pictures in your mind will never be the same. People go, others arrive to take their place, and even those who endure have changed—grown or diminished—from what you remember. So let them all remain as I have described.

It was a war in another life beneath a visiting moon.

> *Forebear to judge, for we are sinners all.*
> *Close up his eyes, and draw the curtain close;*
> *And let us all to meditation.*
>
> *William Shakespeare*
> *—Henry VI, Part 3, iii.31*

Glossary

AK-47 – Soviet-designed assault rifle firing a 7.62x39mm rimless round.

AKM – version of AK-47 with folding stock.

Alouette – the French Aérospatiale Alouette III was used extensively by the South African Air Force in both the gunship and casualty evacuation roles.

B-10 – Soviet-designed recoilless gun firing a projectile with approximately the same destructive power as an 82mm mortar round. Occasionally used by Swapo as a stand-off weapon.

Bakkie – pickup truck in Afrikaans; literally, a bucket.

Blesbok – a mine-protected supply vehicle built on the same monocoque V-hull as the Casspir. Each Ops K group of four Casspirs was accompanied by one Blesbok.

Bliksem – literally "lightning" in Afrikaans, but in its vernacular an exclamation or verb with a variety of meanings, depending on context.

Boer – Afrikaans for "farmer," but a generic term for Afrikaners.

Bosbok – the Italian Aermacchi AM.3 tandem-seat, light-observation aircraft used by the South African Air Force in the aerial reconnaissance role.

Braai – Afrikaans for barbecue.

C-130 – Lockheed Hercules four-engined transport and cargo aircraft, nicknamed "Flossie."

CANU – Caprivi African National Union, a liberation movement formed in 1962 and allied with Swapo. Dedicated to the independence of South West Africa/Namibia, many of its members who crossed into Angola and Zambia eventually were imprisoned by Swapo for tribal reasons.

Caprivi (Or Caprivi Strip) – a strip of land once claimed by imperial Germany with an eye to connecting German West Africa with German East Africa (now Tanzania) via the Zambezi River.

Casevac – casualty evacuation.

Casspir – a mine-protected armoured personnel carrier originally designed for the South African Police (SAP) and used by both Koevoet and the SWATF 101 Battalion on counterinsurgency operations in Namibia. The name is an acronym derived from the Casspir's designers – the Council for Scientific and Industrial Research (CSIR) – and South African

Police (SAP). The latest generation of Mine Resistant Ambush Protected (MRAP) armoured fighting vehicles used by the US military are direct descendants of the Casspir.

CCN – Council of Churches of Namibia, which supported Swapo's efforts to liberate South West Africa/Namibia.

Cheese mine – Yugoslavian TMA-3 "minimum metal anti-tank blast mine," a 6.5kg block of yellow TNT moulded in the shape of a cheese wheel.

COIN – counterinsurgency.

COMOPS – Communications Operations, a "hearts-and-minds" programme designed to draw the local population away from Swapo and to engender support for the government and security forces.

Cuca shop – a small shop selling a limited selection of such items such as canned goods and beer. Named after a legendary but no longer available Portuguese-Angolan beer.

Cutline – a cleared strip that marked the border between South West Africa/Namibia and Angola. *see* Yati.

Eenhana – a company-sized permanent base occupied by 53 Battalion, an SAAF helicopter detachment, and a Koevoet communications/operations centre.

Etale – SADF base located on the west side of the tar road about 7km south of Ohangwena. Pronounced Ee-tah´-lee.

Goeie môre – Afrikaans for "good morning."

FAPLA – Popular Armed Forces for the Liberation of Angola, the Angolan Army of the Soviet and Cuban-backed MPLA government.

Heatstrim – South Africa security forces' nickname for the Yugoslavian M-60 high-explosive antitank rifle grenade. STRIM is the acronym for "Societe Technique de Recherches Industrielles et Mecaniques," the French arms manufacturer that produced the original rifle grenade purchased by the SADF for use with the R1 (or FN/FAL) rifle. STRIM became the slang for any rifle grenade, regardless of its origin.

Hoe gaan dit? – Afrikaans for "How goes it?"

Kamachona – Oshivambo for herd boy.

Kaokoveld – a dry and mountainous desert lying west of Ovamboland, bordered on the north by Angola and to the east by the Atlantic Ocean.

Katima Mulilo – a small town at the end of the Eastern Caprivi and Sector 70 HQ

Kavango – tribal area of the Kavango tribe, lying east of Ovamboland and south of Angola.

Klick – kilometre.

Koevoet – pronounced "koo-foot," Afrikaans for "crowbar." The name signified prying the Swapo insurgents from the thick bush. The official name was South West African Police Counterinsurgency Unit (SWAPOLCOIN).

Kolodio – Oshivambo for "right."

Kolomosho – Oshivambo for "left."

Komesho – Oshivambo for "forward."

Kraal – an enclosure of sharpened logs set on end surrounding the traditional branch and woven-grass huts of an Ovambo family.

Lekker slaap – Afrikaans for "Sleep well."

MPLA – Popular Movement for the Liberation of Angola, the Angolan Marxist government supported by the Soviet Union, East Germany, and Cuba.

Mohango – the Ovambo staple crop of grain sorghum.

Ohangwena – Kwanyama tribal headquarters and location of 21D, a permanent South African Police Security Branch base.

Omega Base – headquarters for the SWATF 201 "Bushman" Battalion.

Okave – Z1 – Koevoet base in Oshakati. Pronounced Oh-ka´-vee.

Onaimwandi – Z3 – Investigative centre next to Okave.

Ondangwa – the second-largest town in Ovamboland and the location of the major South African Air Force base in the operational area. It was also the location of the primary trauma centre.

Operational area – the northern area of South West Africa/Namibia that bordered on Angola. This included the Kaokoveld and Ovamboland of Sector 10, the Kavango and Western Caprivi of Sector 20, and the Eastern Caprivi of Sector 70.

Opuwa – western-most Koevoet base, located in Kaokoveld.

Ops K – *see* Koevoet.

Oshakati – the largest town in Ovamboland and the location of Koevoet and SWATF headquarters.

Oshivambo – language of the Ovambo people.

Ovambo – the largest ethnic group in Namibia, comprising over 55 percent of the country's population. The Ovambo people are made up of seven distinct sub-tribes: Kwanyama, Ndonga, Kwambi, Ngandjera, Mbalantu, Kwaluudhi, and Nkolonkhadi-Eunda, each with its own dialect.

Ovamboland (or Ovambo) – that area of South West Africa/Namibia that traditionally has been the home of the Ovambo people. Part of Sector 10, together with the Kaokoveld.

Pencilstrim – South African security forces nickname for the slender anti-personnel version of the Yugoslavian M-60 rifle grenade. *see* Heatstrim.

PB – Plaaslike bevolking; Afrikaans for "local population."

PKM – Soviet-designed, general purpose machine gun firing a rimmed 7.62x54mm round. Capable of firing amour-piercing ammunition, it was rarely encountered by Koevoet.

PLAN – People's Liberation Army of Namibia, the official armed wing of Swapo.

POM-Z – "Pom-zed," Soviet-designed anti-personnel stake mine triggered by a trip wire.

R5 – short-barrelled version of the Armscor R4, the 5.56-mm automatic rifle based on the Israeli Galil, based in turn on the AK-47.

Rev – an attack on a base.

Romeo Mike – Reaksiemag, Afrikaans for "reaction force." Used to designate 101 Battalion's teams using Casspirs in Ovamboland.

RPD – Soviet-designed light machine gun.

RPG-7 – rocket-propelled grenade capable of penetrating up to 6 inches of laminated steel armour.

RPG-75 – telescoping, one-shot rocket launcher, similar to the American M72 LAW (Light Anti-tank Weapon). The first one seen outside the East bloc was in Ovamboland.

Rundu – small town in the Kavango located seven kilometres south of Angola. It was headquarters for Sector 20 as well as the eastern-most Koevoet base.

RV–rendezvous, "romeo victor," used to designate a grid reference.

SAAF – South African Air Force.

SACC – South African Cape Corps, a unit within the SADF, manned by Coloured (mixed race) South Africans.

SADF – South African Defence Force.

SAMS – South African Medical Service, part of the SADF.

Santie – Oshivambo for sergeant.

Shona – a low area that fills with water during the rainy season.

Shirumbu – Oshivambo for "white man."

SKS – Soviet-designed semi-automatic rifle. Obsolete by modern standards, but still in common use by Swapo during the bush war.

SPLA – Sudan Peoples Liberation Army, the armed wing of the Sudan Peoples Liberation Movement.

Spoor – in the context of this account, tracks left by Swapo insurgents.

Spoorsnyer–Afrikaans for tracker – literally "track cutter."

SWAPO – South West Africa People's Organization, the Soviet-backed liberation movement dedicated to wresting control of South West Africa/ Namibia from the South Africans.

SWAPOL – South West African Police.

SWAPOLCOIN – South West African Police Counterinsurgency Unit, the official name for Koevoet. The Afrikaans version was SWAPOLTIN for *Teen Insurgensie.*

Strandwolf – mine-protected supply vehicle based on same basic design as Wolf Turbo. Used exclusively by Koevoet.

SWATF – South West Africa Territory Force.

Tate'Nkulu – Oshivambo for "grandfather," used as polite form of address for a respected elder.

Tati – Oshivambo for "father" or "uncle," used as a polite form of address between men of similar age and station.

TB – tydelike bevolking, Afrikaans for "temporary base."

TGNU – Transitional Government of National Unity, a black majority government in South West Africa/Namibia appointed by the South Africans.

Tracker – usually an Ovambo special constable highly skilled in following the spoor of Swapo insurgents. *see* Spoorsnyer.

UNR 435 – United Nations Resolution 435, which called for United Nations-supervised elections in South West Africa/Namibia.

Veld – generic Afrikaans word for wilderness or bush. Pronounced "feld."

Victor Yankee – from the first two letter of "vyand," Afrikaans for enemy.

Voorsny – literally "ahead cutting" in Afrikaans, better translated as 'leapfrogging'.

Walking stick – a trimmed branch the trackers used to point out spoor. Some of the Ovambos believed that pointing a finger at a track would send a message to the insurgents' feet to run faster – thus the more neutral stick.

Windhoek – capital of Namibia and overall army and police headquarters.

Wolf Turbo – mine-protected armoured personnel carrier, designed and built by Windhoek Maschinen Fabrik in South West Africa/Namibia. It was used exclusively by Koevoet.

Yati – cleared strip of border between Namibia and Angola. *see* Cutline.

Zulu 1 – SWAPOLCOIN headquarters in Oshakati.

Zulu 2 – SWAPOLCOIN communications centre in Eenhana.

Zulu 3 – SWAPOLCOIN investigation centre adjacent to Zulu One.

Zulu 4 – SWAPOLCOIN base at Rundu in the Kavango.

Zulu 5 – SWAPOLCOIN base at Opuwa in the Kaokoveld.

Zulu 12 – SWAPOLCOIN vehicle maintenance and repair facility in Oshakati. Also referred to as "Blue Bells" for the blue coveralls worn by the mechanics.

Index

Related titles published by Helion & Company and GG Books

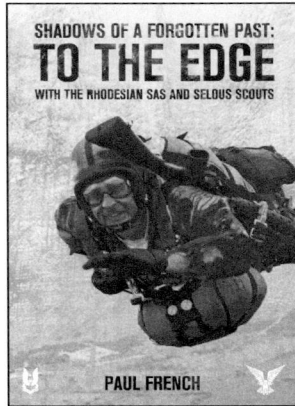

SHADOWS OF A FORGOTTEN PAST:
TO THE EDGE
WITH THE RHODESIAN SAS AND SELOUS SCOUTS

PAUL FRENCH

Shadows of a Forgotten Past: To the Edge with the Rhodesian SAS and Selous Scouts
Paul French
220pp Paperback
ISBN 978-1-908916-60-0

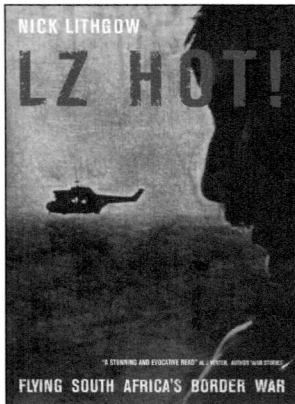

NICK LITHGOW
LZ HOT!
"A STUNNING AND EVOCATIVE READ" *AL J VENTER, AUTHOR 'WAR STORIES'*
FLYING SOUTH AFRICA'S BORDER WAR

LZ Hot! Flying South Africa's Border War
Nick Lithgow
176pp Paperback
ISBN 978-1-908916-59-4

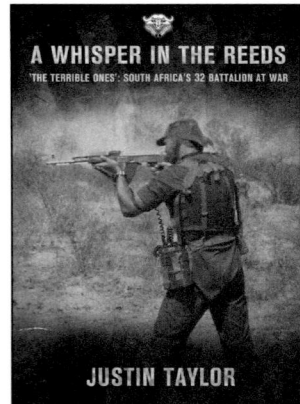

A WHISPER IN THE REEDS
'THE TERRIBLE ONES': SOUTH AFRICA'S 32 BATTALION AT WAR

JUSTIN TAYLOR

A Whisper in the Reeds. Nine Charlie
32: Signalling 'The Terrible Ones'
Justin Taylor
172pp Paperback
ISBN 978-1-908916-58-7

HELION & COMPANY
26 Willow Road, Solihull, West Midlands B91 1UE, England
Telephone 0121 705 3393   Fax 0121 711 4075
Website: http://www.helion.co.uk